Matthew Arnold

Passages From the Prose Writings of Matthew Arnold

Matthew Arnold

Passages From the Prose Writings of Matthew Arnold

ISBN/EAN: 9783744685405

Printed in Europe, USA, Canada, Australia, Japan

Cover: Foto ©Thomas Meinert / pixelio.de

More available books at **www.hansebooks.com**

PASSAGES FROM

THE PROSE WRITINGS

OF

MATTHEW ARNOLD

NEW YORK

MACMILLAN AND · CO.,

1880

CONTENTS.

I. LITERATURE.

II. POLITICS AND SOCIETY.

Contents.

III. PHILOSOPHY AND RELIGION.

I.

LITERATURE.

MODERN times find themselves with an immense system of institutions, established facts, accredited dogmas, customs, rules, which have come to them from times not modern. In this system their life has to be carried forward ; yet they have a sense that this system is not of their own creation, that it by no means corresponds exactly with the wants of their actual life, that, for them, it is customary, not rational. The awakening of this sense is the awakening of the modern spirit. The modern spirit is now awake almost everywhere ; the sense of want of correspondence between the forms of modern Europe and its spirit, between the new wine of the eighteenth and nineteenth centuries, and the old bottles of the eleventh and twelfth centuries, or even of the sixteenth and seventeenth, almost every one now perceives ; it is no longer dangerous to affirm that this want of correspondence exists ; people are even beginning to be shy of denying it. To remove this want of correspondence is beginning to be the settled endeavour of most persons of good sense. Dissolvents of the old European system of dominant ideas and facts we must all be, all of us who have any power of working ; what we have to study is that we may not be acrid dissolvents of it.—*Essays in Criticism.*

RANGE OF MODERN CRITICISM.

THE criticism which, throughout Europe, is at the present day meant, when so much stress is laid on the importance of criticism and the critical spirit,—is a criticism which regards Europe as being, for intellectual and spiritual purposes, one great confederation, bound to a joint action and working to a common result ; and whose members have, for their common outfit, a knowledge of Greek, Roman, and Eastern antiquity, and of one another. Special, local, and temporary advantages being put out of account, that modern nation will in the intellectual and spiritual sphere make most progress, which most thoroughly carries out this programme. And what is that but saying that we too, all of us, as individuals, the more thoroughly we carry it out, shall make the more progress ?—*Essays in Criticism.*

PHILISTINISM.

Philistinism !—we have not the expression in English. Perhaps we have not the word because we have so much of the thing. At Soli, I imagine, they did not talk of solecisms ; and here, at the very head-quarters of Goliath, nobody talks of Philistinism. The French have adopted the term *épicier* (grocer), to designate the sort of being whom the Germans designate by the term Philistine ; but the French term,—besides that it casts a slur upon a respectable class, composed of living and susceptible members, while the original Philistines are dead and buried long ago,—is really, I think, in itself much less apt and expressive than the German term. Efforts have been made to obtain in English some term equivalent to *Philister* or *épicier* ; Mr. Carlyle has made several such efforts : 'respectability with its thousand gigs,' he says ; —well, the occupant of every one of these gigs is, Mr. Carlyle means, a Philistine. However, the word *respectable* is far too valuable a word to be thus perverted from its proper meaning ; if the English are ever to have a word for the thing we are speaking of,—and so prodigious are the changes which the modern spirit is introducing, that even we English shall perhaps one day come to want such a word,—I think we had much better take the term *Philistine* itself.

Philistine must have originally meant, in the mind of those who invented the nickname, a strong, dogged, unenlightened opponent of the chosen people, of the children of the light. The party of change, the would-be remodellers of the old traditional European order, the invokers of reason against custom, the representatives of the modern spirit in every sphere where it is applicable, regarded themselves, with the robust self-confidence natural to reformers, as a chosen people, as children of the light. They regarded their adversaries as humdrum people, slaves to routine, enemies to light; stupid and oppressive, but at the same time very strong. This explains the love which Heine, that Paladin of the modern spirit, has for France; it explains the preference which he gives to France over Germany : 'the French,' he says, 'are the chosen people of the new religion, its first gospels and dogmas have been drawn up in their language ; Paris is the new Jerusalem, and the Rhine is the Jordan which divides the consecrated land of freedom from the land of the Philistines.' He means that the French, as a people, have shown more accessibility to ideas than any other people ; that prescription and routine have had less hold upon them than upon any other people ; that they have shown most readiness to move and to alter at the bidding (real or supposed) of reason. This explains, too, the detestation which Heine had for the English : ' I might settle in England,' he says, in his exile, ' if it were not that I should find there two things, coal-smoke and Englishmen ; I cannot abide either.' What he hated in the English was the 'ächt-brittische Beschränktheit,' as he calls ·it,—the *genuine British narrowness.* In truth, the English, profoundly as they have modified the old Middle-Age order, great as is the liberty which they have secured for themselves, have in all their changes proceeded, to use a familiar expression, by the rule of thumb ; what was intolerably inconvenient to them they have suppressed, and as they have suppressed it, not because it was irrational, but because it was practically inconvenient, they have seldom in suppressing it appealed to reason, but always, if possible, to some precedent, or form, or letter, which served as a convenient instrument for their purpose, and which saved them from the necessity of recurring to general principles. They have thus become, in a certain sense, of all people the most inaccessible to ideas and the most impatient of them ; inaccessible to them, because of their want of familiarity with them ; and impatient of them, because they have got on so well without them, that they despise those who, not having got on as well as themselves, still make a fuss for what they themselves have done so well without. But there has certainly followed from hence, in this country, somewhat of a general depression of pure intelligence : Philistia has come to be thought by us the true Land of Promise, and it is anything but that ; the born lover of ideas, the born hater of commonplaces, must feel in this country, that the sky over his head is of brass and iron.—*Essays in Criticism.*

ENGLISH LITERARY OPINION.

I THINK that in England, partly from the want of an Academy, partly from a national habit of intellect to which that want of an Academy is itself due, there exists too little of what I may call a public force of correct literary opinion, possessing within certain limits a clear sense of what is right and wrong, sound and unsound, and sharply recalling men of ability and learning from any flagrant misdirection of these their advantages. I think, even, that in our country a powerful misdirection of this kind is often more likely to subjugate and pervert opinion, than to be checked and corrected by it. Hence a chaos of false tendencies, wasted efforts, impotent conclusions, works which ought never to have been undertaken. Anyone who can introduce a little order into this chaos by establishing in any quarter a single sound rule of criticism, a single rule which clearly marks what is right as right, and what is wrong as wrong, does a good deed ; and his deed is so much the better the greater force he counteracts of learning and ability applied to thicken the chaos.—*Last Words on Translating Homer.*

ENGLISH ECCENTRICITY.

THE eccentricity, the arbitrariness, of which Professor Francis Newman's conception of Homer offers so signal an example, are not a peculiar failing of Mr. Newman's own ; in varying degrees, they are the great defect of English intellect, the great blemish of English literature. Our literature of the eighteenth century, the literature of the school of Dryden, Addison, Pope, Johnson, is a long reaction against this eccentricity, this arbitrariness : that reaction perished by its own faults, and its enemies are left once more masters of the field. Our present literature, which is very far, certainly, from having the spirit and power of Elizabethan genius, yet has in its own way these faults, eccentricity and arbitrariness, quite as much as the Elizabethan literature ever had. They are the cause, that while upon none, perhaps, of the modern literatures has so great a sum of force been expended as upon the English literature, at the present hour this literature, regarded not as an object of mere literary interest but as a living intellectual instrument, ranks only third in European effect and importance among the literatures of Europe ; it ranks after the literatures of France and Germany. Of these two literatures, as of the intellect of Europe in general, the main effort, for now many years, has been a *critical* effort ; the endeavour, in all branches of knowledge—theology, philosophy, history, art, science—to see the object as in itself it really is. But, owing to the presence in English literature of this eccentric and arbitrary spirit, owing to the strong tendency of English writers to bring to the consideration of their object some individual fancy, almost the last thing for which one would come to English literature is just that very thing which now Europe most desires : *criticism.—Lectures on Translating Homer.*

LITERARY CONSCIENCE.

' IN France,' says M. Sainte-Beuve, 'the first consideration for us is not whether we are amused and pleased by a work of art or mind, nor is it whether we are touched by it. What we seek above all to learn is, whether *we were right* in being amused with it, and in applauding it, and in being moved by it.' Those are very remarkable words, and they are, I believe, in the main quite true. A Frenchman has, to a considerable degree, what one may call a conscience in intellectual matters ; he has an active belief that there is a right and a wrong in them, that he is bound to honour and obey the right, that he is disgraced by cleaving to the wrong. All the world has, or professes to have, this conscience in moral matters. The word *conscience* has become almost confined, in popular use, to the moral sphere, because this lively susceptibility of feeling is, in the moral sphere, so far more common than in the intellectual sphere. The livelier, in the moral sphere, this susceptibility is, the greater becomes a man's readiness to admit a high standard of action, an ideal authoritatively correcting his everyday moral habits ; here, such willing admission of authority is due to sensitiveness of conscience. And a like deference to a standard higher than one's own habitual standard in intellectual matters, a like respectful recognition of a superior ideal, is caused, in the intellectual sphere, by sensitiveness of intelligence. Those whose intelligence is quickest, openest, most sensitive, are readiest with this deference ; those whose intelligence is less delicate and sensitive are less disposed to it.—*Essays in Criticism.*

DISTINCTION.

OF this quality the world is impatient ; it chafes against it, rails at it, insults it, hates it ;—it ends by receiving its influence, and by undergoing its law. This quality at last inexorably corrects the world's blunders, and fixes the world's ideals. It procures that the popular poet shall not finally pass for a Pindar, nor the popular historian for a Tacitus, nor the popular preacher for a Bossuet.—*Essays in Criticism.*

CURIOSITY.

THE notion of the free play of the mind upon all subjects being a pleasure in itself, being an object of desire, being an essential provider of elements without which a nation's spirit, whatever compensations it may have for them, must, in the long run, die of inanition, hardly enters into an Englishman's thoughts. It is noticeable that the word *curiosity,* which in other languages is used in a good sense, to mean, as a high and fine quality of man's nature, just this disinterested love of a free play of the mind on all subjects for its own sake,—it is noticeable, I say, that this word has in our language no sense of the kind, no sense but a rather bad and disparaging one. But criticism, real criticism, is essentially the exercise of this very quality. It obeys an instinct prompting it to try to know the best that is known and thought in the world, irrespectively of practice, politics, and everything of the kind ; and to value knowledge and thought as they approach this best, without the intrusion of any other considerations whatever. This is an instinct for which there is, I think, lit·le original sympathy in the practical English nature, and what there was of it has undergone a long benumbing period of blight and suppression in the epoch of concentration which followed the French Revolution.—*Essays in Criticism.*

SYSTEMATIC JUDGMENTS.

MANY and diverse must be the judgments passed upon every great poet, upon every considerable writer. There is the judgment of enthusiasm and admiration, which proceeds from ardent youth, easily fired, eager to find a hero and to worship him. There is the judgment of gratitude and sympathy, which proceeds from those who find in an author what helps them, what they want, and who rate him at a very high value accordingly. There is the judgment of ignorance, the judgment of incompatibility, the judgment of envy and jealousy. Finally, there is the systematic judgment, and this judgment is the most worthless of all. The sharp scrutiny of envy and jealousy may bring real faults to light. The judgments of incompatibility and ignorance are instructive, whether they reveal necessary clefts of separation between the experiences of different sorts of people, or reveal simply the narrowness and bounded view of those who judge. But the systematic judgment is altogether unprofitable. Its author has not really his eye upon the professed object of his criticism at all, but upon something else which he wants to prove by means of that object. He neither really tells us, therefore, anything about the object, nor anything about his own ignorance of the object. He never fairly looks at it, he is looking at something else. Perhaps if he looked at it straight and full, looked at it simply, he might be able to pass a good judgment on it. As it is, all he tells us is that he is no genuine critic, but a man with a system, an advocate.

Here is the fault of Professor Hermann Grimm, and of his Berlin lectures on Goethe. The professor is a man with a system ; the lectures are a piece of advocacy. Professor Grimm is not looking straight at ‘the greatest poet of all times and of all peoples ;’ he is looking at the necessities, as to literary glory, of the new German empire.—*Mixed Essays.*

THE *JOURNEYMAN-WORK OF LITERATURE.*

EDUCATED opinion exists here as in France ; but in France the Academy serves as a sort of centre and rallying-point to it, and gives it a force which it has not got here. Why is all the *journeyman-work* of literature, as I may call it, so much worse done here than it is in France ? I do not wish to hurt any one's feelings ; but surely this is so. Think of the difference between our books of reference and those of the French, between our biographical dictionaries (to take a striking instance) and theirs ; think of the difference between the translations of the classics turned out for Mr. Bohn's library and those turned out for M. Nisard's collection ! As a general rule, hardly any one amongst us, who knows French and German well, would use an English book of reference when he could get a French or German one ; or would look at an English prose translation of an ancient author when he could get a French or German one. It is not that there do not exist in England, as in France, a number of people perfectly well able to discern what is good, in these things, from what is bad, and preferring what is good ; but they are isolated, they form no powerful body of opinion, they are not strong enough to set a standard up to which even the journeyman-work of literature must be brought, if it is to be vendible. Ignorance and charlatanism in work of this kind are always trying to pass off their wares as excellent, and to cry down criticism as the voice of an insignificant, over-fastidious minority ; they easily persuade the multitude that this is so when the minority is scattered about as it is here ; not so easily when it is banded together as in the French Academy.—*Essays in Criticism.*

THE NOTE OF PROVINCIALITY.

IN a production which we have all been reading lately, a production stamped throughout with a literary quality very rare in this country,—*urbanity*; in this production, the work of a man never to be named by any son of Oxford without sympathy, a man who alone in Oxford of his generation, alone of many generations, conveyed to us in his genius that same charm, that same ineffable senti-ment, which this exquisite place itself conveys,—I mean Dr. Newman,—an expression is frequently used which is more common in theological than in literary language, but which seems to me fitted to be of general service ; the *note* of so and so, the note of catholicity, the note of antiquity, the note of sanctity, and so on. Adopting this expressive word, I say that in the bulk of the intellectual work of a nation which has no centre, no intellectual metropolis like an Academy, like M. Sainte-Beuve's ' sovereign organ of opinion,' like M. Renan's ' recog-nised authority in matters of tone and taste,'—there is observable a *note of provinciality.* Now, to get rid of provinciality is a certain stage of culture; a stage the positive result of which we must not make of too much importance, but which is, nevertheless, indispensable; for it brings us on to the platform where alone the best and highest intellectual work can be fairly said to begin. Work done after men have reached this platform is *classical*; and that is the only work which, in the long run, can stand. All the *scoriæ* in the work of men of great genius who have not lived on this platform, are due to their not having lived on it. Genius raises them to it by moments, and the portions of their work which are immortal are done at these moments; but more of it would have been immortal if they had not reached this platform at moments only, if they had had the culture which makes men live there.—*Essays in Criticism.*

AN ENGLISH ACADEMY.

NATIONS have their own modes of acting, and these modes are not easily changed; they are even consecrated, when great things have been done in them. When a literature has produced Shakspeare and Milton, when it has even produced Swift and Burke, it cannot well abandon its traditions; it can hardly begin, at this late time of day, with an institution like the French Academy. I think academies with a limited, special, scientific scope, in the various lines of intellectual work,—academies like that of Berlin, for instance,—we with time may, and probably shall, establish. And no doubt they will do good; no doubt the presence of such influential centres of correct information will tend to raise the standard amongst us for what I have called the *journeyman-work* of literature, and to free us from the scandal of such biographical dictionaries as Chalmers's, or such translations as a recent one of Spinoza, or perhaps, such philological freaks as Mr. Forster's about the one primeval language. But an academy quite like the French Academy, a sovereign organ of the highest literary opinion, a recognised authority in matters of intellectual tone and taste, we shall hardly have, and perhaps we ought not to wish to have it. But then every one amongst us with any turn for literature will do well to remember to what shortcomings and excesses, which such an academy tends to correct, we are liable; and the more liable, of course, for not having it.—*Essays in Criticism.*

THE SAME.

Because I have freely pointed out the dangers and inconveniences to which our literature is exposed in the absence of any centre of taste and authority like the French Academy, it is constantly said that I want to introduce here in England an institution like the French Academy. I have, indeed, expressly declared that I wanted no such thing. But let me notice how it is just our worship of machinery, and of external doing, which leads to this

C

charge being brought; and how the inwardness of culture would make us seize, for watching and cure, the faults to which our want of an Academy inclines us, and yet prevent us from trusting to an arm of flesh, as the Puritans say,—from blindly flying to this outward machinery of an Academy in order to help ourselves. For the very same culture and free inward play of thought which shows how the Corinthian style, or the whimsies about the One Primeval Language, are generated and strengthened in the absence of an Academy, shows us, too, how little any Academy, such as we should be likely to get, would cure them. Every one who knows the characteristics of our national life, knows exactly what an English Academy would be like. One can see the happy family in one's mind's eye as distinctly as if it were already constituted. Lord Stanhope,[1] the Dean of St. Paul's,[2] the Bishop of Oxford,[3] Lord Houghton, Mr. Gladstone, the Dean of Westminster, Mr. Froude, Mr. Henry Reeve,—everything which is influential, accomplished, and distinguished; and then, some fine morning, a dissatisfaction of the public mind with this brilliant and select coterie, a flight of Corinthian leading articles, and an irruption of Mr. G. A. Sala. Clearly, this is not what will do us good. The very same faults,—the want of sensitiveness of intellectual conscience, the disbelief in

---

[1] The late Lord Stanhope.   [2] The late Dean Milman.
[3] The late Bishop Wilberforce.

right reason, the dislike of authority,—which have hindered our having an Academy and have worked injuriously in our literature, would also hinder us from making our Academy, if we established it, one which would really correct them.—*Culture and Anarchy.*

CREATIVE EPOCHS.

THE grand work of literary genius is a work of synthesis and exposition, not of analysis and discovery ; its gift lies in the faculty of being happily inspired by a certain intellectual and spiritual atmosphere, by a certain order of ideas, when it finds itself in them ; of dealing divinely with these ideas, presenting them in the most effective and attractive combinations,—making beautiful works with them, in short. But it must have the atmosphere, it must find itself amidst the order of ideas, in order to work freely ; and these it is not so easy to command. This is why great creative epochs in literature are so rare, this is why there is so much that is unsatisfactory in the productions of many men of real genius ;—because for the creation of a master-work of literature two powers must concur, the power of the man and the power of the moment, and the man is not enough without the moment ; the creative power has, for its happy exercise, appointed elements, and those elements are not in its own control. —*Essays in Criticism.*

GENIUS OF HOMER.

HOMER has not only the English vigour, he has the Greek grace ; and when one observes the boisterous, rollicking way, in which his English admirers,—even men of genius, like the late Professor Wilson,—love to talk of Homer and his poetry, one cannot help feeling that there is no very deep community of nature between them and the object of their enthusiasm. 'It is all very well, my good friends,' I always imagine Homer saying to them, if he could hear them : 'you do me a great deal of honour, but somehow or other you praise me too like barbarians.' For Homer's grandeur is not the mixed and turbid grandeur of the great poets of the north, of the authors of Othello and Faust ; it is a perfect, a lovely grandeur. Certainly his poetry has all the energy and power of the poetry of our ruder climates ; but it has, besides, the pure lines of an Ionian horizon, the liquid clearness of an Ionian sky.—*Lectures on Translating Homer.*

HOMER AND THE BIBLE.

WE shall find one English book and one only, where, as in the Iliad itself, perfect plainness of speech is allied with perfect nobleness ; and that book is the Bible. No one could see this more clearly than Pope saw it. 'This pure and noble simplicity,' he says, 'is nowhere in such perfection as in the Scripture and Homer.' Yet even with Pope a woman is a 'fair,' a father is a 'sire,' and an old man a 'reverend sage,' and so on through all the phrases of that pseudo-Augustan, and most unbiblical, vocabulary. The Bible, however, is undoubtedly the grand mine of diction for the translator of Homer ; and, if he knows how to discriminate truly between what will suit him and what will not, the Bible may afford him also invaluable lessons of style.—*Lectures on Translating Homer.*

HOMER AND THE ELIZABETHANS.

As eminently as Homer is plain, so eminently is the Elizabethan literature in general, and Chapman in particular, fanciful. Steeped in humours and fantasticality up to its very lips, the Elizabethan age, newly arrived at the free use of the human faculties after their long term of bondage, and delighting to exercise them freely, suffers from its own extravagance in this first exercise of them, can hardly bring itself to see an object quietly or to describe it temperately. Happily, in the translation of the Bible, the sacred character of their original inspired the translators with such respect, that they did not dare to give the rein to their own fancies in dealing with it. But, in dealing with works of profane literature, in dealing with poetical works above all, which highly stimulated them, one may say that the minds of the Elizabethan translators were *too* active ; that they could not forbear importing so much of their own, and this of a most peculiar and Elizabethan character, into their original, that they effaced the character of the original itself.—*Lectures on Translating Homer.*

HOMER, SPENSER, AND KEATS.

SPENSER's verse is fluid and rapid, no doubt, but there are more ways than one of being fluid and rapid, and Homer is fluid and rapid in quite another way than Spenser. Spenser's manner is no more Homeric than is the manner of the one modern inheritor of Spenser's beautiful gift ; the poet, who evidently caught from Spenser his sweet and easy-slipping movement, and who has exquisitely employed it ; a Spenserian genius, nay, a genius by natural endowment richer probably than even Spenser ; that light which shines so unexpected and without fellow in our century, an Elizabethan born too late, the early lost and admirably gifted Keats.—*Lectures on Translating Homer.*

HOMER AND SCOTT.

THE poetic style of Scott is,—(it becomes necessary to say so when it is proposed to 'translate Homer into the melodies of Marmion'),—it is, tried by the highest standards, a bastard epic style ; and that is why, out of his own powerful hands, it has had so little success. It is a less natural, and therefore a less good style, than the original ballad-style ; while it shares with the ballad-style the inherent incapacity of rising into the grand style, of adequately rendering Homer. Scott is certainly at his best in his battles. Of Homer you could not say this ; he is not better in his battles than elsewhere ; but even between the battle-pieces of the two there exists all the difference which there is between an able work and a masterpiece.

> Tunstall lies dead upon the field,
> His life-blood stains the spotless shield :
> Edmund is down—my life is reft—
> The Admiral alone is left.—

—' For not in the hands of Diomede the son of Tydeus rages the spear, to ward off destruction from the Danaans ; neither as yet have I heard the voice of the son of Atreus, shouting from out his hated mouth ; but the voice of Hector the slayer of men bursts round me, as he cheers on the Trojans ; and they with their yellings fill all the plain, overcoming the Achaians in the battle.'—I protest that, to my feeling, Homer's performance, even through that pale and far-off shadow of a prose translation, still has a hundred times more of the grand manner about it, than the original poetry of Scott.—*Lectures on Translating Homer.*

HOMER AND THE BALLADISTS.

But, after all, Homer is not a better poet than the balladists, because he has taken in the hexameter a better instrument ; he took this instrument because he was a *different* poet from them ; so different,—not only so much better, but so essentially different,—that he is not to be classed with them at all. Poets receive their distinctive character, not from their subject, but from their application to that subject of the ideas (to quote the 'Recluse')

> On man, on nature, and on human life,

which they have acquired for themselves. In the ballad-poets in general, as in men of a rude and early stage of the world, in whom their humanity is not yet variously and fully developed, the stock of these ideas is scanty, and the ideas themselves not very effective or profound. In them the narrative itself is the great matter, not the spirit and significance which underlies the narrative. Even in later times of richly developed life and thought, poets appear who have what may be called a *balladist's mind* ; in whom a fresh and lively curiosity for the outward spectacle of the world is much more strong than their sense of the inward significance of that spectacle. When they apply ideas to their narrative of human events, you feel that they are, so to speak, travelling out of their own province : in the best of them you feel this perceptibly, but in those of a lower order you feel it very strongly. Even Sir Walter Scott's efforts of this kind,— even, for instance, the

> Breathes there the man with soul so dead . . . .

or the

> Oh woman ! in our hours of ease . . . .

even these leave, I think, as high poetry, much to be
desired; far more than the same poet's descriptions of a
hunt or a battle.   But Lord Macaulay's

> Then out spake brave Horatius,
>   The captain of the gate :
> ' To all the men upon this earth
>   Death cometh soon or late.' . . .

(and here, since I have been reproached with under-
valuing Lord Macaulay's Lays of Ancient Rome, let me
frankly say that, to my mind, a man's power to detect the
ring of false metal in those Lays is a good measure of his
fitness to give an opinion about poetical matters at all),—
I say, Lord Macaulay's

> To all the men upon this earth
> Death cometh soon or late . . . .

it is hard to read without a cry of pain.   But with Homer
it is very different.   This 'noble barbarian,' this 'savage
with the lively eye,'—whose verse, Mr. Newman thinks,
would affect us, if we could hear the living Homer, 'like
an elegant and simple melody from an African of the
Gold Coast,'—is never more at home, never more nobly
himself, than in applying profound ideas to his narrative.
As a poet he belongs,—narrative as is his poetry, and
early as is his date,—to an incomparably more developed

spiritual and intellectual order than the balladists, or than Scott and Macaulay; he is here as much to be distinguished from them, and in the same way, as Milton is to be distinguished from them.   He is, indeed, rather to be classed with Milton than with the balladists and Scott; for what he has in common with Milton,—the noble and profound application of ideas to life,—is the most essential part of poetic greatness.—*Last Words on Translating Homer.*

KEY-NOTE TO THE ILIAD.

'From Homer and Polygnotus I every day learn more clearly,' says Goethe, 'that in our life here above ground we have, properly speaking, to enact Hell:' —if the student must absolutely have a key-note to the Iliad, let him take this of Goethe, and see what he can do with it.—*Lectures on Translating Homer.*

EXHILARATION OF HEBREW PROPHECY.

To make a great work pass into the popular mind is not easy; but the series of chapters at the end of the Book of Isaiah, the chapters containing the great prophecy of Israel's restoration,—have, as has Hebrew prophecy in general, but to a still higher degree than anything else in Hebrew prophecy, one quality which facilitates this passage for them : their boundless exhilaration.   Much good poetry is profoundly melancholy ; now, the life of the people is such that in literature they require joy.   If ever that 'good time coming,' for which they long, was presented with energy and magnificence, it is in these chapters ; it is impossible to read them without catching its glow.—*A Bible Reading for Schools.*

THE CELTIC GENIUS.

SENTIMENTAL,—*always ready to react against the despotism of fact* ; that is the description which a great friend [1] of the Celt gives of him. And it is not a bad description of the sentimental temperament ; it lets us into the secret of its dangers and of its habitual want of success. Balance, measure, and patience, these are the eternal conditions, even supposing the happiest temperament to start with, of high success ; and balance, measure, and patience are just what the Celt has never had. Even in the world of spiritual creation, he has never, in spite of his admirable gifts of quick perception and warm emotion, succeeded perfectly, because he never has had steadiness, patience, sanity enough to comply with the conditions under which alone can expression be perfectly given to the finest perceptions and emotions. The Greek has the same perceptive, emotional temperament as the Celt ; but he adds to this temperament the sense of *measure* ; hence his admirable success in the plastic arts, in which the Celtic genius, with its chafing against the despotism of fact, its perpetual straining after mere emotion,

---

[1] M. Henri Martin.

has accomplished nothing. In the comparatively petty art of ornamentation, in rings, brooches, crosiers, relic-cases, and so on, he has done just enough to show his delicacy of taste, his happy temperament ; but the grand difficulties of painting and sculpture, the prolonged dealings of spirit with matter, he has never had patience for. Take the more spiritual arts of music and poetry. All which emotion alone can do in music the Celt has done ; the very soul of emotion breathes in the Scotch and Irish airs ; but with all this power of musical feeling, what has the Celt, so eager for emotion that he has not patience for science, effected in music, to be compared with what the less emotional German, steadily developing his musical feeling with the science of a Sebastian Bach or a Beethoven, has effected ? In poetry, again,—poetry which the Celt has so passionately, so nobly loved ; poetry where emotion counts for so much, but where reason, too, reason, measure, sanity, also count for so much, —the Celt has shown genius, indeed, splendid genius ; but even here his faults have clung to him, and have hindered him from producing great works such as other nations with a genius for poetry,—the Greeks, say, or the Italians,—have produced. The Celt has not produced great poetical works, he has only produced poetry with an air of greatness investing it all, and sometimes giving, moreover, to short pieces, or to passages, lines, and snatches of long pieces, singular beauty and power. And yet he loved poetry so much that he grudged no pains to it; but the true art, the *architectonicé* which shapes great works, such as the 'Agamemnon' or the 'Divine Comedy,' comes only after a steady, deep-searching survey, a firm conception of the facts of human life, which the Celt has not patience for. So he runs off into technic, where he employs the utmost elaboration, and attains astonishing skill; but in the contents of his poetry you have only so much interpretation of the world as the first dash of a quick, strong perception, and then sentiment, infinite sentiment, can bring you. Here, too, his want of sanity and steadfastness has kept the Celt back from the highest success.

If his rebellion against fact has thus lamed the Celt even in spiritual work, how much more must it have lamed him in the world of business and politics! The skilful and resolute appliance of means to ends which is needed both to make progress in material civilisation, and also to form powerful states, is just what the Celt has least turn for. He is sensual, or at least sensuous; loves bright colours, company, and pleasure; and here he is like the Greek and Latin races. But compare the talent the Greek and Latin (or Latinised) races have shown for gratifying their senses, for procuring an outward life rich, luxurious, splendid, with the Celt's failure to reach any material civilisation sound and satisfying, and not out at elbows, poor, slovenly, and half-barbarous. The sensuousness of the Greek made Sybaris and Corinth, the sensuousness of the Latin made Rome and Baiæ, the sensuousness of the Latinised Frenchman makes Paris ; the sensuousness of the Celt proper has made Ireland. Even in his ideal heroic times, his gay and sensuous nature cannot carry him, in the appliances of his favourite life of sociability and pleasure, beyond the gross and creeping Saxon whom he despises ; the regent Breas, we are told in the ' Battle of Moytura of the Fomorians,' became unpopular because 'the knives of his people were not greased at his table, nor did their breath smell of ale at the banquet.' In its grossness and barbarousness is not that Saxon, as Saxon as it can be ? just what the Latinised Norman, sensuous and sociable like the Celt, but with the talent to make this bent of his serve to a practical embellishment of his mode of living, found so disgusting in the Saxon.

And as in material civilisation he has been ineffectual, so has the Celt been ineffectual in politics. This colossal, impetuous, adventurous wanderer, the Titan of the early world, who in primitive times fills so large a place on earth's scene, dwindles and dwindles as history goes on, and at last is shrunk to what we now see him. For ages and ages the world has been constantly slipping, ever more and more, out of the Celt's grasp. 'They went forth to the war,' Ossian says most truly, '*but they always fell.*'—*Study of Celtic Literature.*

NATURAL MAGIC.

THE Celt's quick feeling for what is noble and distinguished gave to his poetry style ; his indomitable personality gave it pride and passion ; his sensibility and nervous exaltation gave it a better gift still, the gift of rendering with wonderful felicity the magical charm of nature. The forest solitude, the bubbling spring, the wild flowers, are everywhere in romance. They have a mysterious life and grace there ; they are nature's own children, and utter her secret in a way which makes them something quite different from the woods, waters, and plants of Greek and Latin poetry. Now, of this delicate natural magic Celtic romance is so pre-eminent a mistress, that it seems impossible to believe the power did not come into romance from the Celts.[1] Magic is just the word for it,—the magic of nature ; not merely the beauty of nature,—that the Greeks and Latins had ; not merely an honest smack of the soil, a faithful realism,—that the Germans had ; but the intimate life of nature, her weird power and her fairy charm. As the Saxon names of places, with the pleasant wholesome smack of the soil in them, —Weathersfield, Thaxted, Shalford,—are to the Celtic

---

[1] Rhyme,—the most striking characteristic of our modern poetry as distinguished from that of the ancients, and a main source, to our poetry, of its magic and charm, of what we call its *romantic element*,—rhyme itself, all the weight of evidence tends to show, comes into our poetry from the Celts.

names of places, with their penetrating, lofty beauty,—
Velindra, Tyntagel, Caernarvon,—so is the homely realism of German and Norse nature to the fairy-like loveli-　.
ness of Celtic nature.　Gwydion wants a wife for his
pupil : 'Well,' says Math, 'we will seek, I and thou,
by charms and illusions, to form a wife for him out of
flowers.　So they took the blossoms of the oak, and the
blossoms of the broom, and the blossoms of the meadow-
sweet, and produced from them a maiden, the fairest
and most graceful that man ever saw.　And they baptised her, and gave her the name of Flower-Aspect.'
Celtic romance is full of exquisite touches like that,
showing the delicacy of the Celt's feeling in these matters,
and how deeply nature lets him come into her secrets.—
Study of Celtic Literature.

HOW POETRY INTERPRETS.

POETRY interprets in two ways ; it interprets by expressing with magical felicity the physiognomy and movement
of the outward world, and it interprets by expressing
with inspired conviction the ideas and laws of the inward
world of man's moral and spiritual nature.　In other
words, poetry is interpretative both by having *natural
magic* in it, and by having *moral profundity*.　In both
ways it illuminates man ; it gives to him a satisfying sense
of reality ; it reconciles him with himself and the universe.

Thus Æschylus's ' δράσαντι παθεῖν ' and his ' ἀνήριθμον γέλασμα ' are alike interpretative. Shakspeare interprets both when he says :

> Full many a glorious morning have I seen,
> Flatter the mountain-tops with sovran eye ;

and when he says :

> There's a divinity that shapes our ends,
> Rough-hew them as we will.

These great poets unite in themselves the faculty of both kinds of interpretation, the naturalistic and the moral. But it is observable that in the poets who unite both kinds, the latter (the moral) usually ends by making itself the master.—*Essays in Criticism.*

SHAKSPEARE.

IT is not quite sound and sober criticism to say, as Mr. Stopford Brooke does of Shakspeare: 'He was altogether, from end to end, an artist, and the greatest artist the modern world has known.' Or again : ' In the unchangeableness of pure art-power Shakspeare stands entirely alone.' There is a peculiarity in Mr. Stopford Brooke's use of the words *art, artist.* He means by an artist one whose aim in writing is not to reveal himself, but to give pleasure ; he says most truly that Shakspeare's aim was to please, that Shakspeare 'made men and women whose dramatic action on each other and towards a catastrophe was intended to please the public, not to reveal himself.' This is indeed the true temper of the artist. But when we call a man emphatically *artist*, a *great artist*, we mean something more than this temper in which he works ; we mean by art, not merely an aim to please, but also, and more, a law of pure and flawless workmanship. As living always under the sway of *this* law, and as, therefore, a perfect artist, we do not con-ceive of Shakspeare. His workmanship is often far from being pure and flawless.

> Till that Bellona's bridegroom, lapp'd in proof,
> Confronted him with self-comparisons—

there is but one name for such writing as that, if Shakspeare had signed it a thousand times,—it is detestable. And it is too frequent in Shakspeare. We ought not, therefore, to speak of Shakspeare as 'alto-gether, from end to end, an artist ;' as 'standing entirely alone in the unchangeableness of pure art-power.' He is the richest, the most wonderful, the most powerful, the most delightful of poets ; he is not altogether, nor even eminently, an artist.—*Mixed Essays.*

MILTON'S POWER OF STYLE.

MILTON'S true distinction as a poet is undoubtedly his 'unfailing level of style.' Milton has always the sure, strong touch of the master. His power both of diction and of rhythm is unsurpassable, and it is characterised by being always present ;—not depending on an access of emotion, not intermittent, but, like the grace of Raphael, working in its possessor as a constant gift of nature. Milton's style, moreover, has the same propriety and soundness in presenting plain matters, as in the comparatively smooth task for a poet of presenting grand ones. His rhythm is as admirable where, as in the line

> And Tiresias and Phineus, prophets old——

it is unusual, as in such lines as—

> With dreadful faces throng'd and fiery arms——

where it is simplest. And what high praise this is, we may best appreciate by considering the ever-recurring failure, both in rhythm and in diction, which we find in the so-called Miltonic blank verse of Thomson, Cowper, Wordsworth. What leagues of lumbering movement ! what desperate endeavours, as in Wordsworth's

> And at the ' Hoop ' alighted, famous inn,

to render a platitude endurable by making it pompous ! Shakspeare himself, divine as are his gifts, has not, of the marks of the master, this one : perfect sureness of hand in his style. Alone of English poets, alone in English art, Milton has it ; he is our great artist in style, our one first-rate master in the grand style. He is as truly a master in this style as the great Greeks are, or Virgil, or Dante. The number of such masters is so limited that a man acquires a world-rank in poetry and art, instead of a mere local rank, by being counted among them. But Milton's importance to us Englishmen, by virtue of this distinction of his, is incalculable. The charm of a master's unfailing touch in diction and in rhythm, no one, after all, can feel so intimately, so profoundly, as his own countrymen. Invention, plan, wit, pathos, thought, all of them are in great measure capable of being detached from the original work itself, and of being exported for admiration abroad. Diction and rhythm are not. Even when a foreigner can read the work in its own language, they are not, perhaps, easily appreciable by him. It shows M. Scherer's thorough knowledge of English, and his critical sagacity also, that he has felt the force of them in Milton. We natives must naturally feel it yet more powerfully. Be it remembered, too, that English literature, full of vigour and genius as it is, is peculiarly impaired by gropings and inadequacies in form. And the same with English art. Therefore for the English artist in any line, if he is a true artist, the study of Milton may well have an indescribable attraction. It gives him lessons which nowhere else from an Englishman's work can he obtain, and feeds a sense which English work, in general, seems bent on disappointing and baffling. And this sense is yet so deep-seated in human nature,—this sense of style,—that probably not for artists alone, but for all intelligent Englishmen who read him, its gratification by Milton's poetry is a large, though often not fully recognised, part

of his charm, and a very wholesome and fruitful one.
—*Mixed Essays.*

DANTE, SHAKSPEARE, GOETHE.

THE natural magic of Keats and Wordsworth, Byron's vigour of style and Titanic personality, may be wanting to Goethe's poetry ; but see what it has accomplished without them ! How much more than Byron with his style and personality, and Keats and Wordsworth with their natural magic ! Why, for the immense, serious task it had to perform, the steadiness of German poetry, its going near the ground, its patient fidelity to nature, its using great plainness of speech, poetical drawbacks in one point of view, were safeguards and helps in another. The plainness and earnestness of these two lines from Goethe :

> Es bildet ein Talent sich in der Stille,
> Sich ein Character in dem Strom der Welt—

compared with the play and power of Shakspeare's style or Dante's, suggest at once the difference between Goethe's task and theirs, and the fitness of the faithful laborious German spirit for its own task. Dante's task was to set forth the lesson of the world from the point of view of mediæval Catholicism ; the basis of spiritual life was given, Dante had not to make this anew. Shakspeare's task was to set forth the spectacle of the world when man's spirit re-awoke to the possession of the world at the Renascence. The spectacle of human life, left to bear its own significance and tell its own story, but shown in all its fulness, variety, and power, is at that moment the great matter ; but, if we are to press deeper, the basis of spiritual life is still at that time the traditional religion, reformed or unreformed, of Christendom, and Shakspeare has not to supply a new basis. But when Goethe came, Europe had lost her basis of spiritual life ; she had to find it again ; Goethe's task was,—the inevitable task for the modern poet henceforth is,—as it was for the Greek poet in the days of Pericles, not to preach a sublime sermon on a traditional text like Dante, not to exhibit all the kingdoms of human life and the glory of them like Shakspeare, but to interpret human life afresh, and to supply a new spiritual basis to it. This is not only a work for style, eloquence, charm, poetry ; it is a work for science ; and the scientific, serious German spirit, not carried away by this and that intoxication of ear, and eye, and self-will, has peculiar aptitudes for it.—*Study of Celtic Literature.*

GOETHE'S NATURALISM.

GOETHE'S profound, imperturbable naturalism is absolutely fatal to all routine-thinking. He puts the standard, once for all, inside every man instead of outside him. When Goethe is told, such a thing must be so, there is immense authority and custom in favour of its being so,

it has been held to be so for a thousand years, he answers
with Olympian politeness : ' But *is* it so? is it so to *me ?* '
Nothing could be more really subversive of the foundations on which the old European order rested ; and it
may be remarked that no persons are so radically detached from this order, no persons so thoroughly modern,
as those who have felt Goethe's influence most deeply.
If it is said that Goethe professes to have in this way
deeply influenced but a few persons, and those persons
poets, one may answer that he could have taken no
better way to secure, in the end, the ear of the world ; for
poetry is simply the most beautiful, impressive, and widely
effective mode of saying things, and hence its importance.—*Essays in Criticism.*

GOETHE'S GREATNESS.

It is by no means as the greatest of all poets that Goethe
may rightly call forth the pride and praise of his German
countrymen.   It is as the clearest, the largest, the most
helpful thinker of modern times.   It is not principally in
his published works, it is in the immense Goethe-litera-
ture of letter, journal, and conversation, in the volumes
of Riemer, Falk, Eckermann, the Chancellor von Müller,
in the letters to Merck and Madame von Stein and many
others, in the correspondence with Schiller, the correspondence with Zelter, that the elements for an impression
of the truly great, the truly significant Goethe are to be

found.   Goethe is the greatest poet of modern times, not because he is one of the half-dozen human beings who in the history of our race have shown the most signal gift for poetry, but because, having a very considerable gift for poetry, he was at the same time, in the width, depth, and richness of his criticism of life, by far our greatest modern man.   He may be precious and important to us on this account above men of other and more alien times, who as poets rank higher.   Nay, his preciousness and importance as a clear and profound modern spirit, as a master-critic of modern life, must communicate a worth of their own to his poetry, and may well make it erroneously seem to have a positive value and perfectness as poetry, more than it has.   It is most pardonable for a student of Goethe, and may even for a time be serviceable, to fall into this error.   Nevertheless, poetical defects, where they are present, subsist, and are what they are.   And the same with defects of character.   Time and attention bring them to light; and when they are brought to light, it is not good for us, it is obstructing and retarding, to refuse to see them.   Goethe himself would have warned us against doing so.—*Mixed Essays.*

GOETHE'S FOUNDATION.

PINDAR and Sophocles,—as we all say so glibly, and often with so little discernment of the real import of what we are saying,—had not many books; Shakspeare was no deep reader. True ; but in the Greece of Pindar and Sophocles, in the England of Shakspeare, the poet lived in a current of ideas in the highest degree animating and nourishing to the creative power ; society was, in the fullest measure, permeated by fresh thought, intelligent and alive. And this state of things is the true basis for the creative power's exercise, in this it finds its data, its materials, truly ready for its hand ; all the books and reading in the world are only valuable as they are helps to this. Even when this does not actually exist, books and reading may enable a man to construct a kind of semblance of it in his own mind, a world of knowledge and intelligence in which he may live and work. This is by no means an equivalent, to the artist, for the nationally diffused life and thought of the epochs of Sophocles or Shakspeare ; but, besides that it may be a means of preparation for such epochs, it does really constitute, if many share in it, a quickening and sustaining atmosphere of great value. Such an atmosphere the many-sided learning and the long and widely-combined critical effort of Germany formed for Goethe, when he lived and worked. There was no national glow of life and thought there, as in the Athens of Pericles, or the England of Elizabeth. That was the poet's weakness. But there was a sort of equivalent for it in the complete culture and unfettered thinking of a large body of Germans. That was his strength. In the England of the first quarter of this century, there was neither a national glow of life and thought, such as we had in the age of Elizabeth, nor yet a culture and a force of learning and criticism, such as were to be found in Germany. Therefore the creative power of poetry wanted, for success in the highest sense, materials and a basis ; a thorough interpretation of the world was necessarily denied to it.—*Essays in Criticism.*

OUR 1800–1830.

WE in England, in our great burst of literature during the first thirty years of the present century, had no manifestation of the modern spirit, as this spirit manifests itself in Goethe's works or Heine's. And the reason is not far to seek. We had neither the German wealth of ideas, nor the French enthusiasm for applying ideas. There reigned in the mass of the nation that inveterate inaccessibility to ideas, that Philistinism,—to use the German nickname,—which reacts even on the individual genius that is exempt from it. In our greatest literary epoch, that of the Elizabethan age, English society at large was accessible to ideas, was permeated by them, was vivified by them, to a degree which has never been reached in England since. Hence the unique greatness in English literature of Shakspeare and his contemporaries. They were powerfully upheld by the intellectual life of their nation ; they applied freely in literature the then modern ideas,—the ideas of the Renascence and the Reformation. A few years afterwards, the great English middle class, the kernel of the nation, the class whose intelligent sympathy had upheld a Shakspeare, entered the prison of Puritanism, and had the key turned upon its spirit there for two hundred years. *He enlargeth a nation*, says Job, *and straiteneth it again.*

In the literary movement of the beginning of the nineteenth century the signal attempt to apply freely the modern spirit was made in England by two members of the aristocratic class, Byron and Shelley. Aristocracies are, as such, naturally impenetrable by ideas ; but their individual members have a high courage and a turn for breaking bounds ; and a man of genius, who is the born child of the idea, happening to be born in the aristocratic ranks, chafes against the obstacles which prevent him from freely developing it. But Byron and Shelley did not succeed in their attempt freely to apply the modern spirit in English literature ; they could not succeed in it ; the resistance to baffle them, the want of intelligent sympathy to guide and uphold them, were too great. Their literary creation, compared with the literary creation of Shakspeare and Spenser, compared with the literary creation of Goethe and Heine, is a failure. The best literary creation of that time in England proceeded from men who did not make the same bold attempt as Byron and Shelley. What, in fact, was the career of the chief English men of letters, their contemporaries ? The greatest of them, Wordsworth, retired (in Middle-Age phrase) into a monastery. I mean, he plunged himself in the inward life, he voluntarily cut himself off from the modern spirit. Coleridge took to opium. Scott became the historiographer royal of feudalism. Keats passionately gave himself up to a sensuous genius, to his faculty for interpreting nature ; and he died of consumption at twenty-five. Wordsworth, Scott, and Keats have left admirable works ; far more solid and complete works than those which Byron and Shelley have left. But their works have this defect ;—they do not belong to that which is the main current of the literature of modern epochs, they do not apply modern ideas to life ; they constitute, therefore, *minor currents*, and all other literary work of our day, however popular, which has the same defect, also constitutes but a minor current. Byron and Shelley will long be remembered, long after the inadequacy of their actual work is clearly recognised, for their passionate, their Titanic effort to flow in the main stream of modern literature ; their names will be greater than their writings ; *stat magni nominis umbra.—Essays in Criticism.*

PRODIGALITY OF NATURE.

WHAT a spendthrift, one is tempted to cry, is Nature ! With what prodigality, in the march of generations, she employs human power, content to gather almost always little result from it, sometimes none ! Look at Byron, that Byron whom the present generation of Englishmen are forgetting ; Byron, the greatest natural force, the greatest elementary power, I cannot but think, which has appeared in our literature since Shakspeare. And what became of this wonderful production of nature? He shattered himself, he inevitably shattered himself to pieces, against the huge, black, cloud-topped, interminable precipice of British Philistinism. But Byron, it may be said, was eminent only by his genius, only by his inborn force and fire ; he had not the intellectual equipment of a supreme modern poet ; except for his genius he was an ordinary nineteenth-century English gentleman, with little culture and with no ideas. Well, then, look at Heine. Heine had all the culture of Germany ; in his head fermented all the ideas of modern Europe. And what have we got from Heine? A half-result, for want of moral balance, and of nobleness of soul and character. That is what I say ; there is so much power, so many seem able to run well, so many give promise of running well ; —so few reach the goal, so few are chosen. *Many are called, few chosen.—Essays in Criticism.*

SYMBOLISM IN POETRY.

THE first part of 'Faust' is undoubtedly Goethe's best work in poetry. And it is so for the plain reason that, except his 'Gedichte,' it is his most straightforward

work in poetry.   Mr. Hayward's is the best of the translations of 'Faust' for the same reason,—because it is the
most straightforward.   To be simple and straightforward
is, as Milton saw and said, of the essence of first-rate
poetry.   All that M. Scherer says of the ruinousness, to
a poet, of 'symbols, hieroglyphics, mystifications,' is just.
When Mr. Carlyle praises the 'Helena' for being 'not a
type of one thing, but a vague, fluctuating, fitful adum-
bration of many,' he praises it for what is in truth its fatal
defect. The 'Mährchen,' again, on which Mr. Carlyle heaps
such praise, calling it 'one of the notablest performances
produced for the last thousand years,' a performance 'in
such a style of grandeur and celestial brilliancy and life as
the Western imagination has not elsewhere reached ;' the
'Mährchen,' woven throughout of 'symbol, hieroglyphic,
mystification,' is by that very reason a piece of solemn
inanity, on which a man of Goethe's powers could never
have wasted his time, but for his lot having been cast in
a nation which has never lived.—*Mixed Essays.*

GOETHE'S CORPORALISM.

LET us remark that it was not 'snobbishness' in Goethe,
as M. Scherer harshly calls it, which made him take so
seriously the potentate who loved Lola Montes ; it was
simply his German 'corporalism.' A disciplinable and
much-disciplined people, with little humour, and without
the experience of a great national life, regards its official

authorities in this devout and awe-struck way. To a German it seems profane and licentious to smile at his Dogberry. He takes Dogberry seriously and solemnly, takes him at his own valuation.—*Mixed Essays.*

SIMPLICITY AND 'SIMPLESSE.'

FRENCH criticism, richer in its vocabulary than ours, has invented a useful word to distinguish the. semblance of simplicity from the real quality. The real quality it calls *simplicité*, the semblance *simplesse*. The one is natural simplicity, the other is artificial simplicity. What is called simplicity in the productions of a genius essentially not simple, is in truth *simplesse*. The two are distinguishable from one another the moment they appear in company. For instance, let us take the opening of the narrative in Wordsworth's 'Michael :'

> Upon the forest-side in Grasmere Vale
> There dwelt a shepherd, Michael was his name;
> An old man, stout of heart, and strong of limb.
> His bodily frame had been from youth to age
> Of an unusual strength ; his mind was keen,
> Intense, and frugal, apt for all affairs ;
> And in his shepherd's calling he was prompt
> And watchful more than ordinary men.

Now let us take the opening of the narrative in Mr. Tennyson's 'Dora :'

> With Farmer Allan at the farm abode
> William and Dora. William was his son,
> And she his niece. He often look'd at them,
> And often thought, ' I'll make them man and wife '

The simplicity of the first of these passages is *simplicité*; that of the second, *simplesse.—Last Words on Translating Homer.*

HYMNS, ENGLISH AND GERMAN.

OUR German kinsmen and we are the great people for hymns. The Germans are very proud of their hymns, and we are very proud of ours; but it is hard to say which of the two, the German hymn-book or ours, has least poetical worth in itself, or does least to prove genuine poetical power in the people producing it. I have not a word to say against Sir Roundell Palmer's choice and arrangement of materials for his ‘Book of Praise;’ I am content to put them on a level (and that is giving them the highest possible rank) with Mr. Palgrave's choice and arrangement of materials for his ‘Golden Treasury;’ but yet no sound critic can doubt that, so far as poetry is concerned, while the ‘Golden Treasury’ is a monument of a nation's strength, the ‘Book of Praise’ is a monument of a nation's weakness. Only the German race, with its want of quick instinctive tact, of delicate, sure perception, could have invented the hymn as the Germans and we have it; and our non-German turn for style,—style, of which the very essence is a certain happy fineness and truth of poetical perception,—could not but desert us when our German nature carried us into a kind of composition which can please only when the perception is somewhat blunt. Scarcely any one of us ever judges our hymns fairly, because works of this kind have two sides,—their side for religion and their side for poetry. Everything which has helped a man in his religious life, everything which associates itself in his mind with the growth of that life, is beautiful and venerable to him ; in this way, productions of little or no poetical value, like the German hymns and ours, may come to be regarded as very precious. Their worth in this sense, as means by which we have been edified, I do not for a moment hold cheap ; but there is an edification proper to all our stages of development, the highest as well as the lowest, and it is for man to press on towards the highest stages of his development, with the certainty that for those stages, too, means of edification will not be found wanting. Now certainly it is a higher state of development when our poetical perception is keen than when it is blunt.—*Study of Celtic Literature.*

HYMNS AGAIN.

HYMNS, such as we know them, are a sort of composition which I do not at all admire. I freely say so now, as I have often said it before. I regret their prevalence and popularity amongst us. Taking man in his totality and in the long run, bad music and bad poetry, to whatever good and useful purposes a man may often manage to turn them, are in themselves mischievous and deteriorating

E

to him. Somewhere and somehow, and at some time or other, he has to pay a penalty and to suffer a loss for taking delight in them. It is bad for people to hear such words and such a tune as the words or tune of, *O happy place! when shall I be, my God, with thee, to see thy face?* —worse for them to take pleasure in it. And the time will come, I hope, when we shall feel the unsatisfactoriness of our present hymns, and they will disappear from our religious services. But that time has not come yet, and will not be brought about soon or suddenly.—*Last Essays.*

. LATIN HYMNS AND THE 'IMITATION.'

It is worth noticing that in our Indo-European Christendom the best productions of the pure religious sentiment have been works like the 'Imitation,' the 'Dies Iræ,' the 'Stabat Mater,'—works clothing themselves in the Middle-Age Latin, the genuine native voice of none of us. The perfection of their kind, but that kind not perfectly legitimate, they take a language not perfectly legitimate; as if to show, that when mankind's Semitic age is once passed, the age which produced the great incomparable monuments of the pure religious sentiment, the books of Job and Isaiah, the Psalms,—works truly to be called inspired, because the same divine power which worked in those who produced them works no longer,—as if to show us, that, after this primitive age, we Indo-Europeans must feel these works without attempting to remake them ; and that our poetry, if it tries to make itself simply the organ of the religious sentiment, leaves the true course, and must conceal this by not speaking a living language. The moment it speaks a living language, and still makes itself the organ of the religious sentiment only, as in the German and English hymns, it betrays weakness ;—the weakness of all false tendency.—*Study of Celtic Literature.*

GERMAN STYLE.

ENGLISHMEN and Frenchmen have alike the same instinctive sense rebelling against what is verbose, ponderous, roundabout, inane,—in one word, *niais* or silly, – in German literature.

This ground of sympathy between Englishmen and Frenchmen has not been enough remarked, but it is a very real one. They owe it to their having alike had a long-continued national life, a long-continued literary activity, such as no other modern nation has had. This course of practical experience does of itself beget a turn for directness and clearness of speech, a dislike for futility and fumbling, such as without it we shall rarely find general. Dr. Wiese, in his recent useful work on English schools, expresses surprise that the French language and literature should find more favour in Teutonic England than the German. But community of practice is more telling than community of origin. While English and French are printed alike, and while an English and a French sentence each of them says what it has to say in the same direct fashion, a German newspaper is still printed in black letter, and a German sentence is framed in the style of this which we quote from Dr. Wiese himself: 'Die Engländer einer grossen, in allen Erdtheilen eine Achtung gebietende Stellung einnehmenden Nation angehören!' The Italians are a Latin race, with a clear-cut language ; but much of their modern prose has all the circuitousness and slowness of the German, and from the same cause : the want of the pressure of a great national life, with its practical discipline, its ever-active traditions ; its literature, for centuries past, powerful and incessant. England has these in common with France. —*Mixed Essays.*

BLENDING OF TEMPERAMENTS.

JUST what constitutes special power and genius in a man seems often to be his blending, with the basis of his national temperament, some additional gift or grace not proper to that temperament. Shakspeare's greatness is thus in his blending an openness and flexibility of spirit, not English, with the English basis ; Addison's, in his blending a moderation and delicacy, not English, with the English basis ; Burke's, in his blending a largeness of view and richness of thought, not English, with the English basis. In Germany itself, in the same way, the greatness of their great Frederic lies in his blending a rapidity and clearness, not German, with the German basis ; the greatness of Goethe in his blending a love of form, nobility, and dignity,—the grand style,—with the German basis. But the quick, sure, instinctive perception of the incongruous and absurd not even genius seems to give in Germany ; at least, I can think of only one German of genius, Lessing (for Heine was a Jew, and the Jewish temperament is quite another thing from the German), who shows it in an eminent degree.—*Study of Celtic Literature.*

OUR ENGLISH MIXTURE.

IT is not a sheer advantage to have several strings to one's bow ! if we had been all German, we might have had the science of Germany ; if we had been all Celtic, we might have been popular and agreeable ; if we had been all Latinised, we might have governed Ireland as the French govern Alsace, without getting ourselves detested. But now we have Germanism enough to make us Philistines, and Latinised Normanism enough to make us imperious, and Celtism enough to make us self-conscious and awkward ; but German fidelity to Nature, and Latin precision and clear reason, and Celtic quick-wittedness and spirituality, we fall short of. Nay, perhaps, if we are doomed to perish (Heaven avert the omen !), we shall perish by our Celtism, by our self-will and want of patience with ideas, our inability to see the way the world is going ; and yet those very Celts, by our affinity with whom we are perishing, will be hating and upbraiding us all the time.—*Study of Celtic Literature.*

ENGLISH PROSE AND POETRY.

POETRY, no doubt, is more excellent in itself than prose. In poetry man finds the highest and most beautiful expression of that which is in him. We had a far better poetry than the poetry of the eighteenth century before that century arrived, we have had a better since it departed. Like the Greeks, and unlike the French, we can point to an age of poetry anterior to our age of prose, eclipsing our age of prose in glory, and fixing the future character and conditions of our literature. We do well to place our pride in the Elizabethan age and Shakspeare, as the Greeks placed theirs in Homer. We did well to return in the present century to the poetry of that older age for illumination and inspiration, and to put aside, in a great measure, the poetry and poets intervening between Milton and Wordsworth. Milton, in whom our great poetic age expired, was the last of the immortals. The glory of English literature is in poetry, and in poetry the strength of the eighteenth century does not lie.

Nevertheless, the eighteenth century accomplished for us an immense literary progress, and its very shortcomings in poetry were an instrument to that progress, and served it. The example of Germany may show us what a nation loses from having no prose style. The practical genius of our people could not but urge irresistibly to the production of a real prose style, because for the purposes of modern life the old English prose, the prose of Milton and Taylor, is cumbersome, unavailable, impossible. A style of regularity, uniformity, precision, balance, was wanted. These are the qualities of a serviceable prose style. Poetry has a different *logic*, as Coleridge said, from prose ; poetical style follows another law of evolution than the style of prose. But there is no doubt that a style of regularity, uniformity, precision, balance, will acquire a yet stronger hold upon the mind of a nation, if it is adopted in poetry as well as in prose, and so comes to govern both. This is what happened in France. To the practical, modern, and social genius of the French, a true prose was indispensable. They produced one of conspicuous excellence,—a prose marked in the highest degree by the qualities of regularity, uniformity, precision, balance. With little opposition from any deep-seated and imperious poetic instincts, the French made their poetry also conform to the law which was moulding their prose. French poetry became marked with the qualities of regularity, uniformity, precision, balance. This may have been bad for French poetry, but it was good for French prose. It heightened the perfection with which those qualities, the true qualities of prose, were impressed upon it. When England, at the Restoration, desired a modern prose, and began to create it, our writers turned naturally to French literature, which had just accomplished the very process which engaged them. The King's acuteness and taste helped. Indeed, to the admission of French influence of all kinds, Charles the Second's character and that of his court were but too favourable. But the influence of the French writers was at that moment on the whole fortunate, and seconded what was a vital and necessary effort in our literature. Our literature required a prose which conformed to the true law of prose ; and that it might acquire this the more surely, it compelled poetry, as in France, to conform itself to the law of prose likewise. The classic verse of French poetry was the Alexandrine, a measure favourable to the qualities of regularity, uniformity, precision, balance. Gradually a measure favourable to those very same qualities,—the ten-syllable couplet,—established itself as the classic verse of England, until in the eighteenth century it had b come the ruling form of our poetry. Poetry, or rather the use of verse, entered in a remarkable degree, during that century, into the whole of the daily life of the civilised classes ; and the poetry of the century was a perpetual school of the qualities requisite for a good prose, the qualities of regularity, uniformity, precision, balance. This may have been of no great service to English poetry, although to say that it has been of no service at all, to say that the eighteenth century has in no respect changed the conditions for English poetical style, or that it has changed them for the worse, would be untrue. But it was undeniably of signal service to that which was the great want and work of the hour, English prose.

Do not let us, therefore, hastily despise Johnson and his century for their defective poetry and criticism of poetry. True, Johnson is capable of saying : 'Surely no man could have fancied that he read Lycidas with pleasure had he not known the author ! ' True, he is capable of maintaining that 'the description of the temple in Congreve's " Mourning Bride " was the finest poetical passage he had ever read—he recollected none in Shakspeare equal to it.' But we are to conceive of Johnson and of his century as having a special task committed to them, the establishment of English prose ; and as capable of being warped and narrowed in their judgments of poetry by this exclusive task. Such is the common course and law of progress ; one thing is done at a time, and other things are sacrificed to it. We must be thankful for the thing done, if it is valuable, and we must put up with the temporary sacrifice of other things to this one.—*Preface to Johnson's ' Six Chief Lives.'*

BURKE.

IT is the fashion to treat Burke's writings on the French Revolution as superannuated and proved wrong by the event ; as the eloquent but unphilosophical tirades of bigotry and prejudice. I will not deny that they are often disfigured by the violence and passion of the moment, and that in some directions Burke's view was bounded, and his observation therefore at fault. But on the whole, and for those who can make the needful corrections, what distinguishes these writings is their profound; permanent, fruitful, philosophical truth. They contain the true philosophy of an epoch of concentration, dissipate the heavy atmosphere which its own nature is apt to engender round it, and make its resistance rational instead of mechanical.

But Burke is so great because, almost alone in England, he brings thought to bear upon politics, he saturates politics with thought. It is his accident that his ideas were at the service of an epoch of concentration, not of an epoch of expansion ; it is his characteristic that he so lived by ideas, and had such a source of them welling up within him, that he could float even an epoch of concentration and English Tory politics with them. It does not hurt him that Dr. Price and the Liberals were enraged with him ; it does not even hurt him that George the Third and the Tories were enchanted with him. His greatness is that he lived in a world which neither English Liberalism nor English Toryism is apt to enter ; —the world of ideas, not the world of catchwords and party habits. So far is it from being really true of him that he 'to party gave up what was meant for mankind, that at the very end of his fierce struggle with the French Revolution, after all his invectives against its false pretensions, hollowness, and madness, with his sincere conviction of its mischievousness, he can close a memorandum on the best means of combating it, some of the last pages he ever wrote,—the 'Thoughts on French Affairs,' in December 1791,—with these striking words : ··

' The evil is stated, in my opinion, as it exists. The remedy must be where power, wisdom, and information, I hope, are more united with good intentions than they can be with me. I have done with this subject, I believe, for ever. It has given me many anxious moments for the last two years. *If a great change is to be made in human affairs, the minds of men will be fitted to it ; the general opinions and feelings will draw that way. Every fear, every hope will forward it ; and then they who persist in opposing this mighty current in human affairs, will appear rather to resist the decrees of Providence itself, than the mere designs of men. They will not be resolute and firm, but perverse and obstinate.'*

That return of Burke upon himself has always seemed to me one of the finest things in English literature, or

indeed in any literature. That is what I call living by
ideas : when one side of a question has long had your
earnest support, when all your feelings are engaged, when
you hear all round you no language but one, when your
party talks this language like a steam-engine and can
imagine no other,—still to be able to think, still to be
irresistibly carried, if so it be, by the current of thought
to the opposite side of the question, and, like Balaam, to
be unable to speak anything *but what the Lord has put
in your mouth.* I know nothing more striking, and I must
add that I know nothing more un-English.—*Essays in
Criticism.*

COLERIDGE.

COLERIDGE had less delicacy and penetration than Joubert, but more richness and power ; his production,
though far inferior to what his nature at first seemed to
promise, was abundant and varied. Yet in all his production how much is there to dissatisfy us ! How many
reserves must be made in praising either his poetry, or
his criticism, or his philosophy ! How little either of
his poetry, or of his criticism, or of his philosophy, can
we expect permanently to stand ! But that which will
stand of Coleridge is this : the stimulus of his continual
effort,—not a moral effort, for he had no morals,—but of
his continual instinctive effort, crowned often with rich
success, to get at and to lay bare the real truth of his

matter in hand, whether that matter were literary, or philosophical, or political, or religious ; and this in a country where at that moment such an effort was almost unknown ; where the most powerful minds threw themselves upon poetry, which conveys truth, indeed, but conveys it indirectly ; and where ordinary minds were so habituated to do without thinking altogether, to regard considerations of established routine and practical convenience as paramount, that any attempt to introduce within .the domain of these the disturbing element of thought, they were prompt to resent as an outrage. Coleridge's great usefulness lay in his supplying in England, for many years and under critical circumstances, by the spectacle of this effort of his, a stimulus to all minds capable of profiting by it in the generation which grew up around him. His action will still be felt as long as the need for it continues. When, with the cessation of the need, the action too has ceased, Coleridge's memory, in spite of the disesteem,—nay, repugnance,—which his character may and must inspire, will yet for ever remain invested with that interest and gratitude which invests the memory of founders.—*Essays in Criticism.*

JOUBERT AND JEFFREY.

JOUBERT was not famous while he lived, and he will not be famous now that he is dead. But, before we pity him for this, let us be sure what we mean, in literature, by

famous.   There are the famous men of genius in literature,—the Homers, Dantes, Shakspeares ; of them we
need not speak ; their praise is for ever and ever.   Then
there are the famous men of ability in literature : their
praise is in their own generation.   And what makes this
difference ?   The work of the two orders of men is at
bottom the same,—*a criticism of. life.*   The end and
aim of all literature, if one considers it attentively, is, in
truth, nothing but that.   But the criticism which the men
of genius pass upon human life is permanently acceptable
to mankind ; the criticism which the men of ability pass
upon human life is transitorily acceptable.   Between
Shakspeare's criticism of human life and Scribe's the
difference is there !—the one is permanently acceptable,
the other transitorily.   Whence then, I repeat, this difference ?   It is that the acceptableness of Shakspeare's
criticism depends upon its inherent truth : the acceptableness of Scribe's upon its suiting itself, by its subject-
matter, ideas, mode of treatment, to the taste of the
generation that hears it.   But the taste and ideas of one
generation are not those of the next.   This next generation in its turn arrives ;—first its sharpshooters, its
quick-witted, audacious light troops ; then the elephantine
main body.   The imposing array of its predecessor it
confidently assails, riddles it with bullets, passes over its
body.   It goes hard then with many once popular re-
putations, with many authorities once oracular.   Only

two kinds of authors are safe in the general havoc. The first kind are the great abounding fountains of truth, whose criticism of life is a source of illumination and joy to the whole human race for ever,—the Homers, the Shakspeares. These are the sacred personages, whom all civilised warfare respects. The second are those whom the out-skirmishers of the new generation, its forerunners, —quick-witted soldiers, as I have said, the select of the army,—recognise, though the bulk of their comrades behind might not, as of the same family and character with the sacred personages, exercising like them an immortal function, and like them inspiring a permanent interest. They snatch them up, and set them in a place of shelter, where the on-coming multitude may not overwhelm them. These are the Jouberts. They will never, like the Shakspeares, command the homage of the multitude ; but they are safe ; the multitude will not trample them down. Except these two kinds, no author is safe. Let us consider, for example, Joubert's famous contemporary, Lord Jeffrey. All his vivacity and accomplishment avail him nothing ; of the true critic he had in an eminent degree no quality, except one,—curiosity. Curiosity he had, but he had no gift for truth ; he cannot illuminate and rejoice us ; no intelligent out-skirmisher of the new generation cares about him, cares to put him in safety ; at this moment we are all passing over his body. Let us consider a greater than Jeffrey, a critic whose reputation still stands firm,—will stand, many people think, for ever,—the great apostle of the Philistines, Lord Macaulay. Lord Macaulay was, as I have somewhere said, a born rhetorician ; a splendid rhetorician doubtless, and, beyond that, an *English* rhetorician also, an *honest* rhetorician ; still, beyond the apparent rhetorical truth of things he never could penetrate ; for their vital truth, for what the French call the *vraie vérité*, he had absolutely no organ ; therefore his reputation, brilliant as it is, is not secure. Rhetoric so good as his excites and gives pleasure ; but by pleasure alone you cannot permanently bind men's spirits to you.   Truth illuminates and gives joy, and it is by the bond of joy, not of pleasure, that men's spirits are indissolubly held.   As Lord Macaulay's own generation dies out, as a new generation arrives, without those ideas and tendencies of its predecessor which Lord Macaulay so deeply shared and so happily satisfied, will he give the same pleasure ? and, if he ceases to give this, has he enough of light in him to make him last ?   Pleasure the new generation will get from its own novel ideas and tendencies ; but light is another and a rarer thing, and must be treasured wherever it can be found.   Will Macaulay be saved, in the sweep and pressure of time, for his light's sake, as Johnson has already been saved by two generations, Joubert by one ?   I think it very doubt‑ful.   But, for a spirit of any delicacy and dignity, what a fate, if he could foresee it ! to be an oracle for one generation, and then of little or no account for ever. How far better, to pass with scant notice through one's own generation, but to be singled out and preserved by the very iconoclasts of the next, then in their turn by those of the next, and so, like the lamp of life itself, to be handed on from one generation to another in safety! This is Joubert's lot, and it is a very enviable one. The new men of the new generations, while they let the dust deepen upon a thousand Laharpes, will say of him : ' He lived in the Philistine's day, in a place and time when almost every idea current in literature had the mark of Dagon upon it, and not the mark of the children of light. Nay, the children of light were as yet hardly so much as heard of ; the Canaanite was then in the land. Still, there were even then a few, who, nourished on some secret tradition, or illumined, perhaps, by a divine inspiration, kept aloof from the reigning superstitions, never bowed the knee to the gods of Canaan ; and one of these few was called *Joubert.*'—*Essays in Criticism.*

MIDDLE-CLASS MACAULAYESE.

'You ask me,' said Arminius, 'why I call Mr. Hepworth Dixon's style middle-class Macaulayese. I call it Macaulayese because it has the same internal and external characteristics as Macaulay's style ; the external characteristic being a hard metallic movement with nothing of the soft play of life, and the internal characteristic being a perpetual semblance of hitting the right nail on the head without the reality. And I call it middle-class Macaulayese, because it has these faults without the compensation of great studies and of conversance with great affairs, by which Macaulay partly redeemed them.'—*Friendship's Garland.*

MACAULAY'S PLACE IN CIVILISATION.

HUMAN progress consists in a continual increase in the number of those, who, ceasing to live by the animal life alone and to feel the pleasures of sense only, come to participate in the intellectual life also, and to find enjoyment in the things of the mind. The enjoyment is not at first very discriminating. Rhetoric, brilliant writing, gives to such persons pleasure for its own sake; but it gives them pleasure, still more, when it is employed in commendation of a view of life which is on the whole theirs, and of men and causes with which they are naturally in sympathy. The immense popularity of Macaulay is due to his being pre-eminently fitted to give pleasure to all who are beginning to feel enjoyment in the things of the mind. It is said that the traveller in Australia, visiting one settler's hut after another, finds again and again that the settler's third book, after the Bible and Shakspeare, is some work by Macaulay. Nothing can be more natural. The Bible and Shakspeare may be said to be imposed upon an Englishman as objects of his admiration ; but as soon as the common Englishman, desiring culture, begins to choose for himself, he chooses Macaulay. Macaulay's view of things is, on the whole, the view of them which he feels to be his own also ; the persons and causes praised are those which he himself is disposed to admire ; the persons and causes blamed are those with which he himself is out of sympathy ; and the rhetoric employed to praise or to blame them is animating and excellent. Macaulay is thus a great civiliser. In hundreds of men he hits their nascent taste for the things of the mind, possesses himself of it and stimulates it, draws it powerfully forth and confirms it.

But, with the increasing number of those who awake to the intellectual life, the number of those also increases, who, having awoke to it, go on with it, follow where it leads them. And it leads them to see that it is their business to learn the real truth about the important men, and things, and books, which interest the human mind. For thus is gradually to be acquired a stock of sound ideas, in which the mind will habitually move, and which alone can give to our judgments security and solidity. To be satisfied with fine writing about the object of one's study, with having it praised or blamed in accordance with one's own likes or dislikes, with any conventional treatment of it whatever, is at this stage of growth seen to be futile. At this stage, rhetoric, even when it is so

good as Macaulay's, dissatisfies. And the number of
people who have reached this stage of mental growth is
constantly, as things are now, increasing ; increasing by
the very same law of progress which plants the beginnings
of mental life in more and more persons who, until now,
have never known mental life at all. So that while the
number of those who are delighted with rhetoric such as
Macaulay's is always increasing, the number of those
who are dissatisfied with it is always increasing too.—
Mixed Essays.

GEORGE SAND'S NOVELS.

Even three or four only out of George Sand's many books
might suffice to show her to us, if they were well chosen ;
let us say, the 'Lettres d'un Voyageur,' 'Mauprat,' 'Fran-
çois le Champi,' and a story which I was glad to see Mr.
Myers, in his appreciative notice of Madame Sand, single
out for praise,—'Valvèdre.' In these may be found all
the principal elements of their author's strain : the cry of
agony and revolt, the trust in nature and beauty, the
aspiration towards a purged and renewed human society.

Of George Sand's strain, during forty years, these are
the grand elements.   Now it is one of them which appears
most prominently, now it is another. The cry of agony
and revolt is in her earlier work only, and passes away in
her later. But in the evolution of these three elements,
—the passion of agony and revolt, the consolation from

nature and from beauty, the ideas of social renewal,—in the evolution of these is George Sand and George Sand's life and power. Through their evolution her constant motive declares and unfolds itself, and that motive is this : '*the sentiment of the ideal life, which is none other than man's normal life as we shall one day know it.*' This is the motive, and through these elements is its evolution ; an evolution pursued, moreover, with the most unfailing resolve, the most absolute sincerity.—*Mixed Essays.*

GEORGE SAND.

WHETHER or not the number of George Sand's works,—always fresh, always attractive, but poured out too lavishly and rapidly,—is likely to prove a hindrance to her fame, I do not care to consider. Posterity, alarmed at the rate at which its literary baggage grows upon it, always seeks to throw away as much as it can, as much as it dares,—everything but masterpieces. But the immense vibration of George Sand's voice upon the ear of Europe will not soon die away. Her passions and her errors have been abundantly talked of. She left them behind her, and men's memory of her will leave them behind also. There will remain of her to mankind the sense of benefit and stimulus from the passage upon earth of that large and frank nature, of that large and pure utte.ance,—the *large utterance of the early gods.* There will remain an admiring and ever widening report of that great and ingenuous soul, simple, affectionate, without vanity, without pedantry, human, equitable, patient, kind. She believed herself, she said, 'to be in sympathy, across time and space, with a multitude of honest wills which interrogate their conscience and try to put themselves in accord with it.'   This chain of sympathy will extend more and more.

It is silent, that eloquent voice ! it is sunk, that noble, that speaking head ! we sum up, as we can, what she said to us, and we bid her adieu.   From many hearts in many lands a troop of tender and grateful regrets converge towards her humble churchyard in Berry.   Let them be joined by these words of sad homage from one of a nation which she esteemed, and which knew her very little and very ill.   Her guiding thought, the guiding thought which she did her best to make ours too, 'the sentiment of the ideal life, which is none other than man's normal life as we shall one day know it,' is in harmony with words and promises familiar to that sacred place where she lies.   *Exspectat resurrectionem mortu-orum, et vitam venturi sæculi.—Mixed Essays.*

THE OXFORD MOVEMENT.

OXFORD, the Oxford of the past, has many faults ; and she has heavily paid for them in defeat, in isolation, in want of hold upon the modern world. Yet we in Oxford, brought up amidst the beauty and sweetness of that beautiful place, have not failed to seize one truth :— the truth that beauty and sweetness are essential characters of a complete human perfection. When I insist on this, I am all in the faith and tradition of Oxford. I say boldly that this our sentiment for beauty and sweetness, our sentiment against hideousness and rawness, has been at the bottom of our attachment to so many beaten causes, of our opposition to so many triumphant movements. And the sentiment is true, and has never been wholly defeated, and has shown its power even in its defeat. We have not won our political battles, we have not carried our main points, we have not stopped our adversaries' advance, we have not marched victoriously with the modern world ; but we have told silently upon literature and upon the mind of the country, we have prepared currents of feeling which sap our adversaries' position when it seems gained, we have kept up our own communications with the future. Look at the course of the great movement which shook Oxford to its centre some thirty years ago ! It was directed, as any one who reads Dr. Newman's 'Apology' may see, against what in

one word may be called ‘Liberalism.’ Liberalism prevailed ; it was the appointed force to do the work of the
hour ; it was necessary, it was inevitable that it should
prevail. The Oxford movement was broken, it failed ;
our wrecks are scattered on every shore :—

Quæ regio in terris nostri non plena laboris ?

But what was it, this liberalism, as Dr. Newman saw it,
and as it really broke the Oxford movement ? It was
the great middle-class liberalism, which had for the
cardinal points of its belief the Reform Bill of 1832, and
local self-government, in politics ; in the social sphere,
free-trade, unrestricted competition, and the making of
large industrial fortunes ; in the religious sphere, the
Dissidence of Dissent and the Protestantism of the
Protestant religion. I do not say that other and more
intelligent forces than this were not opposed to the
Oxford movement : but this was the force which really
beat it ; this was the force which Dr. Newman felt himself to be fighting with ; this was the force which till only
the other day seemed to be the paramount force in this
country, and to be in possession of the future ; this was
the force whose achievements fill Mr. Lowe or Mr.
Bright with such inexpressible admiration, and of whose
rule they cry : *Esto perpetua /* And where is this great
force of Philistinism now ? It is thrust into the second
rank, it is become a power of yesterday, it has lost the

future. A new power has made its appearance, a power which it is impossible yet to judge fully, but which is certainly a wholly different force from middle-class liberalism ; different in its cardinal points of belief, different in its tendencies in every sphere. It loves and admires neither the legislation of middle-class Parliaments, nor the local self-government of middle-class vestries, nor the unrestricted competition of middle-class industrialists, nor the dissidence of middle-class Dissent and the Protestantism of middle-class Protestant religion. I am not now praising this new force, or saying that its own ideals are better ; all I say is, that they are wholly different. And who will estimate how much the currents of feeling created by Dr. Newman's movements, the keen desire for beauty and sweetness which it nourished, the deep aversion it manifested to the hardness and vulgarity of middle-class liberalism, the strong light it turned on the hideous and grotesque illusions of middle-class Protestantism,—who will estimate how much all these contributed to swell the tide of secret dissatisfaction which has mined the ground under the self-confident liberalism of the last thirty years, and has prepared the way for its sudden collapse and supersession ? It is, in this manner that the sentiment of Oxford for beauty and sweetness conquers, and in this manner long may it continue to conquer !—*Culture and Anarchy.*

OXFORD.

BEAUTIFUL city,—so venerable, so lovely, so unravaged
by the fierce intellectual life of our century, so serene !

There are our young barbarians, all at play !

And yet, steeped in sentiment as she lies, spreading her
gardens to the moonlight, and whispering from her towers
the last enchantments of the Middle Age, who will deny
that Oxford, by her ineffable charm, keeps ever calling us
nearer to the true goal of all of us, to the ideal, to perfection,—to beauty, in a word, which is only truth seen
from another side ?—nearer, perhaps, than all the science
of Tübingen.　Adorable dreamer, whose heart has been
so romantic ! who hast given thyself so prodigally, given
thyself to sides and to heroes not mine, only never to the
Philistines ! home of lost causes, and forsaken beliefs,
and unpopular names, and impossible loyalties ! what
example could ever so inspire us to keep down the Philistine in ourselves, what teacher could ever so save us
from that bondage to which we are all prone, that bondage
which Goethe, in his incomparable lines on the death of
Schiller, makes it his friend's highest praise (and nobly
did Schiller deserve the praise) to have left miles out of
sight behind him ;—the bondage of ' *was uns alle bändigt,*
DAS GEMEINE ! ' Oxford will forgive me, even if I have
unwittingly drawn upon her a shot or two aimed at her

unworthy son ; for she is generous, and the cause in which I fight is, after all, hers. Apparitions of a day, what is our puny warfare against the Philistines, compared with the warfare which this queen of romance has been waging against them for centuries, and will wage after we are gone ?—*Essays in Criticism.*

A CHAIR OF CELTIC AT OXFORD.

A MAN of exquisite intelligence and charming character, the late Mr. Cobden, used to fancy that a better acquaintance with the United States was the grand panacea for us ; and once in a speech he bewailed the inattention of our seats of learning to them, and seemed to think that if our ingenuous youth at Oxford were taught a little less about the Ilissus, and a little more about Chicago, we should all be the better for it. Chicago has its claims upon us, no doubt ; but it is evident that from the point of view to which I have been leading, a stimulation of our Anglo-Saxonism, such as is intended by Mr. Cobden's proposal, does not appear the thing most needful for us ; seeing our American brothers themselves have rather, like us, to try and moderate the flame of Anglo-Saxonism in their own breasts, than to ask us to clap the bellows to it in ours. So I am inclined to beseech Oxford, instead of expiating her over-addiction to the Ilissus by lectures on Chicago, to give us an expounder for a still more remote-looking object than the Ilissus,—the Celtic languages and literature. And yet why should I call it remote? if, as I have been labouring to show, in the spiritual frame of us English ourselves, a Celtic fibre, little as we may have ever thought of tracing it, lives and works. *Aliens in speech, in religion, in blood!* said Lord Lyndhurst; the philologists have set him right about the speech, the physiologists about the blood; and perhaps, taking religion in the wide but true sense of our whole spiritual activity, of poetry as well as of creed, those who follow the matter out will find that the Celt is not so wholly alien to us in religion.

At this moment, when the narrow Philistinism which has long had things all its own way in England, is showing its natural fruits, and we are beginning to feel ashamed, and uneasy, and alarmed at it; at such a moment, it needs some moderation not to be attacking Philistinism by storm, but to mine it through such gradual means as the slow approaches of culture, and the introduction of chairs of Celtic. But the hard unintelligence, which is just now our bane, cannot be conquered by storm; it must be suppled and reduced by culture, by a growth in the variety, fulness, and sweetness of our spiritual life; and this end can only be reached by studying things that are outside of ourselves, and by studying them disinterestedly. Let us reunite ourselves with our better mind and with the world through science; and let it be one of our angelic revenges on the Philistines, who among their other sins are the guilty authors of Fenianism, to found at Oxford a chair of Celtic, and to send, through the gentle ministration of science, a message of peace to Ireland.—*Study of Celtic Literature.*

ARTHUR HUGH CLOUGH.

How can I help remembering what a mind and character we have lost in losing Mr. Clough, whose name has more than once occurred in my lectures on Homer? He, too, was busy with Homer; but it is not on that account that I now speak of him. Nor do I speak of him in order to call attention to his qualities and powers in general, admirable as these were. I mention him because, in so eminent a degree, he possessed these two invaluable literary qualities : a true sense for his object of study, and a single-hearted care for it. He had both; but he had the second even more eminently than the first. He greatly developed the first through means of the second. In the study of art, poetry, or philosophy, he had the most undivided and disinterested love for his object in itself, the greatest aversion to mixing up with it anything accidental or personal. His interest was in literature itself; and it was this which gave so rare a stamp to his character, which kept him so free from all taint of littleness. In the saturnalia of ignoble personal passions, of which the struggle for literary success, in old and crowded communities, offers so sad a spectacle, he never mingled. He had not yet traduced his friends, nor flattered his enemies, nor disparaged what he admired, nor praised what he despised. Those who knew him well had the conviction that, even with time, these literary arts would never be his. His poem, 'The Bothie of Toper-na-Fuosich,' has some admirable Homeric qualities ;—out-of-doors freshness, life, naturalness, buoyant rapidity. Some of the expressions in that poem,—' *Dangerous Corrievreckan. . . . Where roads are unknown to Loch Nevish,*'—come back now to my ear with the true Homeric ring. But that in him of which I think oftenest, is the Homeric simplicity of his literary life.—*Last Words on Translating Homer.*

II.

POLITICS AND SOCIETY.

THE YOUNG LIONS.

MR. WRIGHT would perhaps be more indulgent to my vivacity, if he considered that we are none of us likely to be lively much longer. My vivacity is but the last sparkle of flame before we are all in the dark, the last glimpse of colour before we all go into drab,—the drab of the earnest, prosaic, practical, austerely literal future. Yes, the world will soon be the Philistines' ! and then, with every voice, not of thunder, silenced, and the whole earth filled and ennobled every morning by the magnificent roaring of the young lions of the 'Daily Telegraph,' we shall all yawn in one another's faces with the dismallest, the most unimpeachable gravity.—*Essays in Criticism.*

BRITISH CONSTITUTION.

WHERE shall we find language innocent enough, how shall we make the spotless purity of our intentions evident enough, to enable us to say to the political Englishman, that the British Constitution itself, which, seen from the practical side, looks such a magnificent organ of progress and virtue, seen from the speculative side,—with its compromises, its love of facts, its horror of theory, its studied avoidance of clear thoughts,—that, seen from this side, our august Constitution sometimes looks,—forgive me, shade of Lord Somers !—a colossal machine for the manufacture of Philistines ?—*Essays in Criticism.*

THE LICENSED VICTUALLERS.

EVERY thing in our political life tends to hide from us that there is anything wiser than our ordinary selves, and to prevent our getting the notion of a paramount right reason. Royalty itself, in its idea the expression of the collective nation, and a sort of constituted witness to its best mind, we try to turn into a kind of grand advertising van, meant to give publicity and credit to the inventions, sound or unsound, of the ordinary self of individuals.

I remember, when I was in North Germany, having this very strongly brought to my mind in the matter of schools and their institution. In Prussia, the best schools are Crown patronage schools, as they are called ; schools which have been established and endowed (and new ones are to this day being established and endowed) by the Sovereign himself out of his own revenues, to be under the direct control and management of him or of those representing him, and to serve as types of what schools should be. The Sovereign, as his position raises him above many prejudices and littlenesses, and as he can always have at his disposal the best advice, has evident advantages over private founders in well planning and directing a school ; while at the same time his great means and his great influence secure, to a well-planned school of his, credit and authority. This is what, in North Germany, the governors do in the matter of education for the governed ; and one may say that they thus give the governed a lesson, and draw out in them the idea of a right reason higher than the suggestions of an ordinary man's ordinary self.

But in England how different is the part which in this matter our governors are accustomed to play ! The Licensed Victuallers or the Commercial Travellers propose to make a school for their children ; and I suppose, in the matter of schools, one may call the Licensed Victuallers or the Commercial Travellers ordinary men, with their natural taste for the bathos still strong ; and a Sovereign with the advice of men like Wilhelm von Humboldt or Schleiermacher may, in this matter, be a better judge, and nearer to right reason. And it will be allowed, probably, that right reason would suggest that, to have a sheer school of Licensed Victuallers' children, or a sheer school of Commercial Travellers' children, and to bring them all up, not only at home but at school too, in a kind of odour of licensed victualism or of bagmanism, is not a wise training to give to these children. And in Germany, I have said, the action of the national guides or governors is to suggest and provide a better.

But, in England, the action of the national guides or governors is, for a Royal Prince or a great Minister to go down to the opening of the Licensed Victuallers' or of the Commercial Travellers' school, to take the chair, to extol the energy and self-reliance of the Licensed Victuallers or the Commercial Travellers, to be all of their way of thinking, to predict full success to their schools, and never so much as to hint to them that they are probably doing a very foolish thing, and that the right way to go to work with their children's education is quite different. And it is the same in almost every department of affairs.— *Culture and Anarchy.*

BARBARIANS, PHILISTINES, POPULACE.

For the middle class, for that great body which, as we know, 'has done all the great things that have been done in all departments,' we have a designation which now has become pretty well known, and which we may as well still keep for them,—the designation of Philistines. What this term means I have so often explained that I need not repeat it here. For the aristocratic class we have as yet got no special designation. Almost all my attention has naturally been concentrated on my own class, the middle class, with which I am in closest sympathy, and which has been, besides, the great power of our day, and has had its praises sung by all speakers and newspapers.

Still, the aristocratic class is so important in itself, and the weighty functions which Mr. Carlyle proposes at the present critical time to commit to it must add so much to its importance, that it seems neglectful, and a strong instance of that want of coherent philosophic method for which Mr. Frederic Harrison blames me, to leave the aristocratic class so much without notice and denomination. It may be thought that the characteristic which I have occasionally mentioned as proper to aristo-cracies,—their natural inaccessibility, as children of the established fact, to ideas,—points to our extending to this class also the designation of Philistines; the Philistine being, as is well known, the enemy of the children of light or servants of the idea. Nevertheless, there seems to be an inconvenience in thus giving one and the same designation to two very different classes; and besides, if we look into the thing closely, we shall find that the term Philistine conveys a sense which makes it more peculiarly appropriate to our middle class than to our aristocratic. For *Philistine* gives the notion of something particularly stiff-necked and perverse in the resistance to light and the children of light, and therein it specially suits our middle class, who not only do not pursue sweetness and light, but who even prefer to them that sort of machinery of business, chapels, tea-meetings, and addresses from Mr. Murphy, which makes up the dismal and illiberal life on which I have so often touched. But the aristocratic class has actually, as we have seen, in its well-known politeness, a kind of image or shadow of sweetness ; and as for light, if it does not pursue light, it is not that it perversely cherishes some dismal and illiberal existence in preference to light, but it is lured off from following light by those mighty and eternal seducers of our race which weave for this class their most irresistible charms,—by worldly splendour, security, power, and pleasure. These seducers are exterior goods, but they are goods ; and he who is hindered by them from caring for light and ideas, is not so much doing what is perverse as what is too natural.

Keeping this in view, I have in my own mind often indulged myself with the fancy of employing, in order to designate our aristocratic class, the name of *The Barbarians*. The Barbarians, to whom we all owe so much, and who reinvigorated and renewed our worn-out Europe, had, as is well known, eminent merits ; and in this country, where we are for the most part sprung from the Barbarians, we have never had the prejudice against them which prevails among the races of Latin origin. The Barbarians brought with them that staunch individualism, as the modern phrase is, and that passion for doing as one likes, for the assertion of personal liberty, which appears to Mr. Bright the central idea of English life, and of which we have, at any rate, a very rich supply. The stronghold and natural seat of this passion was in the nobles of whom our aristocratic class are the inheritors ; and this class, accordingly, have signally manifested it, and have done much by their example to recommend it to the body of the nation, who already, indeed, had it in their blood. The Barbarians, again, had the passion for field-sports ; and they have handed it on to our aristocratic class, who of this passion too, as of the passion for asserting one's personal liberty, are the great natural stronghold. The care of the Barbarians for the body, and for all manly exercises ; the vigour, good looks, and fine complexion which they acquired and perpetuated in their families by these means,—all this may be observed still in our aristocratic class. The chivalry of the Barbarians, with its characteristics of high spirit, choice manners, and distinguished bearing,—what is this but the attractive commencement of the politeness of our aristocratic class? In some Barbarian noble, no doubt, one would have admired, if one could have been then alive to see it, the rudiments of our politest peer. Only, all this culture (to call it by that name) of the Barbarians was an exterior culture mainly. It consisted principally in outward gifts and graces, in looks, manners, accomplishments, prowess. The chief inward gifts which had part in it were the most exterior, so to speak, of inward gifts, those which come nearest to outward ones ; they were courage, a high spirit, self-confidence. Far within, and unawakened, lay a whole range of powers of thought and feeling, to which these interesting productions of nature had, from the circumstances of their life, no access. Making allowances for the difference of the times, surely we can observe precisely the same thing now in our aristocratic class. In general its culture is exterior chiefly ; all the exterior graces and accomplishments, and the more external of the inward virtues, seem to be principally its portion. It now, of course, cannot but be often in contact with those studies by which, from the world of thought and feeling, true culture teaches us to fetch sweetness and light ; but its hold upon these very studies appears remarkably external, and unable to exert any deep power upon its spirit. Therefore the one insufficiency which we noted in the perfect mean of this class was an insufficiency of light. And owing to the same causes, does not a subtle criticism lead us to make, even on the good looks and politeness of our aristocratic class, and of even the most fascinating half of that class, the feminine half, the one qualifying remark, that in these charming gifts there should perhaps be, for ideal perfection, a shade more *soul?*

I often, therefore, when I want to distinguish clearly the aristocratic class from the Philistines proper, or middle class, name the former, in my own mind, *The Barbarians.* And when I go through the country, and see this and that beautiful and imposing seat of theirs crowning the landscape, ' There,' I say to myself, ' is a great fortified post of the Barbarians.'—*Culture and Anarchy.*

AMERICA.

OUR society distributes itself into Barbarians, Philistines, and Populace ; and America is just ourselves, with the Barbarians quite left out, and the Populace nearly.   This leaves the Philistines for the great bulk of the nation ;— a livelier sort of Philistine than ours, and with the pressure and false ideal of our Barbarians taken away, but left all the more to himself and to have his full swing. And as we have found that the strongest and most vital part of English Philistinism was the Puritan and Hebraising middle-class, and that its Hebraising keeps it from culture and totality, so it is notorious that the people of the United States issues from this class, and reproduces its tendencies,—its narrow conception of man's spiritual range and of his one thing needful. From Maine to Florida, and back again, all America Hebraises. Difficult as it is to speak of a people merely from what one reads, yet that, I think, one may without much fear of contradiction say.   I mean, when in the United States any spiritual side in man is wakened to activity, it is generally the religious side, and the religious side in a narrow way.   Social reformers go to Moses or St. Paul for their doctrines, and have no notion there is anywhere else to go to ; earnest young men at schools and universities, instead of conceiving salvation as a harmonious perfection only to be won by unreservedly cultivating many sides in us, conceive of it in the old Puritan fashion, and fling themselves ardently upon it in the old, false ways of this fashion, which we know so well, and such as Mr. Hammond, the American revivalist, has lately at Mr. Spurgeon's Tabernacle been refreshing our memory with.—*Culture and Anarchy.*

AMERICA AND FRANCE.

A RECENT French writer, looking for the good points in the old French nobility, remarks that this at any rate is to be said in their favour : they established a high and charming ideal of social intercourse and manners, for a nation formed to profit by such an ideal, and which has profited by it ever since. And in America, perhaps, we see the disadvantages of having social equality before there has been any such high standard of social life and manners formed.—*Mixed Essays.*

THE ENGLISH GENTLEMAN.

HEAVEN forbid that I should speak in dispraise of that unique and most English class which Mr. Charles Sumner extols,—the large class of gentlemen, not of the landed class or of the nobility, but cultivated and refined. They are a seemly product of the energy and of the power to rise in our race. Without, in general, rank and splendour and wealth and luxury to polish them, they have made their own the high standard of life and manners of an aristocratic and refined class. Not having all the dissipations and distractions of this class, they are much more seriously alive to the power of intellect and knowledge, to the power of beauty. The sense of conduct, too, meets with fewer trials in this class. To some extent, however, their contiguousness to the aristocratic class has now the effect of materialising them, as it does the class of newly enriched people. The most palpable action is on the young amongst them, and on their standard of life and enjoyment. But in general, for this whole class, established facts, the materialism which they see regnant, too much block their mental horizon, and limit the possibilities of things to them. They are deficient in openness and flexibility of mind, in free play of ideas, in faith and ardour. Civilised they are, but they are not much of a civilising force; they are somehow bounded and ineffective.—*Mixed Essays.*

THE ALDERMAN-COLONEL.

EVERY one remembers the virtuous Alderman-Colonel, or Colonel-Alderman, who had to lead his militia through the London streets; how the bystanders gathered to see him pass; how the London roughs, asserting an Englishman's best and most blissful right of doing what he likes, robbed and beat the bystanders; and how the blameless warrior-magistrate refused to let his troops interfere. 'The crowd,' he touchingly said afterwards, 'was mostly composed of fine, healthy, strong men, bent on mischief; if he had allowed his soldiers to interfere, they might have been overpowered, their rifles taken from them and used against them by the mob ; a riot, in fact, might have ensued, and been attended with bloodshed, compared with which the assaults and loss of property that actually occurred would have been as nothing.' Honest and affecting testimony of the English middle class to its own inadequacy for the authoritative part one's admiration would sometimes incline one to assign to it ! 'Who are we,' they say by the voice of their Alderman-Colonel, 'that we should not be overpowered if we attempt to cope with social anarchy, our rifles taken from us and used against us by the mob, and we, perhaps, robbed and beaten ourselves? Or what light have we, beyond a free-born Englishman's impulse to do as he likes, which could justify us in preventing, at the cost of bloodshed, other free-born Englishmen from doing as they like, and robbing and beating us as much as they please?'— *Culture and Anarchy.*

THE ROUGH.

THE rough is just asserting his personal liberty a little, going where he likes, assembling where he likes, bawling as he likes, hustling as he likes. Exactly as the rest of us,—as the country squires in the aristocratic class, as the political dissenters in the middle class,—he has no idea of a *State*, of the nation in its collective and corporate character controlling, as government, the free swing of this or that one of its members in the name of the higher reason of all of them, his own as well as that of others.   He sees the rich, the aristocratic class, in occupation of the executive government ; and so, if he is stopped from making Hyde Park a bear-garden or the streets impassable, he cries out that he is being butchered by the aristocracy.

His apparition is somewhat embarrassing, because too many cooks spoil the broth ; because, while the aristocratic and middle classes have long been doing as they like with great vigour, he has been too undeveloped and submissive hitherto to join in the game ; and now, when he does come, he comes in immense numbers, and is rather raw and rough.   But he does not break many laws, or not many at one time ; and, as our laws were made for very different circumstances from our present (but always with an eye to Englishmen doing as they like), and as the clear letter of the law must be against our Englishman who does as he likes, and not only the spirit of the law and public policy, and as Government must neither have any discretionary power nor act resolutely on its own interpretation of the law if any one disputes it, it is evident our laws give our playful giant, in doing as he likes, considerable advantage.—*Culture and Anarchy.*

REQUISITES FOR CIVILISATION.

I PUT first among the elements in human civilisation the instinct of expansion, because it is the basis which man's whole effort to civilise himself presupposes. General civilisation presupposes this instinct, which is inseparable from human nature ; presupposes its being satisfied, not defeated. The basis being given, we may next enumerate the powers which, upon this basis, contribute to build up human civilisation. They are the power of conduct, the power of intellect and knowledge, the power of beauty, the power of social life and manners. Expansion, conduct, science, beauty, manners,—here are the conditions of civilisation, the claimants which man must satisfy before he can be humanised.—*Mixed Essays.*

THE PILGRIM FATHERS.

MEN of culture and poetry, it will be said, are again and again failing, and failing conspicuously, in the necessary first stage to a harmonious perfection, in the subduing of the great obvious faults of our animality, which it is the glory of the religious organisations to have helped us to subdue. True, they do often so fail. They have often been without the virtues as well as the faults of the Puritan ; it has been one of their dangers that they so felt the Puritan's faults that they too much neglected the practice of his virtues. I will not, however, exculpate them at the Puritan's expense. They have often failed in morality, and morality is indispensable. And they have been punished for their failure, as the Puritan has been rewarded for his performance. They have been punished wherein they erred; but their ideal of beauty, of sweetness and light, and a human nature complete on all its sides, remains the true ideal of perfection still ; just as the Puritan's ideal of perfection remains narrow and inadequate, although for what he did well he has been richly rewarded. Notwithstanding the mighty results of the Pilgrim Fathers' voyage, they and their standard of perfection are rightly judged when we figure to ourselves Shakspeare or Virgil,—souls in whom sweetness and light, and all that in human nature is most humane were eminent,—accompanying them on their voyage, and think what intolerable company Shakspeare and Virgil would have found them ! In the same way let us judge the religious organisations which we see all around us. Do not let us deny the good and the happiness which they have accomplished ; but do not let us fail to see clearly that their idea of human perfection is narrow and inadequate, and that the Dissidence of Dissent and the Protestantism of the Protestant religion will never bring humanity to its true goal. As I said with regard to wealth : Let us look at the life of those who live in it and for it,—so I say with regard to the religious organisations. Look at the life imaged in such a newspaper as the 'Nonconformist,'—a life of jealousy of the Establishment, disputes, tea-meetings, openings of chapels, sermons ; and then think of it as an ideal of a human life completing itself on all sides, and aspiring with all its organs after sweetness, light, and perfection !—*Culture and Anarchy.*

THE PURITAN TYPE.

MEN make crude types and try to impose them, but to no purpose. *L'homme s'agite, Dieu le mène,* says Bossuet. 'There are many devices in a man's heart nevertheless, the counsel of the Eternal, that shall stand. Those who offer us the Puritan type of life offer us a religion not true, the claims of intellect and knowledge not satisfied, the claim of beauty not satisfied, the claim of manners not satisfied. In its strong sense for conduct that life touches truth ; but its other imperfections hinder it from employing even this sense aright. The type mastered our nation for a time. Then came the reaction. The nation said : 'This type, at any rate, is amiss ; we are not going to be all like *that !* ' The type retired into our middle class, and fortified itself there. It seeks to endure, to emerge, to deny its own imperfections, to impose itself again ;—impossible ! If we continue to live, we must outgrow it. The very class in which it is rooted,

our middle class, will have to acknowledge the type's inadequacy, will have to acknowledge the hideousness, the
immense ennui of the life which this type has created,
will have to transform itself thoroughly.—*Mixed Essays.*

PURITANISM AND LIBERTY.

Is it certain that of the good which we admittedly have
in our England of to-day,—the seriousness and the
political liberty,—the Puritans and the Puritan triumph
are the authors? The assumption that they are so is
plausible; it is current;—it pervades, let me observe in
passing, Mr. Green's fascinating History. But is the
assumption sound? When one considers the strength,
the boldness, the self-assertion, the instincts of resistance
and independence in the English nature, it is surely
hazardous to affirm that only by the particular means of
the Puritan struggle and the Puritan triumph could we
have become free in our persons and property. When
we consider the character shown, the signal given, in the
thinking of Thomas More and Shakspeare, of Bacon
and Harvey, how shall we say that only at the price of
Puritanism could England have had free thought? When
we consider the seriousness of Spenser, that ideal Puritan
before the fanatical Puritans and without their faults;
when we consider Spenser's seriousness and pureness, in
their revolt against the moral disorder of the Renascence,
and remember the allies which they had in the native

integrity and piety of the English race, shall we even venture to say that only at the price of Puritanism could we have had seriousness?   Puritanism has been one element in our seriousness ; but it is not the whole of our seriousness, nor the best in it.—*Mixed Essays.*

MR. SMITH.

THE newspapers a short time ago contained an account of the suicide of a Mr. Smith, secretary to some insurance company or other, who, it was said, 'laboured under the apprehension that he would come to poverty, and that he was eternally lost.'   And when I read these words, it occurred to me that the poor man who came to such a mournful end was, in truth, a kind of type,— by the selection of his two grand objects of concern, by their isolation from everything else, and their juxtaposition to one another,—of all the strongest, most respectable, and most representative part of our nation.   'He laboured under the apprehension that he would come to poverty, and that he was eternally lost.'   The whole middle-class have a conception of things,—a conception which makes us call them Philistines,—just like that of this poor man ; though we are seldom, of course, shocked by seeing it take the distressing, violently morbid, and fatal turn, which it took with him.   But how generally, with how many of us, are the main concerns of life limited to these two : the concern for making money, and the concern for saving our souls ! And how entirely does the narrow and mechanical conception of our secular business proceed from a narrow and mechanical conception of our religious business. What havoc do the united conceptions make of our lives !—*Culture and Anarchy.*

OUR COAL.

EVERY one must have observed the strange language current during the late discussions as to the possible failure of our supplies of coal. Our coal, thousands of people were saying, is the real basis of our national greatness ; if our coal runs short, there is an end of the greatness of England. But what *is* greatness ?—culture makes us ask. Greatness is a spiritual condition worthy to excite love, interest, and admiration ; and the outward proof of possessing greatness is, that we excite love, interest, and admiration. If England were swallowed up by the sea to-morrow, which of the two, a hundred years hence, would most excite the love, interest, and admiration of mankind,—would most, therefore, show the evidences of having possessed greatness,—the England of the last twenty years, or the England of Elizabeth, of a time of splendid spiritual effort, but when our coal, and our industrial operations depending on coal, were very little developed ? Well, then, what an unsound habit of mind it must be which makes us talk of things like coal or iron as constituting the greatness of England, and how salutary a friend is culture, bent on seeing things as they are, and thus dissipating delusions of this kind and fixing standards of perfection that are real !—*Culture and Anarchy.*

FREE TRADE.

ALL our fellow-men, in the East of London and elsewhere, we must take along with us in the progress towards perfection, if we ourselves really, as we profess, want to be perfect ; and we must not let the worship of any fetish, any machinery, such as manufactures or population,—which are not, like perfection, absolute goods in themselves, though we think them so,—create for us such a multitude of miserable, sunken, and ignorant human beings, that to carry them all along with us is impossible and perforce they must for the most part be left by us in their degradation and wretchedness. But evidently the conception of free-trade, on which our liberal friends vaunt themselves, and in which they think they have found the secret of national prosperity,—evidently, I say, the mere unfettered pursuit of the production of wealth, and the mere mechanical multiplying, for this end, of manufactures and population, threatens to create for us, if it has not created already, those vast, miserable, unmanageable masses of sunken people, to the existence of which we are, I repeat, absolutely forbidden to reconcile ourselves, in spite of all that the philosophy of the

'Times' and the poetry of Mr. Robert Buchanan may say to persuade us.—*Culture and Anarchy.*

SWEETNESS AND LIGHT.

THE Greek word εὐφυΐα, a finely tempered nature, gives exactly the notion of perfection as culture brings us to conceive it : a harmonious perfection, a perfection in which the characters of beauty and intelligence are both present, which unites 'the two noblest of things,'—as Swift, who of one of the two, at any rate, had himself all too little, most happily calls them in his 'Battle of the Books,' —'the two noblest of things, *sweetness and light.*' The εὐφυής, I say, is the man who tends towards sweetness and light ; the ἀφυής, on the other hand, is our Philistine. The immense spiritual significance of the Greeks is due to their having been inspired with this central and happy idea of the essential character of human perfection ; and Mr. Bright's misconception of culture, as a smattering of Greek and Latin, comes itself, after all, from this wonderful significance of the Greeks having affected the very machinery of our education, and is in itself a kind of homage to it.—*Culture and Anarchy.*

ATHENIAN CULTURE.

A FINE culture is the complement of a high reason, and it is in the conjunction of both with character, with energy, that the ideal for men and nations is to be placed.

It is common to hear remarks on the frequent divorce between culture and character, and to infer from this that culture is a mere varnish, and that character only deserves any serious attention. No error can be more fatal. Culture without character is, no doubt, something frivolous, vain, and weak ; but character without culture is, on the other hand, something raw, blind, and dangerous. The most interesting, the most truly glorious peoples, are those in which the alliance of the two has been effected most successfully, and its result spread most widely. This is why the spectacle of ancient Athens has such profound interest for a rational man ; that it is the spectacle of the culture of a *people.* It is not an aristo-cracy, leavening with its own high spirit the multitude which it wields, but leaving it the unformed multitude still ; it is not a democracy, acute and energetic, but tasteless, narrow-minded, and ignoble ; it is the middle and lower classes in the highest development of their humanity that these classes have yet reached. It was the *many* who relished those arts, who were not satisfied with less than those monuments. In the conversations recorded by Plato, or even by the matter-of-fact Xeno-phon, which for the free yet refined discussion of ideas have set the tone for the whole cultivated world, shop-keepers and tradesmen of Athens mingle as speakers. For any one but a pedant, this is why a handful of Athenians of two thousand years ago are more interesting than the millions of most nations our contemporaries. Surely, if they knew this, those friends of progress, who have confidently pronounced the remains of the ancient world to be so much lumber, and a classical education an aristocratic impertinence, might be inclined to reconsider their sentence.—*Mixed Essays.*

FIRE AND STRENGTH.

IT is not at this moment true, what the majority of people tell us, that the world wants fire and strength more than sweetness and light, and that things are for the most part to be settled first and understood afterwards. How much of our present perplexities and ·confusion this untrue notion has caused already, and is tending still to perpetuate ! Therefore the true business of the friends of culture now is, to dissipate this false notion, to spread the belief in right reason and in a firm intelligible law of things, and to get men to try, in preference to staunchly acting with imperfect knowledge, fo obtain some sounder basis of knowledge on which to act. This is what the friends and lovers of culture have to do, however the believers in action may grow impatient with us for saying so, and may insist on our lending a hand to their practical operations and showing a commendable interest in them.—*Culture and Anarchy.*

ANTI-POLITICS.

IT is our business, as we have seen, to get the present believers in action, and lovers of political talking and doing, to make a return upon their own minds, scrutinise their stock notions and habits much more, value their present talking and doing much less ; in order that, by learning to think more clearly, they may come at last to act less confusedly.   But how shall we persuade our Barbarian to hold lightly to his feudal usages ; how shall we persuade our Nonconformist that his time spent in agitating for the abolition of church-establishments would have been better spent in getting worthier ideas of God and the ordering of the world, or his time spent in battling for voluntaryism in education better spent in learning to value and found a public and national culture ; how shall we persuade, finally, our Alderman-Colonel not to be content with sitting in the hall of judgment or marching at the head of his men of war, without some knowledge how to perform judgment and how to direct men of war,—how, I say, shall we persuade all these of this, if our Alderman-Colonel can say that we want to get his leading-staff and his scales of justice for our own hands ; or the Nonconformist, that we want for ourselves his platform ; or the Barbarian, that we want for ourselves his pre-eminency and function ?   Certainly they will be less slow to believe, as we want them to believe, that the intelligible law of things has in itself something desirable and precious, and that all place, function, and bustle are hollow goods without it, if they see that we ourselves can content ourselves with this law and find in it our satisfaction, without making it an instrument to give us for ourselves place, function, and bustle.

At this exciting juncture, then, while so many of the lovers of new ideas, somewhat weary, as we too are, of the stock performances of our Liberal friends upon the political stage, are disposed to rush valiantly upon this public stage themselves, we cannot at all think that for a wise lover of new ideas this stage is the fitting place. Plenty of people there will be without us,—country gentlemen in search of a club, demagogues in search of a tub, lawyers in search of a post, industrialists in search of gentility,—who will come from the east and from the west, and will sit down at that Thyestean banquet of clap-trap which English public life for these many years past has been. So long as those old organisations, of which we have seen the insufficiency,—those expressions of our ordinary self, Barbarian or Philistine,—have force anywhere, they will have force in Parliament. There the man whom the Barbarians send, cannot but be impelled to please the Barbarians' ordinary self, and their natural taste for the bathos; and the man whom the Philistines send cannot but be impelled to please those of the Philistines. But through the length and breadth of our nation a sense, —vague and obscure as yet,—of weariness with the old organisations, of desire for their transformation, works and grows. In the House of Commons the old organisations must inevitably, as I have already urged, be most enduring and strongest, the transformation must inevitably be longest in showing itself; and it may truly be averred, therefore, that at the present juncture the centre of movement is not in the House of Commons. It is in the fermenting mind of the nation; and his is for the next twenty years the real influence who can address himself to this.

Every one is now boasting of what he has done to educate men's minds and to give things the course they are taking. Mr. Disraeli educates, Mr. Bright educates, Mr. Beales educates. We, indeed, pretend to educate no one, for we are still engaged in trying to clear and educate ourselves. But we are sure that the endeavour to reach, through culture, the firm intelligible law of things, we are sure that the detaching ourselves from our stock notions and habits, that a more free play of consciousness, an increased desire for sweetness and light, and all the bent which we call Hellenising, is the master-impulse even now of the life of our nation and of humanity,—somewhat obscurely perhaps for this actual moment, but decisively and certainly for the immediate future; and that those who work for this are the sovereign educators. Docile echoes of the eternal voice, pliant organs of the infinite will, such workers are going along with the essential movement of the world ; and this is their strength, and their happy and divine fortune.— *Culture and Anarchy.*

THE SPOTTED DOG.

THE old recipe, to think a little more. and bustle a little less, seems to me still the best recipe to follow. So I take comfort when I find the 'Guardian' reproaching me with having no influence ; for I know what influence means,—a party, practical proposals, action ; and I say to myself: 'Even supposing I could get some followers, and assemble them, brimming with affectionate enthusiasm, in a committee-room at some inn ; what on earth should I say to them ? what resolutions could I propose ? I could only propose the old Socratic commonplace, *Know thyself;* and how black they would all look at that !' No ; to inquire, perhaps too curiously, what that present state of English development and civilisation is, which according to Mr. Lowe is so perfect that to give votes to the working class is stark madness ; and, on the other hand, to be less sanguine about the divine and saving effect of a vote on its possessor than my friends in the committee-room at the 'Spotted Dog,'— that is my inevitable portion. To bring things under the light of one's intelligence, to see how they look there, to accustom oneself simply to regard the Marylebone Vestry, or the Educational Home, or our Divorce Court, or our gin-palaces open on Sunday and the Crystal Palace shut, as absurdities,—that is, I am sure, invaluable exercise for us just at present.   Let all persist in it who can, and steadily set their desires on introducing, with time, a little more soul and spirit into the too, too solid flesh of English society.—*Friendship's Garland.*

YOUNG LIBERALS.

BECAUSE machinery is the one concern of our actual politics, and an inward working, and not machinery, is what we most want, we keep advising our ardent young Liberal friends to think less of machinery, to stand more aloof from the arena of politics at present, and rather to try and promote, with us, an inward working.   They do not listen to us, and they rush into the arena of politics, where their merits, indeed, seem to be little appreciated as yet; and then they complain of the reformed constituencies, and call the new Parliament a Philistine Parliament.   As if a nation, nourished and reared as ours has been, could give us, just yet, anything but a Philistine Parliament !—and would a Barbarian Parliament be even so good, or a Populace Parliament ?   For our part, we rejoice to see our dear old friends, the Hebraising Philistines, gathered in force in the Valley of Jehoshaphat previous to their final conversion, which will certainly come. But, to attain this conversion, we must not try to oust them from their places and to contend for machinery with them ; no, we must work on them inwardly and cure their spirit. Ousted they will not be, but transformed. Ousted they do not deserve to be, and will not be.—*Culture and Anarchy.*

HUMANE INDIVIDUALS.

IN each class there are born a certain number of natures with a curiosity about their best self, with a bent for seeing things as they are, for disentangling themselves from machinery, for simply concerning themselves with reason and the will of God, and doing their best to make these prevail ;—for the pursuit, in a word, of perfection. To certain manifestations of this love for perfection mankind have accustomed themselves to give the name of genius ; implying by this name, something original and heaven-bestowed in the passion. But the passion is to be found far beyond those manifestations of it to which the world usually gives the name of genius, and in which there is, for the most part, a *talent* of some kind or other, a special and striking faculty of execution informed by the heaven-bestowed ardour, or genius. It is to be found in many manifestations besides these, and may best be called, as we have called it, the love and pursuit of perfection ; culture being the true nurse of the pursuing love, and sweetness and light the true characters of the pursued perfection. Natures with this bent emerge in all classes,

—among the Barbarians, among the Philistines, among the Populace. And this bent always tends to take them out of their class, and to make their distinguishing characteristic not their Barbarianism or their Philistinism, but their *humanity*. They have, in general, a rough time of it in their lives ; but they are sown more abundantly than one might think, they appear where and when one least expects it, they set up a fire which enfilades, so to speak, the class with which they are ranked ; and, in general, by the extrication of their best self as the self to develope, and by the simplicity of the ends fixed by them as paramount, they hinder the unchecked predominance of that class-life which is the affirmation of our ordinary self, and seasonably disconcert mankind in their worship of machinery.

Therefore, when we speak of ourselves as divided into Barbarians, Philistines, and Populace, we must be understood always to imply that within each of these classes there are a certain number of *aliens*, if we may so call them,—persons who are mainly led, not by their class spirit, but by a general *humane* spirit, by the love of human perfection ; and that this number is capable of being diminished or augmented.—*Culture and Anarchy.*

THE GREATEST HAPPINESS OF THE GREATEST NUMBER.

THE well-being of the many comes out more and more distinctly, in proportion as time goes on, as the object we must pursue. An individual or a class, concentrating their efforts upon their own well-being exclusively, do but beget troubles both for others and for themselves also. No individual life can be truly prosperous, passed, as Obermann says, in the midst of men who suffer ; *passée au milieu des générations qui souffrent.* To the noble soul, it cannot be happy ; to the ignoble, it cannot be secure. Socialistic and communistic schemes have generally, however, a fatal defect; they are content with too low and material a standard of well-being. That instinct of perfection, which is the master-power in humanity, always rebels at this, and frustrates the work. Many are to be made partakers of well-being, true ; but the ideal of well-being is not to be, on that account, lowered and coarsened. —*Mixed Essays.*

THE SOCIAL IDEA.

CULTURE looks beyond machinery, culture hates hatred ; culture has one great passion, the passion for sweetness and light. It has one even yet greater !—the passion for making them *prevail.* It is not satisfied till we *all* come to a perfect man ; it knows that the sweetness and light of the few must be imperfect until the raw and unkindled masses of humanity are touched with sweetness and light. If I have not shrunk from saying that we must work for sweetness and light, so neither have I shrunk from saying that we must have a broad basis, must have sweetness and light for as many as possible. Again and again I have insisted how those are the happy moments of humanity, how those are the marking epochs of a people's life, how those are the flowering times for literature and art and all the creative power of genius, when there is a *national* glow of life and thought, when the whole of society is in the fullest measure permeated by thought, sensible to beauty, intelligent and alive. Only it must be *real* thought and *real* beauty ; *real* sweetness and *real* light. Plenty of people will try to give the masses, as they call them, an intellectual food prepared and adapted in the way they think proper for the actual condition of the masses. The ordinary popular literature is an example of this way of working on the masses. Plenty of people will try to indoctrinate the masses with the set of ideas and judgments constituting the creed of their own profession or party. Our religious and political organisations give an example of this way of working on the masses. I condemn neither way ; but culture works differently. It does not try to teach down to the level of inferior classes; it does not try to win them for this or that sect of its own, with ready-made judgments and watch-words.

It seeks to do away with classes and sects; to make the best that has been thought and known in the world current everywhere; to make all men live in an atmosphere of sweetness and light, where they may use ideas, as it uses them itself, freely,—nourished, and not bound by them.

This is the *social idea*; and the men of culture are the true apostles of equality.—*Culture and Anarchy.*

CULTURE.

THE poor require culture as much as the rich; and at present their education, even when they get education, gives them hardly anything of it. Yet hardly less of it, perhaps, than the education of the rich gives to the rich. For when we say that culture is : *To know the best that has been thought and said in the world*, we imply that, for culture, a system directly tending to this end is necessary in our reading. Now, there is no such system yet present to guide the reading of the rich, any more than of the poor. Such a system is hardly even thought of ; a man who wants it must make it for himself. And our reading being so without purpose as it is, nothing can be truer than what Butler says, that really, in general, no part of our time is more idly spent than the time spent in reading.

Still, culture is indispensably necessary, and culture implies reading ; but reading with a purpose to guide it, and with system. He does a good work who does anything to help this ; indeed, it is the one essential service now to be rendered to education.   And the plea, that this or that man has no time for culture, will vanish as soon as we desire culture so much that we begin to examine seriously our present use of our time.   It has often been said, and cannot be said too often : Give to any man all the time that he now wastes, not only on his vices (when he has them), but on useless business, wearisome or deteriorating amusements, trivial letter-writing, random reading ; and he will have plenty of time for culture. ' *Die Zeit ist unendlich lang,*' says Goethe ; and so it really is.   Some of us waste all of it, most of us waste much, but all of us waste some.—*Literature and Dogma.*

LETTERS AND THE MASSES.

I AM persuaded that the transformation of religion, which is essential for its perpetuance, can be accomplished only by carrying the qualities of flexibility, perceptiveness, and judgment, which are the best fruits of letters, to whole classes of the community which now know next to nothing of them, and by procuring the application of those qualities to matters where they are never applied now.—*Last Essays.*

PRIESTHOODS AND ARISTOCRACIES.

THE proud day of priesthoods and aristocracies is over; but in their day they have undoubtedly been, as the law was to the Jews, schoolmasters to the nations of Europe, schoolmasters to bring them to modern society ;—and so dull a learner is man, so rugged and hard to teach, that perhaps those nations which keep their schoolmasters longest are the most enviable. The great ecclesiastical institutions of Europe, with their stately cathedrals, their imposing ceremonial, their affecting services ; the great aristocracies of Europe, with their lustre of descent, their splendour of wealth, their reputation for grace and refinement,—have undoubtedly for centuries served as ideals to ennoble and elevate the sentiment of the European masses. Assuredly, churches and aristocracies often lacked the sanctity or the refinement ascribed to them. But their effect as distant ideals was still the same ; they remained above the individual, a beacon to the imagination of thousands ; they stood, lofty and grand objects, ever present before the eyes of masses of men in whose daily avocations there was little which was lofty, little which was grand ; and they preserved these masses from any danger of over-rating with vulgar self-satisfaction an inferior culture, however broadly sown, by the exhibition of a standard of dignity and refinement still far above them.—*Popular Education in France.*

GOOD OF ARISTOCRACY.

ONE strong and beneficial influence a vigorous and high-minded aristocracy is calculated to exert upon a robust and sound people. I have had occasion, in speaking of Homer, to say very often, and with much emphasis, that he is *in the grand style.* It is the chief virtue of a healthy and uncorrupted aristocracy, that it is, in general, in this grand style. That elevation of character, that noble way of thinking and behaving, which is an eminent gift of nature to some individuals, is also often generated in whole classes of men (at least when these come of a strong and good race) by the possession of power, by the importance and responsibility of high station, by habitual dealing with great things, by being placed above the necessity of constantly struggling for little things. And it is the source of great virtues. It may go along with a not very quick or open intelligence ; but it cannot well go along with a conduct vulgar and ignoble. A governing class imbued with it may not be capable of intelligently leading the masses of a people to the highest pitch of welfare for them ; but it sets them an invaluable example of qualities without which no really high welfare can exist. This has been done for their nation by the best aristocracies. The Roman aristocracy did it; the English aristocracy has done it. They each fostered in the mass of the peoples they governed,—peoples of sturdy moral constitution and apt to learn such lessons,—a greatness of spirit, the natural growth of the condition of magnates and rulers, but not the natural growth of the condition of the common people. They made, the one of the Roman, the other of the English people, in spite of all the shortcomings of each, great peoples, peoples *in the grand style.* And this they did, while wielding the people according to their own notions, and in the direction which seemed good to them ; not as servants and instruments of the people, but as its commanders and heads ; solicitous for the good of their country, indeed, but taking for granted that of that good they themselves were the supreme judges, and were to fix the conditions.—*Mixed Essays.*

WEAK SIDE OF ARISTOCRACY.

IT is because aristocracies almost inevitably fail to appreciate justly, or even to take into their mind, the instinct pushing the masses towards expansion and fuller life, that they lose their hold over them. It is the old story of the incapacity of aristocracies for ideas,—the secret of their want of success in modern epochs. The people treats them with flagrant injustice, when it denies all obligation to them. They can, and often do, impart a high spirit, a fine idea, of grandeur, to the people ; thus they lay the foundations of a great nation. But they leave the people still the multitude, the crowd ; they have small belief in the power of the ideas which are its life. Themselves a power reposing on all which is most solid, material, and visible, they are slow to attach any great importance to influences impalpable, spiritual, and viewless. Although, therefore, a disinterested looker-on might often be dis-

posed, seeing what has actually been achieved by aristocracies, to wish to retain or replace them in their pre-
ponderance, rather than commit a nation to the hazards
of a new and untried future ; yet the masses instinctively
feel that they can never consent to this without re-
nouncing the inmost impulse of their being ; and that
they should make such a renunciation cannot seriously
be expected of them.   Except on conditions which make
its expansion, in the sense understood by itself, fully
possible, democracy will never frankly ally itself with
aristocracy ; and on these conditions perhaps no aristocracy will ever frankly ally itself with it.   Even the English aristocracy, so politic, so capable of compromises,
has shown no signs of being able so to transform itself as
to render such an alliance possible.   The reception given
by the Peers to the bill for establishing life-peerages was,
in this respect, of ill omen.   The separation between
aristocracy and democracy will probably, therefore, go on
still widening.

And it must in fairness be added, that as in one most
important part of general human culture,—openness to
ideas and ardour for them,—aristocracy is less advanced
than democracy, to replace or keep the latter under the
tutelage of the former would on the whole be actually
unfavourable to the progress of the world.   At epochs
when new ideas are powerfully fermenting in a society,
and profoundly changing its spirit, aristocracies, as they

are in general not long suffered to guide it without question, so are they by nature not well fitted to guide it
intelligently.—*Mixed Essays.*

ARISTOCRACIES IN EPOCHS OF EXPANSION.

ARISTOCRACIES, those children of the established fact,
are for epochs of concentration. In epochs of expansion,
epochs such as that in which we now live, epochs when
always the warning voice is again heard, *Now is the
judgment of this world,*—in such epochs aristocracies
with their natural clinging to the established fact, their
want of sense for the flux of things, for the inevitable
transitoriness of all human institutions, are bewildered
and helpless. Their serenity, their high spirit, their
power of haughty resistance,—the great qualities of an
aristocracy, and the secret of its distinguished manners
and dignity,—these very qualities, in an epoch of ex-.
pansion, turn against their possessors. Again and again
I have said how the refinement of an aristocracy may
be precious and educative to a raw nation as a kind of
shadow of true refinement ; how its serenity and dignified freedom from petty cares may serve as a useful
foil to set off the vulgarity and hideousness of that type
of life which a hard middle class tends to establish, and
to help people to see this vulgarity and hideousness in
their true colours. But the true grace and serenity is that
of which Greece and Greek art suggest the admirable

ideals of perfection,—a serenity which comes from having made order among ideas and harmonised them ; whereas the serenity of aristocracies, at least the peculiar serenity of aristocracies of Teutonic origin, appears to come from their never having had any ideas to trouble them. And so, in a time of expansion like the present, a time for ideas, one gets, perhaps, in regarding an aristocracy, even more than the idea of serenity, the idea of futility and sterility.

One has often wondered whether upon the whole earth there is anything so unintelligent, so unapt to perceive how the world is really going, as an ordinary young Englishman of our upper class. Ideas he has not, and neither has he that seriousness of our middle class, which is, as I have often said, the great strength of this class, and may become its salvation. Why, a man may hear a young Dives of the aristocratic class, when the whim takes him to sing the praises of wealth and material comfort, sing them with a cynicism from which the conscience of the veriest Philistine of our industrial middle class would recoil in affright. And when, with the natural sympathy of aristocracies for firm dealing with the multitude, and his uneasiness at our feeble dealing with it at home, an unvarnished young Englishman of our aristocratic class applauds the absolute rulers on the Continent, he in general manages completely to miss the grounds of reason and intelligence which alone can give any colour of justification, any possibility of existence, to those rulers, and applauds them on grounds which it would make their own hair stand on end to listen to.—*Culture and Anarchy.*

DEMOCRATIC EQUALITY.

FOR its seeking after equality, democracy is often, in this country above all, vehemently and scornfully blamed ; its temper contrasted with that worthier temper which can magnanimously endure social distinctions ; its operations all referred, as of course, to the stirrings of a base and malignant envy. No doubt there is a gross and vulgar spirit of envy, prompting the hearts of many of those who cry for equality. No doubt there are ignoble natures which prefer equality to liberty. But what we have to ask is, when the life of democracy is admitted as something natural and inevitable, whether this or that product of democracy is a necessary growth from its parent stock, or merely an excrescence upon it. If it be the latter, certainly it may be due to the meanest and most culpable passions. But if it be the former, then this product, however base and blameworthy the passions which it may sometimes be made to serve, can in itself be no more reprchensible than the vital impulse of democracy is in itself reprehensible ; and this impulse is, as has been shown, identical with the ceaseless vital effort of human nature itself.

Now, can it be denied, that a certain approach to equality, at any rate a certain reduction of signal inequalities, is a natural, instinctive demand of that impulse which drives society as a whole,—no longer individuals and limited classes only, but the mass of a community,—to develope itself with the utmost possible fulness and freedom? Can it be denied, that to live in a society of equals tends in general to make a man's spirits expand, and his faculties work easily and actively; while, to live in a society of superiors, although it may occasionally be a very good discipline, yet in general tends to tame the spirits and to make the play of the faculties less secure and active? Can it be denied, that to be heavily overshadowed, to be profoundly insignificant, has, on the whole, a depressing and benumbing effect on the character? I know that some individuals react against the strongest impediments, and owe success and greatness to the efforts which they are thus forced to make. But the question is not about individuals. The question is about the common bulk of mankind, persons without extraordinary gifts or exceptional energy, and who will ever require, in order to make the best of themselves, encouragement and directly favouring circumstances. Can any one deny, that for these the spectacle, when they would rise, of a condition of splendour, grandeur, and culture, which they cannot possibly reach, has the effect of making them flag in spirit, and of disposing them to sink despondingly back into their own condition? Can any one deny, that the knowledge how poor and insignificant the best condition of improvement and culture attainable by them must be esteemed by a class incomparably richer-endowed, tends to cheapen this modest possible amelioration in the account of those classes also for whom it would be relatively a real progress, and to disen chant their imaginations with it? It seems to me impossible to deny this. And therefore a philosophic observer,[1] with no love for democracy, but rather with a terror of it, has been constrained to remark, that 'the common people is more uncivilised in aristocratic countries than in any others ;' because there 'the lowly and the poor feel themselves, as it were, overwhelmed with the weight of their own inferiority.' He has been con strained to remark,[2] that 'there is such a thing as a manly and legitimate passion for equality, prompting men to desire to be, *all* of them, in the enjoyment of power and consideration.' And, in France, that very equality, which is by us so impetuously decried, while it has by no means

---

[1] M. de Tocqueville. See his *Démocratie en Amérique* (edit. of 1835), vol. i, p. 11. 'Le peuple est plus grossier dans les pays aristocratiques que partout ailleurs. Dans ces lieux, où se rencontrent des hommes si forts et si riches, les faibles et les pauvres se sentent comme accablés de leur bassesse ; ne découvrant aucun point par lequel ils puissent regagner l'égalité, ils désespèrent entièrement d'eux-mêmes, et se laissent tomber au-dessous de la dignité humaine.'

[2] *Démocratie en Amérique*, vol. i, p. 60.

improved (it is said) the upper classes of French society, has undoubtedly given to the lower classes, to the body of the common people, a self-respect, an enlargement of spirit, a consciousness of counting for something in their country's action, which has raised them in the scale of humanity. The common people, in France, seems to me the soundest part of the French nation. They seem to me more free from the two opposite degradations of multitudes, brutality and servility, to have a more developed human life, more of what distinguishes elsewhere the cultured classes from the vulgar, than the common people in any other country with which I am acquainted.— *Mixed Essays.*

FRUITS OF INEQUALITY.

SURELY it is easy to see that the shortcomings in our English civilisation are due to our inequality ; or, in other words, that the great inequality of classes and property, which came to us from the Middle Age and which we maintain because we have the religion of inequality,—that this constitution of things, I say, has the natural and necessary effect, under present circumstances, of materialising our upper class, vulgarising our middle class, and brutalising our lower class. And this is to fail in civilisation.—*Mixed Essays.*

ARMINIUS ON THE MIDDLE-CLASS ERA.

'THE era of aristocracies is over,' said Arminius; 'nations must now stand or fall by the intelligence of their middle class and their people. The people with you is still an embryo; no one can yet quite say what it will come to. You lean, therefore, with your whole weight upon the intelligence of your middle class. And intelligence, in the true sense of the word, your middle class has absolutely none.'—*Friendship's Garland.*

OUR MIDDLE-CLASS EDUCATION.

NEITHER is the secondary and superior instruction given in England so good on the whole, if we regard the whole number of those to whom it is due, as that given in Germany or France, nor is it given in schools of so good a standing. Of course, what good instruction there is, and what schools of good standing there are to get it in, fall chiefly to the lot of the upper class. It is on the middle class that the injury, such as it is, of getting inferior instruction, and of getting it in schools of inferior standing, mainly comes. This injury, as it strikes one after seeing attentively the schools of the Continent, has two aspects. It has a social aspect, and it has an intellectual aspect.

The social injury is this. On the Continent the upper and middle class are brought up on one and the same plane. In England the middle class, as a rule, *is brought*

up on the second plane.   One hears many discussions as
to the limits between the middle and the upper class in
England.   From a social and educational point of view
these limits are perfectly clear.   Ten or a dozen famous
schools, Oxford or Cambridge, the church or the bar, the
army or navy, and those posts in the public service supposed to be posts for gentlemen,—these are the lines of
training, all or any of which give a cast of ideas, a stamp
or habit, which make a sort of association of all those
who share them ; and this association is the upper class.
Except by one of these modes of access, an Englishman
does not, unless by some special play of aptitude or of
circumstances, become a vital part of this association, for
he does not bring with him the cast of ideas in which its
bond of union lies.   This cast of ideas is naturally in the
main that of the most powerful and prominent part of
the association,—the aristocracy.   The professions furnish
the more numerous but the less prominent part ; in no
country, accordingly, do the professions so naturally and
generally share the cast of ideas of the aristocracy as in
England.   Judged from its bad side, this cast of ideas is
characterised by over-reverence for things established, by
an estrangement from the powers of reason and science.
Judged from its good side, it is characterised by a high
spirit, by dignity, by a just sense of the greatness of great
affairs,—all of them governing qualities ; and the professions have accordingly long recruited the governing

force of the aristocracy, and assisted it to rule. But they are separate, to a degree unknown on the Continent, from the commercial and industrial classes with which in social standing they are naturally on a level. So we have amongst us the spectacle of a middle class cut in two in a way unexampled anywhere else ; of a professional class brought up on the first plane, with fine and governing qualities, but disinclined to rely on reason and science ; while that immense business class, which is becoming so important a power in all countries, on which the future so much depends, and which in the great public schools of other countries fills so large a place, is in England brought up on the second plane, cut off from the aristocracy and the professions, and without governing qualities.

If only, in compensation, it had science, systematic knowledge, reason ! But here comes in the intellectual mischief of the bad condition of the mass of our secondary schools. In England the business class is not only inferior to the professions and aristocracy in the social stamp of its places of training ; it is actually inferior to them, maimed and incomplete as their development of reason is, in its development of reason. Short as the off-spring of our public schools and universities come of the idea of science and systematic knowledge, the offspring of our middle-class academies probably come, if that be possible, even shorter. What these academies fail to give

in social and governing qualities, they do not make up
for in intellectual power. Their intellectual result is as
faulty as their social result.

If this be true, then that our middle class does not
yet itself see the defects of its own education, is not conscious of the injury to itself from them, and is satisfied
with things as they are, is no reason for regarding this
state of things without disquietude.—*Schools and Universities on the Continent.*

PARIS AND LONDON.

WHAT makes me look at France and the French with
such inexhaustible curiosity and indulgence is this,—their
faults are not of the same kind as ours, so we are not likely
to catch them ; their merits are not of the same kind as
ours, so we are not likely to become idle and self-sufficient
from studying them.   It is not that I so envy my Orleanist
critic, ' Horace,' his Paris as it is ;—I no longer dance,
nor look well when dressed up as the angel Gabriel, so
what should I now do in Paris?—but I find such interest and instruction in considering a city so near
London, and yet so unlike it !   It is not that I so envy
' Horace ' his café-haunting, dominoes-playing *bourgeois* ;
but when I go through Saint Pancras, I like to compare
our vestry-haunting, resolution-passing *bourgeois* with the
Frenchman, and to say to myself : ' This, then, is what
comes of not frequenting cafés nor playing dominoes !

My countrymen here have got no cafés, and have never learnt dominoes, and see the mischief Satan has found for their idle hands to do!' Still, I do not wish them to be the café-haunting, dominoes-playing Frenchmen, but rather some third thing, neither the Frenchmen nor their present selves.—*Friendship's Garland.*

DEMANDS ON LIFE.

IF we consider the beauty and the ever-advancing perfection of Paris,—nay, and the same holds good, in its degree, of all the other great French cities also,—if we consider the theatre there, if we consider the pleasures, recreations, even the eating and drinking, if we consider the whole range of resources for instruction and for delight and for the conveniences of a humane life generally, and if we then think of London, and Liverpool, and Glasgow, and of the life of English towns generally, we shall find that the advantage of France arises from its immense middle class making the same sort of demands upon life which only a comparatively small upper class makes amongst ourselves.

Delicate and gifted single natures are sown in all countries. The French aristocracy will not bear a moment's comparison for splendour and importance with ours, neither have the French our exceptional class, registered by Mr. Charles Sumner, of gentlemen. But these are, after all, only two relatively small divisions broken off from the top of that whole great class which does not live by the labour of its hands. These small divisions make upon life the demands of humane and civilised men. But they are too small and too weak to create a civilisation, to make a Paris. The great bulk of the class from which they are broken off makes, as is well known, no such demands upon life. London, Liverpool, and Glasgow, with their kind of building, physiognomy and effects, with their theatres, pleasures, recreations, and resources in general of delight and convenience for a humane life, are the result. But in France the whole middle class makes, I say, upon life the demands of civilised men, and this immense demand creates the civilisation we see. And the joy of this civilisation creates the passionate delight and pride in France which we find in Frenchmen. Life is so good and agreeable a thing there, and for so many.—*Mixed Essays.*

FRENCH REVOLUTION.

THAT a whole nation should have been penetrated with an enthusiasm for pure reason, and with an ardent zeal for making its prescriptions triumph, is a very remarkable thing, when we consider how little of mind, or of anything so worthy and quickening as mind, comes into the motives which alone, in general, impel great masses of men. In spite of the extravagant direction given to this enthusiasm, in spite of the crimes and follies in which it lost itself, the French Revolution derives from the force, truth, and universality of the ideas which it took for its law, and from the passion with which it could inspire a multitude for these ideas, a unique and still living power ; it is,—it will probably long remain,—the greatest, the most animating event in history. And, as no sincere passion for the things of the mind, even though it turn out in many respects an unfortunate passion, is ever quite thrown away and quite barren of good, France has reaped from hers one fruit,—the natural and legitimate fruit, though not precisely the grand fruit she expected : she is the country in Europe where *the people* is most alive.— *Essays in Criticism.*

ENGLAND AND THE CELTS.

THERE is nothing like love and admiration for bringing people to a likeness with what they love and admire ; but the Englishman seems never to dream of employing these influences upon a race he wants to fuse with him- self. He employs simply material interests for his work of fusion ; and, beyond these, nothing except scorn and rebuke. Accordingly there is no vital union between him and the races he has annexed ; and while France can truly boast of her 'magnificent unity,' a unity of spirit no less than of name between all the people who compose her, in our country the Englishman proper is in union of spirit with no one except other Englishmen proper like himself. His Welsh and Irish fellow-citizens are hardly more amalgamated with him now than they were when Wales and Ireland were first conquered, and the true unity of even these small islands has yet to be achieved. When my lucubrations on the Celtic genius and literature first appeared in the 'Cornhill Magazine,' they brought me, as was natural, many communications from Welshmen and Irishmen having an interest in the subject ; and one could not but be painfully struck, in reading these communications, to see how profound a feeling of aversion and severance from the English they in general manifested. Who can be surprised at it, when he observes the strain of the 'Times' in commenting on a Welsh Eisteddfod, and remembers that this is the characteristic strain of the Englishman in commenting on whatsoever is not himself? And then, with our boundless faith in machinery, we English expect the Welshman as a matter of course to grow attached to us, because we invite him to do business with us, and let him hold any number of public meetings and publish all the newspapers he likes ! When shall we learn, that what attaches people to us is the spirit we are of, and not the machinery we employ ?—*Study of Celtic Literature.*

ENGLAND AND IRELAND.

OUR nation is not deficient in self-esteem, and certainly there is much in our achievements and prospects to give us satisfaction. But even to the most self-satisfied Englishman, Ireland must be an occasion, one would think, from time to time of mortifying thoughts. We may be conscious of nothing but the best intentions towards Ireland, the justest dealings with her. But how little she seems to appreciate them ! We may talk, with the 'Daily Telegraph,' of our 'great and genial policy of conciliation' towards Ireland ; we may say, with Mr. Lowe, that by their Irish policy in 1868 the Liberal Ministry, of whom he was one, 'resolved to knit the hearts of the empire into one harmonious concord, and knitted they were accordingly.' Only, unfortunately, the Irish themselves do not see the matter as we do. All that by our genial policy we seem to have succeeded in inspiring in the Irish themselves is an aversion to us so violent, that for England to incline one way is a sufficient reason to make Ireland incline another ; and the obstruction offered by the Irish members in Parliament is really an expression, above all, of this uncontrollable antipathy. Nothing is more honourable to French civilisation than its success in attaching strongly to France,—France Catholic and Celtic,—the German and Protestant Alsace. What a contrast to the humiliating failure of British civilisation to attach to Germanic and Protestant Great Britain the Celtic and Catholic Ireland !

For my part, I have never affected to be either surprised or indignant at the antipathy of the Irish to us.

What they have had to suffer from us in past times, all the world knows. And now, when we profess to practise 'a great and genial policy of conciliation' towards them, they are really governed by us in deference to the opinion and sentiment of the British middle class, and of the strongest part of this class, the Puritan community. I have pointed out this before, but in a book about schools, and which only those who are concerned with schools are likely to have read. Let me be suffered, therefore, to repeat it here. The opinion and sentiment of our middle class controls the policy of our statesmen towards Ireland. That policy does not represent the real mind of our leading statesmen, but the mind of the British middle class controlling the action of statesmen. The ability of our popular journalists and successful statesmen goes to putting the best colour they can upon the action so controlled. But a disinterested observer will see an action so controlled to be what it is, and will call it what it is. Now the great failure of our actual national life is the imperfect civilisation of our middle class. The great need of our time is the transformation of the British Puritan. Our Puritan middle class presents a defective type of religion, a narrow range of intellect and knowledge, a stunted sense of beauty, a low standard of manners. And yet it is in deference to the opinion and sentiment of such a class that we shape our policy towards Ireland. And we wonder at Ireland's antipathy to us! Nay, we expect Ireland to lend herself to the make-believe of our own journalists and statesmen, and to call our policy 'genial' !—*Mixed Essays.*

MIDDLE CLASS FOREIGN POLICY.

THE foreigners are in no doubt as to the real authors of the policy of modern England. They know that ours is no longer a policy of Pitts and aristocracies, disposing of every movement of the hoodwinked nation to whom they dictate it ; they know that our policy is now dictated by the strong middle part of England,— England happy, as Mr. Lowe, quoting Aristotle, says, in having her middle part strong and her extremes weak; and that, though we are administered by one of our weak extremes, the aristocracy, these managers administer us, as a weak extreme naturally must, with a nervous attention to the wishes of the strong middle part, whose agents they are. It was not the aristocracy which made the Crimean war ; it was the strong middle part—the constituencies. It was the strong middle part which showered abuse and threats on Germany for mishandling Denmark ; and when Germany gruffly answered, *Come and stop us,* slapped its pockets, and vowed that it had never had the slightest notion of pushing matters so far as this. It was the strong middle part which, by the voice of its favourite newspapers, kept threatening Germany, after she had snapped her fingers at us, with a future chastisement from France, just as a smarting school-boy threatens his bully with a drubbing to come from some big boy in the background. It was the strong middle part, speaking through the same newspapers, which was full of coldness, slights, and sermons for the American Federals during their late struggle; and as soon as they had succeeded, discovered that it had always wished them well, and that nothing was so much to be desired as that the United States and we should be the fastest friends possible. Some people will say that the aristocracy was an equal offender in this respect. Very likely; but the behaviour of the strong middle part makes more impression than the behaviour of a weak extreme; and the more so, because from the middle class, their fellows in number-less ways, the Americans expected sympathy, while from the aristocracy they expected none. And, in general, the faults with which foreigners reproach us in the matters named,—rash engagement, intemperate threatening, un-dignified retreat, ill-timed cordiality,—are not the faults of an aristocracy, by nature in such concerns prudent, reticent, dignified, sensitive on the point of honour; they are rather the faults of a rich middle class,—testy, abso-lute, ill-acquainted with foreign matters, a little ignoble, very dull to perceive when it is making itself ridiculous. —*Friendship's Garland.*

THE YOUNG MAN FROM THE COUNTRY.

ENGLISHMEN are often heard complaining of the little gratitude foreign nations show them for their sympathy, their good-will. The reason is, that the foreigners think that an Englishman's good-will to a foreign cause, or dislike to it, is never grounded in a perception of its real merits and bearings, but in some chance circumstance. They say that the Englishman never, in these cases, really comprehends the situation, and so they can never feel him to be in living sympathy with them. I have got into much trouble for calling my countrymen Philistines, and all through these remarks I am determined never to use that word ; but I wonder if there can be anything offensive in calling one's countryman a young man from the country. I hope not ; and if not, I should say, for the benefit of those who have seen Mr. John Parry's amusing entertainment, that England and Englishmen, holding forth on some great crisis in a foreign country,— Poland, say, or Italy,—are apt to have on foreigners very much the effect of the young man from the country, who talks to the nursemaid after she has upset the perambulator. There is a terrible crisis, and the discourse of the young man from the country, excellent in itself, is felt not to touch the crisis vitally. Nevertheless, on he goes ; the perambulator lies a wreck, the child screams, the nursemaid wrings her hands, the old gentleman storms, the policeman gesticulates, the crowd thickens; still, that astonishing young man talks on, serenely unconscious that he is not at the centre of the situation.— *Friendship's Garland.*

THE GREAT WAR WITH FRANCE.

'YOUR "Times" was telling you the other day,' said Arminius to me, 'that instead of being proud of Waterloo and the great war which was closed by it, it really seemed as if you ought rather to feel embarrassed at the recollection of them, since the policy for which they were fought is grown obsolete; the world has taken a turn which was not Lord Castlereagh's, and to look back on the great Tory war is to look back upon an endless account of blood and treasure wasted. Now, that is not so at all. What France had in her head, from the Convention, "faithful to the principles of the sovereignty of the people, which will not permit them to acknowledge anywhere the institutions militating against it," to Napoleon, with his "immense projects for assuring to France the empire of the world,"—what she had in her head, along with many better and sounder notions destined to happier fortune, was *supremacy.* She had always a vision of a sort of federation of the States of Europe under the primacy of France. Now to this the world, whose progress no doubt lies in the direction of more concert and common

purpose among nations, but these nations free, self-impelled, and living each its own life, was not moving. Whoever knocks to pieces a scheme of this sort does the world a service. In antiquity, Roman empire had a scheme of this sort, and much more. The barbarians knocked it to pieces ;—honour to the barbarians. In the Middle Ages Frederick the Second had a scheme of this sort. The Papacy knocked it to pieces ;—honour to the Papacy. In our own century, France had a scheme of this sort. Your fathers knocked it to pieces ;—honour to your fathers. They were just the people to do it. They had a vigorous lower class, a vigorous middle class, and a vigorous aristocracy. The lower class worked and fought, the middle class found the money, and the aristocracy wielded the whole. This aristocracy was high-spirited, reticent, firm, despising frothy declamation. It had all the qualities useful for its task and time ; Lord Grenville's words, as early as 1793 : "England will never consent that France shall arrogate the power of annulling at her pleasure, and under the pretence of a pretended natural right, the political system of Europe,"—these few words, with their lofty strength, contain, as one may say, the prophecy of future success ; you hear the very voice of an aristocracy standing on sure ground, and with the stars in its favour. Well, you succeeded, and in 1815, after Waterloo, you were the first power in Europe.'
—*Friendship's Garland.*

'YOUR great organ, the "Times,"' said Arminius another day, 'not satisfied with itself conveying to other Powers in the most magnificent manner (a duty, to say the truth, it always fulfils) "what England believes to be due from and to her," keeps exhorting your Government to do the same, to speak some brave words, and to speak them "with promptitude and energy."

'I suppose your Government will do so. But forgive me if I tell you that to us disrespectful foreigners it makes very little difference in our estimate of you and of the future whether your Government does so or not. What gives the sense and significance to a Government's declarations is the power which is behind the Government. And what is the power which is behind the Government of England at the present epoch? The Philistines.

'Simply and solely the Philistines, my dear friend, take my word for it ! No, you will say, it is the nation. Pardon me, you have no nation. France is fused into one nation by the military spirit, and by her democracy, the great legacy of 1789, and subsisting even amidst her present corruption. Germany is fused into one nation by her idea of union and of the elevation of her whole people through culture. You are made up, as I have often told you through my poor disciple whom you so well know, of three distinct and unfused bodies,—Barbarians, Philistines, Populace. You call them aristocracy, middle, and lower class. One of these three must be predominant and lead. Your lower class counts as yet for little or nothing. There is among them a small body of workmen with modern ideas, ideas of organisation, who may be a nucleus for the future ; there are more of them Philistines in a small way, Philistines in embryo; but most of them are mere populace, or, to use your own kindly term, *residuum*. Such a class does not lead. Formerly your aristocracy led ; it commanded the politics of the country ; it had an aristocracy's ideas,—limited enough, but the idea of the country's grandeur and dignity was among them ;—it took your middle and lower class along with it, and used them in its own way, and it made the great war which the battle of Waterloo crowned. But countries must outgrow a feudal organisation, and the political command of an aristocracy ; your country has outgrown it. You aristocracy tells upon England socially ; by all the power of example of a class high-placed, rich, idle, self-indulgent, without mental life, it teaches your Philistines how to live fast. But it no longer rules ; at most it but administers ; the Philistines rule. That makes the difference between Lord Grenville and Lord Granville. When Lord Grenville had to speak to Europe in 1793, he had behind him your aristocracy, not indeed fused with your middle and lower class, but wielding them and using their force; and all the world knew what your aristocracy meant, for they knew it themselves. But Lord Granville has behind him, when he speaks to Europe in 1870, your Philistines or middle class ; and how should the world know, or much care, what your middle class mean ? for they do not know it themselves.

'You may be. mortified, but such is the truth. To be consequent and powerful, men must be bottomed on some vital idea or sentiment, which lends strength and certainty to their action. Your aristocracy of seventy years ago had the sentiment of the greatness of the old aristocratical England, and that sentiment gave them force to endure labours, anxiety, danger, disappointment, loss, restrictions of liberty. Your ruling middle class has no such foundation ; hence its imbecility. It would tell you it believes in industrial development and liberty. Examine what it means by these, and you find it means getting rich and not being meddled with. And these it imagines to be self-acting powers for good, and agents of greatness ; so that if more trade is done in England than anywhere else, if your personal independence is without a check, and your newspaper publicity unbounded, your Philistines think they are by the nature of things great, powerful, and admirable, and that their England has only to speak "with promptitude and energy" in order to prevail.

'And this is the power which Lord Granville has behind him, and which is to give the force and meaning to his words. Poor Lord Granville! I imagine he is under no illusions. He knows the British Philistine, with his likes and dislikes, his effusion and confusion, his hot and cold fits, his want of dignity and of the stedfastness which comes from dignity, his want of ideas and of the stedfastness which comes from ideas ;—he has seen him at work already. He has seen the Russian war and the Russian peace ; a war and peace your aristocracy did not make and never would have made,—the British Philistine and his newspapers have the whole merit of it. In your social gatherings I know you have the habit of assuring one another that in some mysterious way the Russian war did you good in the eyes of Europe. Undeceive yourselves ; it did you nothing but harm, and Lord Granville is far too clever a man not to know it. Then, in the Denmark quarrel, your Philistines did not make war, indeed, but they threatened it. Surely in the Denmark case there was no want of brave words ; no failure to speak out "with promptitude and energy." And we all know what came of it. Unique British Philistine ! Is he most to be revered when he makes his wars or when he threatens them ? And at the prompting of this great backer Lord Granville is now to speak ! Probably he will have, as the French say, to execute himself ; only do not suppose that we are under

any delusion as to the sort of force he has behind him.'
—*Friendship's Garland.*

THE BRITISH PHILISTINE AND CONTINENTAL GOVERNMENTS.

'You are a self-governing people,' Arminius went on, 'you are represented by your "strong middle part," youɪ Philistine: and this is what your Government must watch ; this is what it must take its cue from.

'Here, then, is your situation, that your Government does not and cannot really govern, but at present is and must be the mouthpiece of your Philistines ; and that foreign Governments know this very well, know it to their cost. Nothing the best of them would like better than to deal with England seriously and respectfully,— the England of their traditions, the England of history ; nothing, even, they would like better than to deal with the English Government,—as at any time it may happen to stand, composed of a dozen men more or less eminent, —seriously and respectfully. But, good God ! it is not with these dozen men in their natural state that a foreign Government finds it has to deal ; it is with these dozen men sitting in devout expectation to see how the cat will jump,—and that cat the British Philistine !

'What statesman can deal seriously and respectfully with you, when he finds that he is not dealing mind to mind with an intelligent equal, but that he is dealing with a tumult of likes and dislikes, hopes, panics, intrigues, stock-jobbing, quidnuncs, newspapers,—dealing with *ignorance*, in short, for that one word contains it all,—behind his intelligent equal? Whatever he says to a British Minister, however convincing he may be, a foreign statesman knows that he has only half his hearer's attention, that only one of the British Minister's eyes is turned his way ; the other eye is turned anxiously back on the home Philistines and the home press, and according as these finally go the British Minister must go too. This sort of thing demoralises your Ministers themselves in the end, ever your able and honest ones, and makes them impossible to deal with. God forgive me if I do him wrong ! —but I always suspect that your sly old Sir Hamilton Seymour, in his conversations with the Emperor Nicholas before the Crimean war, had at last your Philistines and your press, and their unmistakable bent, in his eye, and did not lead the poor Czar quite straight. If ever there was a man who respected England, and would have gone cordially and easily with a capable British minister, that man was Nicholas. England, Russia, and Austria are the Powers with a real interest in the Eastern question, and it ought to be settled fairly between them. Nicholas wished nothing better. Even if you would not thus settle the question, he would have forborne to any extent sooner than go to war with you, if he could only have known what you were really at. To be sure, as you did not know this yourselves, you could not possibly tell *him*, poor man ! Louis Napoleon, meanwhile, had his prestige to make. France pulled the wires right and left ; your Philistines had a passion for that old acrobat Lord Palmerston, who, clever as he was, had an aristocrat's inaptitude for ideas, and believed in upholding and renovating the Grand Turk ; Lord Aberdeen knew better, but his eye was nervously fixed on the British Philistine and the British press. The British Philistine learnt that he was being treated with rudeness and must make his voice heard 'with promptitude and energy.' There was the usual explosion of passions, prejudices, stock-jobbing, newspaper-articles, chatter, and general ignorance, and the Czar found he must either submit to have capital made out of him by French vanity and Bonapartist necessities, or enter into the Crimean war. He entered into the Crimean war, and it broke his heart. France came out of the Crimean war the first Power in Europe, with French vanity and Bonapartist necessities fully served. You came out of it with the British Philistine's *rôle* in European affairs for the first time thoroughly recognised and appreciated.'—*Friendship's Garland.*

THE BLACK SEA QUESTION ILLUSTRATED.

In my immediate neighbourhood here in Cripplegate we have lately had a case which exactly illustrates the present difficulty with Russia as to her use of the

Black Sea. We all do our marketing in Whitecross Street ; and in Whitecross Street is a famous tripe-shop which I always visit before entertaining Arminius, who, like all North Germans, and like our own celebrated Dr. Johnson, is a very gross feeder. Two powerful labourers, who lodge like Arminius in Chequer Alley, and who never could abide one another, used to meet at this tripe-shop and quarrel till it became manifest that the shop could not stand two such customers together, and that one of the couple must give up going there. The fellows' names were Mike and Dennis. It was generally thought the chief blame in the quarrel lay with Mike, who was at any rate much the less plausible man of the two, besides being greatly. the bigger. However that may be, the excellent City Missionary in this quarter, the Rev. *J-hn B-ll* (I forbear to write his name at length for fear of bringing a, blush to his worthy cheek), took Dennis's part in the matter. He and Dennis set, both together upon Mike, and got the best of him. It was Dennis who appeared to do the most in the set-to ; at all events, he got the whole credit, although I have heard the Rev. *J-hn B-ll* (who was undoubtedly a formidable fellow in his old unregenerate days) describe at tea in the Mission Room how he got his stick between Mike's legs at all the critical moments ; how he felt fresher and stronger when the fight ended than when it began ; and how his behaviour had somehow the effect of leaving on the bystanders' minds an impression immensely to his advantage. What is quite certain is, that not only did our reverend friend take part in the engagement, but that also, before, during, and after the struggle, his exhortations and admonitions to Mike, Dennis, the bystanders, and himself, never ceased, and were most edifying. Mike finally, as I said, had to give in, and he was obliged to make a solemn promise to Dennis and the City Missionary that he would use the tripe-shop no more. On this condition a treaty was patched up, and peace reigned in Cripplegate.

And now comes the startling point of resemblance to the present Russian difficulty. A great big hulking German, called Fritz, has been for some time taking a lead in our neighbourhood, and carrying his head a great deal higher in Whitecross Street Market than Dennis liked. At last Dennis could stand it no longer ; he picked a quarrel with Fritz, and they had a battle-royal to prove which was master. In this encounter our City Missionary took no part, though he bestowed, as usual, on both sides good advice and beautiful sentiments in abundance. Dennis had no luck this time ; he got horribly belaboured, and now lies confined to his bed at his lodgings, almost past praying for. But what do you think has been Mike's conduct at this juncture ? Seeing Dennis disabled, he addressed to the City Missionary an indecent scrawl, couched in language with which I will not sully your pages, to the effect that the tripe-shop lay handy to his door (which is true enough) ; and that use it he needs must, and use it he would, in spite of all the Rev. *J-hn B-ll* might say or do to stop him.

The feelings of the worthy Missionary at this communication may be easier imagined than described. He launched at Mike the most indignant moral rebuke ; the brute put his thumb to his nose. To get Mike out of the tripe-shop there is nothing left but physical force. Yet how is our estimable friend to proceed ? Years of outpouring, since he has been engaged in mission-work, have somewhat damaged his wind ; the hospitalities of the more serious-minded citizens of Cripplegate to a man in his position have been, I hope, what they should be ; there are apprehensions, if violent exercise is taken, of gout in the stomach. Dennis can do nothing ; what is worse, Fritz has been seen to wink his eye at Mike in a way to beget grave suspicion that the ruffians have a secret compact together. The general feeling in Cripplegate is that nothing much can be done, and that Mike must be allowed to resort again to the tripe-shop.

But I ask, is this morally defensible? Is it right ? Is it honest ? Has not Lord Shaftesbury's English heart (if it is not presumptuous in me to speak thus of a person in his Lordship's position) guided him true in the precisely similar case of Russia? As Lord Shaftesbury says, a treaty is a promise, and we have a moral right to demand that promises shall be kept. If Mike wanted to use the tripe-shop, he should have waited till Dennis was about again and could talk things over with the City Missionary, and then, perhaps, the two might have been found willing to absolve Mike from his promise. His present conduct is inexcusable ; the only comfort is that the Rev. *J-hn B-ll* has a faith fulpress still to back him, and that Mike is being subjected to a fearful daily castigation in the columns of the ' Band of Hope Review.'—*Friendship's Garland.*

A GERMAN LESSON.

THE last tirade of Arminius to me, before he went off to the wars, was this :—'Your newspapers are every day solemnly saying that the great lesson to be learned from the present war between France and Germany is so and so,—always something which it is not. There are many lessons to be learned from the present war ; I will tell you what is for *you* the great lesson to be learned from it :— *obedience.* That, instead of every man airing his self-consequence, thinking it bliss to talk at random about things, and to put his finger in every pie, you should seriously understand that there is a *right* way of doing things, and that the bliss is, without thinking of one's self-consequence, to do them in that way, or to forward their being done,—this is the great lesson your British public, as you call it, has to learn and may learn, in some degree, from the Germans in this war! Englishmen were once famous for the power of holding their tongues and doing their business, and, therefore, I admire your nation. The business now to be done in the world is harder than ever, and needs far more than has been ever yet needed of thought, study, and seriousness ; miscarry you must, if you let your daily doses of clap-trap make you imagine that liberty and publicity can be any substitute for these.'—*Friendship's Garland.*

REASONS FOR HOPE.

I have a friend who is very sanguine, in spite of the dismal croakings of these foreigners, about the turn things are even now taking amongst us. 'Mean and ignoble as our middle class looks,' he says, 'it has this capital virtue, it has seriousness. With frivolity, cultured or uncultured, you çan do nothing ; but with seriousness there is always hope. Then, too, the present bent of the world towards amusing itself, so perilous to the highest class, is curative and good for our middle class. A piano in a Quaker's drawing-room is a step for him to a more humane life ; nay, perhaps even the penny gaff of the poor East-Londoner is a step for him to a more humane life. It is,—what example shall we choose? it is *Strath-more*, let us say,—it is the one-pound-eleven-and-sixpenny gaff of the young gentlemen of the clubs and the young ladies of Belgravia, that is for them but a step in the primrose path to the everlasting bonfire. Besides, say what you like of the ideallessness of aristocracies, of the vulgarity of our middle class, the immaturity of our lower, and the poor chance which a happy type of modern life has between them, consider this : Of all that makes life liberal and humane,—of light, of ideas, of culture,— every man in every class of society who has a dash of genius in him is the born friend. By his bringing up, by his habits, by his interest, he may be their enemy ; by the primitive, unalterable complexion of his nature, he is their friend.   Therefore, the movement of the modern spirit will be more and more felt among us, it will spread, it will prevaiL   Nay,' this enthusiast often continues, getting excited as he goes on, ' the " Times " itself, which so· stirs some people's indignation,—what is the " Times " but a gigantic Sancho Panza, to borrow a phrase of your friend Heine ;—a gigantic Sancho Panza, following by an attraction he cannot resist that poor, mad, scorned, suffering, sublime enthusiast, the modern spirit ; following it, indeed, with constant grumbling, expostulation, and opposition, with airs of protection, of compassionate superiority, with an incessant by-play of nods, shrugs, and winks addressed to the spectators ; following it, in short, with all the incurable recalcitrancy· of a lower nature, but still following it ?' When my friend talks thus, I always shake my head, and say that this sounds very like the transcendentalism which has already brought me into so many scrapes.—*Friendship's Garland.*

FERMENT.

OUR actual middle class has not yet, certainly, the fine culture, or the living intelligence, which quickened great bodies of men at creative epochs ; but it has the forerunner, the preparer, the indispensable initiator ; it is traversed by a strong intellectual ferment. It is the middle class which has real mental ardour, real curiosity ; it is the middle class which is the great reader ; that immense literature of the day which we see surging up all round us,—literature the absolute value of which it is almost impossible to rate too humbly, literature hardly a word of which will reach, or deserves to reach, the future,—it is the middle class which calls it forth, and its evocation is at least a sign of a widespread mental movement in that class. Will this movement go on and become fruitful : will it conduct the middle class to a high and commanding pitch of culture and intelligence ? That depends on the sensibility which the middle class has for *perfection* ; that depends on its power to *transform itself.—A French Eton.*

'*IS THIS JERUSALEM?*'

IN the Crusade of Peter the Hermit, where the hosts that marched were not filled after the usual composition of armies, but contained along with the fighters whole families of people,—old men, women, and children,—swept by the universal torrent of enthusiasm towards the Holy Land, the marches, as might have been expected, were tedious and painful.   Long before Asia was reached, long before even Europe was half traversed, the little children in that travelling multitude began to fancy, with a natural impatience, that their journey must surely be drawing to an end ; and every evening, as they came in sight of some town which was the destination of that day's march, they cried out eagerly to those who were with them : '*Is this Jerusalem ?*' No, poor children, not this town, nor the next, nor yet the next, is Jerusalem ; Jerusalem is far off, and it needs time, and strength, and much endurance to reach it. Seas and mountains, labour and peril, hunger and thirst, disease and death, are between Jerusalem and you.

So, when one marks the ferment and stir of life in the middle class at this moment, and sees this class impelled to take possession of the world, and to assert itself and its own actual spirit absolutely, one is disposed to exclaim to it : '*Jerusalem is not yet.* Your present spirit is not Jerusalem, is not the goal you have to reach, the place you may be satisfied in.'—*A French Eton.*

THE TRUE JERUSALEM.

THE actual governing class, the English aristocratic class (in the widest sense of the word *aristocratic*),—I cannot wish that the rest of the nation, the new and growing part of the nation, should be transformed in spirit exactly according to the image of that class. The merits and services of that class no one rates higher than I do ; no one appreciates higher than I do the value of the relative standard of elevation, refinement and grandeur, which they have exhibited ; no one would more strenuously oppose the relinquishing of this for any lower standard. But I cannot hide from myself that while modern societies increasingly tend to find their best life in a free and heightened spiritual and intellectual activity, to this tendency aristocracies offer at least a strong passive resistance, by their eternal prejudices, their incurable dearth of ideas. In modern, rich, and industrial societies, they tend to misplace the ideal for the classes below them ; the immaterial chivalrous ideal of high descent and honour is, by the very nature of the case, of force only for aristocracies themselves ; the immaterial modern ideal of spiritual and intellectual perfection through culture, they have not to communicate.. What they can and do communicate is the material ideal of splendour of wealth, and weight of property. And this ideal is the ideal truly operative upon our middle classes at this moment.   To be as rich as they can, that they may reach the splendour of wealth and weight of property, and, with time, the importance, of the actual heads of society, is their ambition.   I do not blame them, or the class from which they get their ideal ; all I say is, that the good ideal for humanity, the true Jerusalem, is an ideal more spiritual than splendid wealth and boundless property, an ideal in which more can participate.   The beloved friends of humanity have been those who made it feel its ideal to be in the things of the mind and spirit, to be in an internal condition separable from wealth and accessible to all,—men like St. Francis, the ardent bridegroom of poverty ; men like the great personages of antiquity, almost all of them, as Lacordaire was so fond of saying, poor.   Therefore, that the middle class should simply take its ideal from the aristocratic class, I do not wish. That the aristocratic class should be able absolutely to assert itself and its own spirit, is not my desire.   No, no ; they are not Jerusalem.

The truth is, the English spirit has to accomplish an immense evolution ; nor, as that spirit at this moment presents itself in any class or description amongst us, can one be perfectly satisfied with it, can one wish it to prevail just as it is.

But in a transformed middle class, in a middle class raised to a higher and more genial culture, we may find, not perhaps Jerusalem, but I am sure, a notable stage towards it.—*A French Eton.*

GOOD OF PHILISTINISM.

ALL tendencies of human nature are in themselves vital and profitable ; when they are blamed, they are only to be blamed relatively, not absolutely. This holds true of the Saxon's phlegm as well as of the Celt's sentiment. Out of the steady humdrum habit of the creeping Saxon, as the Celt calls him,—out of his way of going near the ground,—has come, no doubt, Philistinism, that plant of essentially Germanic growth, flourishing with its genuine marks only in the German fatherland, in Great Britain and her colonies, and in the United States of America ; but what a soul of goodness there is in Philistinism itself ! and this soul of goodness I, who am often supposed to be Philistinism's mortal enemy merely because I do not wish it to have things all its own way, cherish as much as anybody. This steady-going habit leads at last, as we see, up to science, up to the comprehension and interpretation of the world. With us in Great Britain, it is true, it does not seem at present to lead so far as that ; it is in Germany, where the habit is more unmixed, that it leads to science. Here with us it seems at a certain point to meet with a conflicting force, which checks it and prevents its pushing on to science ; but before reaching this point what conquests has it not won ! and all the

more, perhaps, for stopping short at this point, for spending its exertions within a bounded field, the field of plain
sense, of direct practical utility.　How it has augmented
the comforts and conveniences of life for us !　Doors
that open, windows that shut, locks that turn, razors that
shave, coats that wear, watches that go, and a thousand
more of such good things, are the invention of the Philistines.—*Study of Celtic Literature.*

A WORD TO IRELAND.

LET the Celtic members of this empire consider that
they too have to transform themselves ; and though the
summons to transform themselves be often conveyed
harshly and brutally, and with the cry to root up their
wheat as well as their tares, yet that is no reason why the
summons should not be followed so far as their tares are
concerned.　Let them consider that they are inextricably
bound up with us, and that besides, if we look into
the thing closely, we English, alien and uncongenial to
our Celtic partners as we may have hitherto shown
ourselves, have notwithstanding, beyond perhaps any
other nation, a thousand latent springs of possible
sympathy with them.　Let them consider that new ideas
and forces are stirring in England, that day by day
these new ideas and forces gain in power, and that
almost every one of them is the friend of the Celt and
not his enemy.　And, whether our Celtic partners will

consider this or no, at any rate let us ourselves, all of us who are proud of being the ministers of these new ideas, work incessantly to procure for them a wider and more fruitful application ; work to remove the main ground of the Celt's alienation from the Englishman, by substituting, in place of that type of Englishman with whom alone the Celt has too long been familiar, a new type, more intelligent, more gracious, and more humane.—*Study of Celtic Literature.*

REVOLUTION BY DUE COURSE OF LAW.

WE are on our way to what the late Duke of Wellington, with his strong sagacity, foresaw and admirably described as 'a revolution by due course of law.' This is un-doubtedly,—if we are still to live and grow, and this famous nation is not to stagnate and dwindle away on the one hand, or, on the other, to perish miserably in mere anarchy and confusion,—what we are on the way to. Great changes there must be, for a revolution cannot accomplish itself without great changes ; yet order there must be, for without order a revolution cannot accom-plish itself by due course of law. So whatever brings risk of tumult and disorder, multitudinous processions in the streets of our crowded towns, multitudinous meetings in their public places and parks,—demonstrations per-fectly unnecessary in the present course of our affairs,— our best self, or right reason, plainly enjoins us to set our face against. It enjoins us to encourage and uphold the occupants of the executive power, whoever they may be, in firmly prohibiting them. But it does this clearly and resolutely, and is thus a real principle of authority, because it does it with a free conscience ; because, in thus provisionally strengthening the executive power, it knows that it is not doing this merely to enable our Tory aristocrat to affirm himself as against our Radical working man, or our middle-class Dissenter to affirm himself as against both. It knows that it is stablishing *the State*, or organ of our collective best self, of our national right reason. And it has the testimony of conscience that it is stablishing the State on behalf of whatever great changes are needed, just as much as on behalf of order : stablishing it to deal just as stringently, when the time comes, with our Tory aristocrat's prejudices, or with the fanaticism of our middle-class Dissenter, as it deals with our Radical working man's street-processions.— *Culture and Anarchy.*

STATE ACTION.

THE question is, whether, retaining all its power of control over a government which should abuse its trust, the nation may not now find advantage in voluntarily allowing to government purposes somewhat ampler, and limits somewhat wider within which to execute them, than formerly ; whether the nation may not thus acquire in the State an ideal of high reason and right feeling, representing its best self, commanding general respect, and forming a rallying-point for the intelligence and for the worthiest instincts of the community, which will herein find a true bond of union.—*Mixed Essays.*

WHAT IS THE STATE?

THE State,—but what is *the State?* cry many. The State is properly just what Burke called ·it : *the nation in its collective and corporate character.* The State is the representative acting-power of the nation ; the action of the State is the representative action of the nation. It is common to hear the depreciators of State-action run through a string of Ministers' names, and then say : ' Here is really your *State* ; would you accept the action of these men as your own representative action? in what respect is their judgment on national affairs likely to be any better than that of the rest of the world?' In the first place I answer : Even supposing them to be originally no better or wiser than the rest of the world, they have two great advantages from their position : access to almost boundless means of information, and the enlargement of mind which the habit of dealing with great affairs tends to produce. Their position itself, therefore, if they are men of only average honesty and capacity, tends to give them a fitness for acting on behalf of the nation superior to that of other men of equal honesty and capacity who are not in the same position. This fitness may be yet further increased by treating them as persons on whom, indeed, a very grave responsibility has fallen, and from whom very much will be expected ;—nothing less than the representing, each of them in his own department, under the control of Parliament, and aided by the suggestions of public opinion, the collective energy and intelligence of his nation. By treating them as men on whom all this devolves to do, to their honour if they do it well, to their shame if they do it ill, one probably augments their faculty of well-doing ; as it is excellently said : 'To treat men as if they were better than they are, is the surest way to *make* them better than they are.' But to treat them as if they had been shuffled into their places by a lucky accident, were most likely soon to be shuffled out of them again, and meanwhile ought to magnify themselves and their office as little as possible ; to treat them as if they and their functions could without much inconvenience be quite dispensed with, and they ought perpetually to be admiring their own inconceivable good fortune in being permitted to discharge them ;—this is the way to paralyse all high effort in the executive government, to extinguish all lofty sense of responsibility ; to make its members either merely solicitous for the gross advantages, the emolument and self-importance, which they derive from their offices, or else timid, apologetic, and self-mistrustful in filling them ; in either case, formal and inefficient.

But in the second place I answer : If the executive government is really in the hands of men no wiser than the bulk of mankind, of men whose action an intelligent man would be unwilling to accept as representative of his own action, whose fault is that ? It is the fault of the nation itself, which, not being in the hands of a despot or of an oligarchy, being free to control the choice of those who are to sum up and concentrate its action, controls it in such a manner, that it allows to be chosen, agents so little in its confidence, or so mediocre, or so incompetent, that it thinks the best thing that can be done with them is to reduce their action as nearly as possible to a nullity. Hesitating, blundering, unintelligent, inefficacious, the action of the State may be ; but, such as it is, it is the collective action of the nation itself, and the nation is responsible for it. It is our own action which we suffer to be thus unsatisfactory. Nothing can free us from this responsibility. The conduct of our affairs is in our own power. To carry on into its executive proceedings the indecision, conflict, and discordance of its parliamentary debates, may be a natural defect of a free nation, but it is certainly a defect ; it is a dangerous error to call it, as some do, a perfection. The want of concert, reason, and organisation in the State, is the want of concert, reason, and organisation in the collective nation.—*Mixed Essays.*

THE SAME.

Is a citizen's relation to the State that of a dependent to a parental benefactor? By no means ; it is that of a member in a partnership to the whole firm. The citizens of a State, the members of a society, are really a partner- ship ; '*a partnership*,' as Burke nobly says, '*in all science, in all art, in every virtue, in all perfection*.' Towards this great final design of their connexion, they apply the aids which co-operative association can give them.—*A French Eton.*

STATE-HELP NOT DEGRADING.

How vain, then, and how meaningless, to tell a man who, for the instruction of his offspring, receives aid from the State, that he is humiliated ! Humiliated by receiving help for himself as an individual from himself in his cor- porate and associated capacity ! help to which his own money, as a tax-payer, contributes, and for which, as a result of the joint energy and intelligence of the whole community in employing its powers, he himself deserves some of the praise ! He is no more humiliated than one is humiliated by being on the foundation of the Charter- house or of Winchester, or by holding a scholarship or a fellowship at Oxford or Cambridge. Nay (if there be any humiliation here), not so much. For the amount of benefaction, the amount of obligation, the amount, therefore, I suppose, of humiliation, diminishes as the public character of the aid becomes more undeniable. He is no more humiliated than when he crosses London Bridge, or walks down the King's Road, or visits the British Museum. But it is one of the extraordinary inconsistencies of some English people in this matter, that they keep all their cry of humiliation and degradation for help which the State offers. A man is not pauperised, is not degraded, is not oppressively obliged, by taking aid for his son's schooling from Mr. Woodard's subscribers, or from the next squire, or from the next rector, or from the next ironmonger, or from the next druggist ; he is only pauperised when he takes it from the State, when he helps to give it himself !—*A French Eton.*

ANTI-ANARCHY.

EVEN for the sake of the actual present, but far more for the sake of the future, the lovers of culture are unswervingly and with a good conscience the opposers of anarchy. And not as the Barbarians and Philistines, whose honesty and whose sense of humour make them shrink, as we have seen, from treating the State as too serious a thing, and from giving it too much power ;—for indeed the only State they know of, and think they administer, is the expression of their ordinary self. And though the headstrong and violent extreme among them might gladly arm this with full authority, yet their virtuous mean is, as we have said, pricked in conscience at doing this ; and so our Barbarian Secretaries of State let the Park railings be broken down, and our Philistine Alderman-Colonels let the London roughs rob and beat the bystanders. But we, beholding in the State no expression of our ordinary self, but even already, as it were, the appointed frame and prepared vessel of our best self, and, for the future, our best self's powerful, beneficent and sacred expression and organ,—we are willing and resolved, even now, to strengthen against anarchy the trembling hands of our Barbarian Home Secretaries, and the feeble knees of our Philistine Alderman-Colonels ; and to tell them, that it is not really in behalf of their own ordinary self that they are called to protect the Park railings, and to suppress the London roughs, but in behalf of the best self both of themselves and of all of us in the future.— *Culture and Anarchy.*

III.

PHILOSOPHY AND RELIGION.

WE may regard the energy driving at practice, the paramount sense of the obligation of duty, self-control, and work, the earnestness in going manfully with the best light we have, as one force. And we may regard the intelligence driving at those ideas which are, after all, the basis of right practice, the ardent sense for all the new and changing combinations of them which man's development brings with it, the indomitable impulse to know and adjust them perfectly, as another force. And these two forces we may regard as in some sense rivals,—rivals not by the necessity of their own nature, but as exhibited in man and his history,—and rivals dividing the empire of the world between them. And to give these forces names from the two races of men who have supplied the most signal and splendid manifestations of them, we may call them respectively the forces of Hebraism and Hellenism. Hebraism and Hellenism,—between these two points of influence moves our world. At one time it feels more powerfully the attraction of one of them, at another time of the other ; and it ought to be, though it never is, evenly and happily balanced between them.

The final aim of both Hellenism and Hebraism, as of all great spiritual disciplines, is no doubt the same : man's perfection or salvation.   The very language which they both of them use in schooling us to reach this aim is often identical.   Even when their language indicates by variation,— sometimes a broad variation, often a but slight and subtle variation,—the different courses of thought which are uppermost in each discipline, even then the unity of the final end and aim is still apparent. To employ the actual words of that discipline with which we ourselves are all of us most familiar, and the words of which, therefore, come most home to us, that final end and aim is 'that we might be partakers of the divine nature.'   These are the words of a Hebrew apostle; but, of Hellenism and Hebraism alike, this is, I say, the aim.

When the two are confronted, as they very often are confronted, it is nearly always with what I may call a rhetorical purpose ; the speaker's whole design is to exalt and enthrone one of the two, and he uses the other only as a foil and to enable him the better to give effect to his purpose.   Obviously, with us, it is usually Hellenism which is thus reduced to minister to the triumph of Hebraism.   There is a sermon on Greece and the Greek spirit by a man never to be mentioned without interest and respect, Frederick Robertson, in which this rhetorical use of Greece and the Greek spirit, and the inadequate exhibition of them necessarily consequent upon this, is almost ludicrous, and would be censurable if it were not to be explained by the exigencies of a sermon. On the other hand, Heinrich Heine, and other writers of his sort, give us the spectacle of the tables completely turned, and of Hebraism brought in just as a foil and contrast to Hellenism, and to make the superiority of Hellenism more manifest. In both these cases there is injustice and misrepresentation. The aim and end of both Hebraism and Hellenism is, as I have said, one and the same, and this aim and end is august and admirable.

Still, they pursue this aim by very different courses. The uppermost idea with Hellenism is to see things as they really are ; the uppermost idea with Hebraism is conduct and obedience. Nothing can do away with this ineffaceable difference. The Greek quarrel with the body and its desires is, that they hinder right thinking, the Hebrew quarrel with them is, that they hinder right acting. 'He that keepeth the law, happy is he ;' 'Blessed is the man that feareth the Eternal, that delighteth greatly in his commandments ;'—that is the Hebrew notion of felicity ; and, pursued with passion and tenacity, this notion would not let the Hebrew rest till, as is well known, he had at last got out of the law a network of prescriptions to enwrap his whole life, to govern every moment of it, every impulse, every action. The Greek notion of felicity, on the other hand, is perfectly conveyed in these words of a great French moralist : ' *C'est le bonheur des hommes,*'—when? when they abhor that which is evil ?—no ; when they exercise themselves in the law of the Lord day and night?—no ; when they die daily ?—no ; when they walk about the New Jerusalem with palms in their hands?—no ; but when they think aright, when their thought hits, '*quand ils pensent juste.*' At the bottom of both the Greek and the Hebrew notion is the desire, native in man, for reason and the will of God, the feeling after the universal order,—in a word, the love of God. But, while Hebraism seizes upon certain plain, capital intimations of the universal order, and rivets itself, one may say, with unequalled grandeur of earnestness and intensity on the study and observance of them, the bent of Hellenism is to follow, with flexible activity, the whole play of the universal order, to be apprehensive of missing any part of it, of sacrificing one part to another, to slip away from resting in this or that intimation of it, however capital. An unclouded clearness of mind, an unimpeded play of thought, is what this bent drives at. The governing idea of Hellenism is *spontaneity of consciousness* ; that of Hebraism, *strictness of conscience.*— *Culture and Anarchy.*

RENASCENCE AND REFORMATION.

THE Renascence is, in great part, a return towards the pagan spirit, in the special sense in which I have been using the word pagan ;—a return towards the life of the senses and the understanding. The Reformation, on the other hand, is the very opposite to this; in Luther there is nothing Greek or pagan; vehemently as he attacked the adoration of St. Francis, Luther had himself something of St. Francis in him ; he was a thousand times more akin to St. Francis than to Theocritus or to Voltaire. The Reformation,—I do not mean the inferior piece given under that name, by Henry the Eighth and a second-rate company, in this island, but the real Reformation, the German Reformation, Luther's Reformation,—was a reaction of the moral and spiritual sense against the carnal and pagan sense. It was a religious revival like St. Francis's, but this time against the Church of Rome, not within her; for the carnal and pagan sense had now, in the government of the Church of Rome herself, its prime representative. And the grand reaction, once more, against the rule of the heart and imagination, the strong return towards the rule of the senses and understanding, is in the eighteenth century.—*Essays in Criticism.*

HELLENISM.

To get rid of one's ignorance, to see things as they are, and by seeing them as they are to see them in their beauty, is the simple and attractive ideal which Hellenism holds out before human nature. From the simplicity and charm of this ideal, Hellenism, and human life in the hands of Hellenism, is invested with a kind of aërial ease, clearness, and radiancy ; they are full of what we call sweetness and light. Difficulties are kept out of view, and the beauty and rationalness of the ideal have all our thoughts. 'The best man is he who most tries to perfect himself, and the happiest man is he who most feels that he *is* perfecting himself,'—this account of the matter by Socrates, the true Socrates of the 'Memorabilia,' has something so simple, spontaneous, and unsophisticated about it, that it seems to fill us with clearness and hope when we hear it.—*Culture and Anarchy.*

HEBRAISM.

As Hellenism speaks of thinking clearly, seeing things in their essence and beauty, as a grand and precious feat for man to achieve, so Hebraism speaks of becoming conscious of sin, of awakening to a sense of sin, as a feat of this kind. It is obvious to what wide divergence these differing tendencies, actively followed, must lead. As one passes and repasses from Hellenism to Hebraism, from Plato to St Paul, one feels inclined to rub one's eyes and ask oneself whether man is indeed a gentle and simple being, showing the traces of a noble and divine nature ; or an unhappy chained captive, labouring with groanings that cannot be uttered to free himself from the body of this death.

Apparently it was the Hellenic conception of human nature which was unsound, for the world could not live by it. Absolutely to call it unsound, however, is to fall into the common error of its Hebraising enemies ; but it was unsound at that particular moment of man's development, it was premature. The indispensable basis of conduct and self-control, the platform upon which alone the perfection aimed at by Greece can come into bloom, was not to be reached by our race so easily ; centuries of probation and discipline were needed to bring us to it. Therefore the bright promise of Hellenism faded, and Hebraism ruled the world. Then was seen that astonishing spectacle, so well marked by the often quoted words of the prophet Zechariah, when men of all languages and nations took hold of the skirt of him that was a Jew, saying :—' *We will go with you, for we have heard that God is with you.*' And the Hebraism which thus received and ruled a world all gone out of the way and altogether become unprofitable, was, and could not but be, the later, the more spiritual, the more attractive development of Hebraism. It was Christianity ; that is

to say, Hebraism aiming at self-conquest and rescue from the thrall of vile affections, not by obedience to the letter of a law, but by conformity to the image of a self-sacrificing example. To a world stricken with moral enervation Christianity offered its spectacle of an inspired self-sacrifice ; to men who refused themselves nothing, it showed one who refused himself everything :—'*my Saviour banished joy !*' says George Herbert. When the *alma Venus*, the life-giving and joy-giving power of nature, so fondly cherished by the Pagan world, could not save her followers from self-dissatisfaction and ennui, the severe words of the apostle came bracingly and re-freshingly : 'Let no man deceive you with vain words, for because of these things cometh the wrath of God upon the children of disobedience.' Through age after age and generation after generation, our race, or all that part of our race which was most living and progressive, was *baptised into a death* ; and endeavoured, by suffering in the flesh, to cease from sin. Of this endeavour, the animating labours and afflictions of early Christianity, the touching asceticism of mediæval Christianity, are the great historical manifestations. Literary monuments of it, each in its own way incomparable, remain in the Epistles of St. Paul, in St. Augustine's 'Confessions,' and in the two original and simplest books of the 'Imitation.'
—*Culture and Anarchy.*

HEBRAISM OF THE ENGLISH.

EMINENTLY Indo-European by its *humour*, by the power it shows, through this gift, of imaginatively acknowledging the multiform aspects of the problem of life, and of thus getting itself unfixed from its own over-certainty, of smiling at its own over-tenacity, our race has yet (and a great part of its strength lies here), in matters of practical life and moral conduct, a strong share of the assuredness, the tenacity, the intensity of the Hebrews. This turn manifested itself in Puritanism, and has had a great part in shaping our history for the last two hundred years. Undoubtedly it checked and changed amongst us that movement of the Renascence which we see producing in the reign of Elizabeth such wonderful fruits. Undoubtedly it stopped the prominent rule and direct development of that order of ideas which we call by the name of Hellenism, and gave the first rank to a different order of ideas. Apparently, too, as we said of the former defeat of Hellenism, if Hellenism was defeated, this shows that Hellenism was imperfect, and that its ascendency at that moment would not have been for the world's good.

Yet there is a very important difference between the defeat inflicted on Hellenism by Christianity eighteen hundred years ago, and the check given to the Renascence by Puritanism. The greatness of the difference is

well measured by the difference in force, beauty, significance and usefulness, between primitive Christianity and
Protestantism.   Eighteen hundred years ago it was altogether the hour of Hebraism.   Primitive Christianity was
legitimately and truly the ascendent force in the world at
that time, and the way of mankind's progress lay through
its full development.   Another hour in man's development began in the fifteenth century, and the main road
of his progress then lay for a time through Hellenism.
Puritanism was no longer the central current of the
world's progress, it was a side stream crossing the central
current and checking it.   The cross and the check may
have been necessary and salutary, but that does not do
away with the essential difference between the main
stream of man's advance and a cross or side stream.
For more than two hundred years the main stream of
man's advance has moved towards knowing himself and
the world, seeing things as they are, spontaneity of consciousness ; the main impulse of a great part, and that
the strongest part, of our nation, has been towards strictness of conscience.   They have made the secondary the
principal at the wrong moment, and the principal they
have at the wrong moment treated as secondary.
This contravention of the natural order has produced,
as such contravention always must produce, a certain
confusion and false movement, of which we are now
beginning to feel, in almost every direction, the incon-

venience. In all directions our habitual courses of action seem to be losing efficaciousness, credit, and control, both with others and even with ourselves. Everywhere we see the beginnings of confusion, and we want a clue to some sound order and authority. This we can only get by going back upon the actual instincts and forces which rule our life, seeing them as they really are, connecting them with other instincts and forces, and enlarging our whole view and rule of life.—*Culture and Anarchy.*

THE PURITANS AND RELIGION.

Is it contended that the Puritan triumph in the Civil War was the triumph of religion,—of conduct and righteousness? Alas! it was its defeat. So grossly imperfect, so false, was the Puritan conception and presentation of righteousness, so at war with the ancient and inbred integrity, piety, good nature, and good humour of the English people, that it led straight to moral anarchy, the profligacy of the Restoration. It led to the court, the manners, the stage, the literature, which we know. It led to the long discredit of serious things, to the dryness of the eighteenth century, to the 'irreligion' which vexed Butler's righteous soul, to the aversion and incapacity for all deep inquiries concerning religion and its sanctions, to the belief so frequently found now among the followers of natural science that such inquiries are unprofitable. It led, amongst that middle class where religion still lived on to a narrowness, an intellectual poverty, almost incredible. They 'entered the prison of Puritanism, and had the key turned upon their spirit there for two hundred years.' It led to that character of their steady and respectable life which makes one shiver : its hideousness, its immense ennui.—*Mixed Essays.*

FUTURE OF HEBRAISM.

HEBRAISM has its faults and dangers; still, the intense and convinced energy with which the Hebrew, both of the Old and of the New Testament, threw himself upon his ideal of righteousness, and which inspired the incomparable definition of the great Christian virtue, faith,—*the substantiation of things hoped for, the evidence of things not seen,*—this energy of devotion to its ideal has belonged to Hebraism alone. As our idea of perfection widens beyond the narrow limits to which the over-rigour of Hebraising has tended to confine it, we shall yet come again to Hebraism for that devout energy in embracing our ideal, which alone can give to man the happiness of doing what he knows. 'If ye know these things, happy are ye if ye do them !'—the last word for infirm humanity will always be that. For this word, reiterated with a power now sublime, now affecting, but always admirable, our race will, as long as the world lasts, return to Hebraism; and the Bible, which preaches this word, will for ever remain, as Goethe called it, not only a national book, but the Book of the Nations.—*Culture and Anarchy.*

THE LIBERALS AND CHRISTIANITY.

LIBERALS who have no conception of the Christian religion as of a real need of the community, which the community has to satisfy, should learn to fix their view upon the simple source, common to Catholics and Protestants alike, of Christianity's power and permanence. The power and permanence come from Christianity's being a real source of cure for a real bondage and misery. Men have adapted the source to their use according to their lights, often very imperfect;—have piled fantastic buildings around it, carried its healing waters by strange and intricate conduits, done their best to make it no longer recognisable. But, in their fashion, they have used and they do still use it; and whenever their religion is treated, often because of their mishandling and disfigurement of it, as an obsolete nuisance to be discouraged and helped to die out, a profound sentiment in them rebels against such an outrage, because they are conscious not of their vain disfigurements of the Christian religion, but of its genuine curativeness.—*Mixed Essays.*

CATHOLICISM.

IN spite of all the shocks which the feelings of a good Catholic have in this Protestant country inevitably to undergo, in spite of the contemptuous insensibility to the grandeur of Rome which he finds so general and so hard to bear, how much has he to console him, how many acts of homage to the greatness of his religion may he see if he has his eyes open !   I will tell him of one of them. Let him go in London to that delightful spot, that Happy Island in Bloomsbury, the reading-room of the British Museum. Let him visit its sacred quarter, the region where its theological books are placed.   I am almost afraid to say what he will find there, for fear Mr. Spurgeon, like a second Caliph Omar, should give the library to the flames.   He will find an immense Catholic work, the collection of the Abbé Migne, lording it over that whole region, reducing to insignificance the feeble Protestant forces which hang upon its skirts.   Protestantism is duly represented, indeed : the librarian knows his business too well to suffer it to be otherwise. All the varieties of Protestantism are there.   There is the Library of Anglo-Catholic Theology, learned, decorous, exemplary, but a little uninteresting ; there are the works of Calvin, rigid, militant, menacing ; there are the works of Dr. Chalmers, the Scotch thistle valiantly doing duty as the rose of Sharon, but keeping something very Scotch about it all the time; there are the works of Dr. Channing, the last word of religious philosophy in a land where every one has some culture, and where superiorities are discountenanced,— the flower of moral and intelligent mediocrity.   But how are all these divided against one another, and how, though they were all united, are they dwarfed by the Catholic Leviathan, their neighbour! Majestic in its blue and gold unity, this fills shelf after shelf and compartment after compartment, its right mounting up into heaven among the white folios of the 'Acta Sanctorum,' its left plunging down into hell among the yellow octavos of the 'Law Digest.' Everything is there, in that immense 'Patrologiæ Cursus Completus,' in that 'Encyclopédie Théologique,' that 'Nouvelle Encyclopédie Théologique,' that 'Troisième Encyclopédie Théologique;' religion, philosophy, history, biography, arts, sciences, bibliography, gossip. The work embraces the whole range of human interests; like one of the great Middle-Age cathedrals, it is in itself a study for a life. Like the net in Scripture, it drags everything to land, bad and good, lay and ecclesiastical, sacred and profane, so that it be but matter of human concern. Wide-embracing as the power whose product it is! a power, for history at any rate, eminently *the Church*; not, perhaps, the Church of the future, but indisputably the Church of the past, and, in the past, the Church of the multitude.

This is why the man of imagination,—nay, and the philosopher too, in spite of her propensity to burn him,— will always have a weakness for the Catholic Church; because of the rich treasures of human life which have been stored within her pale. The mention of other religious bodies, or of their leaders, at once calls up in our mind the thought of men of a definite type as their adherents ; the mention of Catholicism suggests no such special following. Anglicanism suggests the English episcopate; Calvin's name suggests Dr. Candlish ; Chalmers's, the Duke of Argyll ; Channing's, Boston society ; but Catholicism suggests,—what shall I say?—all the pell-mell of the men and women of Shakspeare's plays. This abundance the Abbé Migne's collection faithfully reflects. —*Essays in Criticism.*

CATHOLICISM TO CATHOLICS.

CATHOLICISM is that form of Christianity which is fullest of human accretions and superstitions, because it is the oldest, the largest, the most popular. It is the religion which has most reached the people. It has been the great popular religion of Christendom, with all the accretions and superstitions inseparable from such a character. The bulk of its superstitions come from its having really plunged so far down into the multitude, and spread so wide among them. If this is a cause of error, it is also a cause of attachment. Who has seen the poor in other churches as they are seen in Catholic churches? Catholicism, besides, enveloped human life ; and Catholics in general feel themselves to have drawn not only their religion from the Church, they feel themselves to have drawn from her, too, their art and poetry and culture.

Her hierarchy, again, originally stamped in their imaginations with the character of a beneficent and orderly authority springing up amidst anarchy, appeared next as offering a career where birth was disregarded and merit regarded, and the things of the mind and the soul were honoured, in the midst of the iron feudal age which worshipped solely birth and force. So thus Catholicism acquired on the·imagination a second hold. And if there is a thing specially alien to religion, it is divisions; if there is a thing specially native to religion, it is peace and union. Hence the original attraction towards unity in Rome, and hence the great charm and power for men's minds of that unity when once attained. All these spells for the heart and imagination has Catholicism to Catholics, in addition to the spell for the conscience of a divine cure for vice and misery. And whoever treats Catholicism as a nuisance, to be helped to die out as soon as possible, has the heart, the imagination, and the conscience of Catholics in just revolt against him.—*Mixed Essays.*

TRUE STRENGTH OF CATHOLICISM.

WHEN Ultramontanism, sacerdotalism, and superstition are gone, Catholicism is not, as some may suppose, gone too. Neither is it left with nothing further but what it possesses in common with all the forms of Christianity, —the curative power of the word, character, and influence of Jesus. It is, indeed, left with this, which is the root of the matter, but it is left with a mighty power besides. It is left with the beauty, the richness, the poetry, the infinite charm for the imagination, of its own age-long growth, a growth such as we have described,— unconscious, popular, profoundly rooted, all-enveloping.

It is the sure sign of a shallow mind, to suppose that the strength of the Catholic Church is really in its tone of absolute certainty concerning its dogmas, in its airs of omniscience. On the contrary, as· experience widens, as the scientific and dogmatic pretensions of the Church become more manifestly illusory, its tone of certitude respecting them, so unguarded, so reiterated, ˆand so grossly calculated for immediate and vulgar effect, will be an embarrassment to it. The gain to-day, the effect upon a certain class of minds, will be found to be more than counterbalanced by the embarrassment to-morrow. Its dogma and its confident assertion of its dogma are no more a real source of strength and permanence to the Catholic Church, than its Ultramontanism. Its real superiority is in its charm for the imagination,—its poetry. I persist in thinking that Catholicism has, from this superiority, a great future before it ; that it will endure while all the Protestant sects (amongst which I do not include the Church of England) dissolve and perish. I persist in thinking that the prevailing form for the Christianity of the future will be the form of Catholicism ;—but a Catholicism purged, opening itself to the light and air, having the consciousness of its own poetry, freed from its sacerdotal despotism and freed from its pseudo-scientific apparatus of superannuated dogma. Its forms will be retained, as symbolising with the force and charm of poetry a few cardinal facts and ideas, simple indeed, but indispensable and inexhaustible, and on which our race could lay hold only by materialising them.—*Mixed Essays.*

THE NEED FOR BEAUTY.

THE need for beauty is a real and now rapidly growing need in man ; Puritanism cannot satisfy it, Catholicism and the English Church can. The needs of intellect and knowledge in him, indeed, neither Puritanism, nor Catholicism, nor the English Church, can at present satisfy. Those needs have to seek satisfaction nowadays elsewhere, —through the modern spirit, science, literature. But, as one drops the false science of the Churches, one perceives that what they had to deal with was so simple that it did not require science. Their beauty remains, investing certain elementary truths of inestimable depth and value, yet of extreme simplicity. But the Puritan Churches have no beauty. This makes the difficulty of maintaining the Established Church of Scotland. Once drop the false science on which successive generations of Scotchmen have so vainly valued themselves, once convince oneself that the Westminster Confession, whatever Principal Tulloch may think, is a document absolutely antiquated, sterile, and worthless, and what remains to the Church of Scotland?   Besides the simple elementary truths present in all forms of Christianity, there remains to the Church of Scotland merely that which remains to the Free Church, to the United Presbyterians, to Puritanism in general,—a religious service which is perhaps the most dismal performance ever invented by man.   It is here that Catholicism and the Church of England have such a real superiority ; and nothing can destroy it, and the present march of things is even favourable to it.   Let Liberals do their best to open Catholicism and the Church of England to all the enlarging influences of the time, to make tyranny and vexatiousness on the part of their clergy impossible ; but do not let them think they are to be destroyed, nor treat them as their natural enemies.— *Mixed Essays.*

MILTON AND ELIZA COOK.

Lord Granville is for admitting, in a public rite, the services of Dissent on the same footing as the services of the Church of England.   But let him accustom himself to attend both, and he will perceive what the difference between the services is.   The difference is really very much the difference between a reading from Milton and a reading from Eliza Cook,—a poetess, I hasten to add, of wide popularity, full of excellent sentiments, of appeals to the love of liberty, country, home.   And for a long while

the English Church, with the State to back her, committed the fatal mistake of trying to compel everybody
to forsake the reading of Eliza Cook and come to the
reading of Milton ; nay, to declare that they utterly ab-
jured Eliza Cook, and that they preferred Milton. And
sometimes, when it would have suited a man to come to
the reading of Milton, they would not let him, if he and
his family had ever preferred Eliza Cook. This was the
time of the strong and fruitful alliance of the Whigs with
Dissent. It may be said to have closed with the death
of a man whom we all admired, Lord Russell. He
established the right of the Dissenters to be not cross-
questioned and persecuted about the preferability of Milton to Eliza Cook ; they were to be free to prefer which
they pleased. Yet Milton remains Milton, and Eliza
Cook remains Eliza Cook. And a public rite, with a
reading of Milton attached to it, is another thing from a
public rite with a reading from Eliza Cook. The general
sentiment has gone heartily with Lord Russell in leaving
the Dissenters perfectly free to prefer and use Eliza Cook
as much as they please ; but is it certain that it will be
found equally to go with Lord Granville in letting them
import her into a public rite ?—*Mixed Essays.*

RATIONALE OF PUBLIC CEREMONIAL.

WHAT is the intention of all forms of public ceremonial
and ministration ? It is, that what is done and said in a

public place, and bears with it a public character, should be done and said worthily. The public is responsible for it. The public gets credit and advantage from it if it is done worthily, is compromised and harmed by it if it is done unworthily. The mode, therefore, of performing public functions in places invested with a public character is not left to the will and pleasure of chance individuals. It is expressly designed to rise above the level which would be thence given. If there is a sort of ignobleness and vulgarity (*was uns alle bändigt, das Gemeine*) which comes out in the crude performance of the mass of mankind left to themselves, public forms, in a higher strain and of recognised worth, are designed to take the place of such crude performance. They are a kind of schooling, which may educate gradually such performance into something better, and meanwhile may prevent it from standing forth, to its own discredit and to that of all of us, as public and representative. This, I say, is evidently the design of all forms for public use on serious and solemn occasions. No one will say that the common Englishman glides off-hand and by nature into a strain pure, noble, and elevated. On the contrary, he falls with great ease into vulgarity. But no people has shown more attachment than the English to old and dignified forms calculated to save us from it.

Such is the origin and such is the defence of the use of a set form of burial-service in our public churchyards. —*Last Essays.*

BURIALS BILL.

THE hearty believers in a man's natural right to have in the parish churchyard a burial to his own liking, do not conceal that they believe also in a man's natural right to have in the parish church a worship to his own liking. 'Let me be honest about it,' said Sir Wilfrid Lawson at Carlisle ; 'if you let the Nonconformist into the churchyard, that is only a step towards letting him into the church.' The two rights do, in fact, stand on precisely the same footing. If the naturalness of a man's wishing to do a thing creates for him a right to do it, then a Dissenter can urge his right to have his own minister say his say over him in the parish churchyard. Equally can he urge his right to have his own minister say his say to him in the parish church.

What bars the right is in both cases just the same thing : the higher right of the community. For the credit and welfare of the community, public forms are appointed to be observed in public places. The will and pleasure of individuals is not to have sway there. This is what bars the Nonconformist's right to have in his life-time what minister and service he likes in the parish church. It is also what bars his right to have after his death what minister and service he likes in the parish churchyard.—
Last Essays.

BURIALS RUBRIC.

In the denial of the burial-office to 'any that die unbaptised ' lies the true source of grievance.

The office is meant for Christians, and this was what the rubric intended, no doubt, to mark; baptism being taken as the stamp common to all Christians. But a large and-well-known sect of Christians, the Baptists, defer baptism until the recipient is of adult age, and their children, therefore, if they die, die unbaptised. To inquire' whether a child presented for burial is a Baptist's child or not, is an inquiry which no judicious and humane clergyman would make. The office was meant for Christians, and Baptists are Christians, for surely they do not cease to be so because of their tenet of adult baptism. Adult baptism was undoubtedly the primitive usage, although the change of usage adopted by the Church was natural and legitimate, and the sticklers (as may so often be said of the sticklers in these questions) would have been wiser had they acquiesced in it. But the rubric dresses the clergyman in an authority for investigating and excluding, which enables a violent and unwise man to play tricks that might, indeed, make the angels weep. Where he has the law on his side, he can refuse the burial-service outright to innocent infants and children the most piously brought up ; he can, under pretence of doubt and inquiry, adjourn, and often withhold it, where he has not.

Such a man does harm to the Church ; but it is not likely that he will have the sense to see this, when he has not eyes to see what harm he does to himself. There may not be many of such men, but a few make a great noise, and do a great deal of mischief. There is no stronger proof of the immense power of inspiring attachment which the Church of England possesses, and of the loveable and admirable qualities shown by many of the clergy, than that the Church should still have so strong a hold upon the affections of the country, in spite of such mischief-makers. If the Church ever loses it and is broken up, it will be by their fault. It was the view of this sort of people with their want of temper and want of judgment, the view of their mischievous action, exerting itself with all the pugnacity and tenacity of the British character, and of their fatal prominence, which moved Clarendon, a sincere friend of the Church of England, to that terrible sentence of his : 'Clergymen, who understand the least, and take the worst measure of human affairs, of all mankind that can write and read !'

The truly desirable, the indispensable change in the regulation of burials, is to remove the power of doing mischief which such persons now enjoy. And the best way to remove it, is to strike out the first rubric to the burial-service altogether.—*Last Essays.*

NATIONAL CHURCHES.

IF there were no national and historic form of church-order in possession of the ground, a genuine Christian would regret having to spend time and thought in shaping one, in having so to encumber himself with *serving*, to busy himself so much about a frame for his religious life as well as about the contents of the frame. After all, a man has only a certain sum of force to spend ; and if he takes a quantity of it for outward things, he has so much the less left for inward things. It is hardly to be believed, how much larger a space the mere affairs of the denomination fill in the time and thoughts of a Dissenter, than in the time and thoughts of a Churchman. Now all machinery-work of this kind is, to a man filled with a real love of the essence of Christianity, something of a hindrance to him in what he most wants to be at, something of a concession to his ordinary self. When an established and historic form exists, such a man should be, therefore, disposed to use it and comply with it. But,—as if it were not satisfied with proving its unprofitableness by corroding us with jealousy and so robbing us of the mildness and sweet reasonableness of Christ which is our mainstay,—political Dissent, Dissent for the sake of church-policy and church-management, proves it, too, by stimulating our ordinary self through over-care for what flatters this. In fact, what is it that the everyday, middle-class Philistine,—not the rare flower of the Dissenters but the common staple,—finds so attrac-tive in Dissent?   Is it not, as to discipline, that his self-importance is fomented by the fuss, bustle, and partisan-ship of a private sect, instead of being lost in the great-ness of a public body?   As to worship, is it not that his taste is pleased by usages and words that come down to *him*, instead of drawing him up to *them*; by services which reflect, instead of the culture of great men of religious genius, the crude culture of himself and his fellows?   And as to doctrine, is it not that his mind is pleased at hearing no opinion but its own, by having all disputed points taken for granted in its own favour, by being urged to no return upon itself, no development? And what is all this but the very feeding and stimulating of our ordinary self, instead of the annulling of it? No doubt it is natural; to indulge our ordinary self is the most natural thing in the world. But Christianity is not natural; and if the flower of Christianity be the grace and peace which comes of annulling our ordinary self, then to this flower it is fatal.—*St. Paul and Protestantism.*

CHURCH AND SECT.

ONE may say that to be reared a member of a national Church is in itself a lesson of religious moderation, and a help towards culture and harmonious perfection. Instead of battling for his own private forms for expressing the inexpressible and defining the undefinable, a man takes those which have commended themselves most to the religious life of his nation; and while he may be sure that within those forms the religious side of his own nature may find its satisfaction, he has leisure and composure to satisfy other sides of his nature as well.

But with the member of a Nonconforming or self-made religious community, how different ! The sectary's *eigene grosse Erfindungen*, as Goethe calls them,—the precious discoveries of himself and his friends for expressing the inexpressible and defining the undefinable in peculiar forms of their own,—cannot but, as he has voluntarily chosen them and is personally responsible for them, fill his whole mind. He is zealous to do battle for them and affirm them ; for in affirming them he affirms himself, and that is what we all like. Other sides of his being are thus neglected, because the religious side, always tending in every serious man to predominance over our other spiritual sides, is in him made quite absorbing and tyrannous by the condition of self-assertion and challenge which he has chosen for himself. And just what is not essential in religion he comes to mistake for essential, and a thousand times the more readily because he has chosen it of himself ; and religious activity he fancies to consist in battling for it.—*Culture and Anarchy.*

PUGILISTIC DISSENT.

THE more the sense of religion grows, and of religion in a large way,—the sense of the beauty and rest of religion, the sense that its charm lies in its grace and peace,—the more will the present attitude, objections, and complaints of the Dissenters indispose men's minds to them. They will, I firmly believe, lose ground ; they will not keep hold of the new generations. In most of the mature Dissenters the spirit of scruple, objection-taking, and division, is, I fear, so ingrained, that in any proffered terms of union they are more likely to seize occasion for fresh cavil than occasion for peace. But the new generations will be otherwise minded. As to the Church's want of grace and peace in disputing the ground with Dissent, the justice of what Barrow says will be more and more felt :—' He that being assaulted is constrained to stand on his defence, may not be said to be in peace ; yet his not being so (involuntarily) is not to be imputed to him.' But the Dissenters have not this, the Church's excuse, for being men of war in a sphere of grace and peace. And they turn themselves into men of war more and more.

Look at one of the ablest of them, who is much before the public, and whose abilities I unfeignedly admire : Mr. Dale. Mr. Dale is really a pugilist, a brilliant pugilist. He has his arena down at Birmingham, where he does his practice with Mr. Chamberlain, and Mr. Jesse Collings, and the rest of his band ; and then from time to time he comes up to the metropolis, to London, and gives a public exhibition here of his skill. And a very powerful performance it often is. And the 'Times' observes, that the chief Dissenting ministers are becoming quite the intellectual equals of the ablest of the clergy. Very likely ; this sort of practice is just the right thing for bracing a man's intellectual muscles. I have no fears concerning Mr. Dale's intellectual muscles ; what I am a little uneasy about is his religious temper. The essence of religion is grace and peace. And though, no doubt, Mr. Dale cultivates grace and peace at other times, when he is not busy with his anti-Church practice, yet his cultivation of grace and peace can be none the better, and must naturally be something the worse, for the time and energy given to his pugilistic interludes. And the more that mankind, instead of placing their religion in all manner of things where it is not, come to place it in sheer goodness, and in grace and peace,—and this is the tendency, I think, with the English people,—the less favourable will public opinion be to the proceedings of the political Dissenters, and the less has the Church to fear from their pugnacious self-assertion.—*Last Essays.*

DISSIDENCE OF DISSENT.

WHETHER the Dissenters will believe it or not, my wish to reconcile them with the Church is from no desire to give their adversaries a victory and them a defeat, but from the conviction that they are on a false line ; from sorrow at seeing their fine qualities and energies thrown away, from hope of signal good to this whole nation if they can be turned to better account. ' The dissidence of Dissent, and the Protestantism of the Protestant religion,' have some of mankind's deepest and truest instincts against them, and cannot finally prevail. If they prevail for a time, that is only a temporary stage in man's history ; they will fail in the end, and will have to confess it.

It is said, and on what seems good authority, that already in America, that Paradise of the sects, there are signs of reaction, and that the multitude of sects there begin to tend to agglomerate themselves into two or three great bodies. It is said, too, that whereas the Church of Rome, in the first year of the present century, had but one in two-hundred of the population of the United States, it has now one in six or seven. This at any rate is certain, that the great and sure gainer by the dissidence of Dissent and the Protestantism of the Protestant religion is the Church of Rome. Unity and continuity in public religious worship are a need of human nature, an eternal aspiration of Christendom ; but unity and continuity in religious worship joined with perfect mental sanity and freedom. A Catholic Church transformed is, I believe, the Church of the future. But what the Dissenters, by their false aims and misused powers, at present effect, is to extend and prolong the reign of a Catholic Church *un*transformed, with all its conflicts, impossibilities, miseries. That, however, is what the Dissenters, in their present state, cannot and will not see. For the growth of insight to recognise it, one must rely, both among the Dissenters themselves and in the nation which has to judge their aims and proceedings, on the help of time and progress ;—time and progress, in alliance with 'the ancient and inbred integrity, piety, good nature, and good humour of the English people.'—*Last Essays.*

COMPREHENSION.

So far am I from being moved, in anything that I do or say in this matter, by ill-will to Puritanism and the Puritans, that it is, on the contrary, just because of my hearty respect for them, and from my strong sense of their value, that I speak as I do. Certainly I consider them to be in the main, at present, an obstacle to progress and to true civilisation. But this is because their worth is, in my opinion, such, that not only must one for their own sakes wish to see it turned to more advantage, but others from whom they are now separated, would greatly gain by conjunction with them, and our whole collective force of growth and progress be thereby immeasurably increased. In short, my own feeling when we regard them, is a feeling, not of ill-will, but of regret at waste of power ; my one desire is a desire of comprehension.— *St. Paul and Protestantism.*

WHAT IS THE CHURCH?

A MAN who has published a good deal which is at variance with the body of theological doctrine commonly received in the Church of England, and commonly preached by its ministers, cannot well, it may be thought, stand up before the clergy as a friend to their cause and to that of the Church. Professed ardent enemies of the Church have assured me that I am really, in their opinion, one of the worst enemies that the Church has,—a much worse enemy than themselves. Perhaps that opinion is shared by some of those who now hear me. I make bold to say that it is totally erroneous. It is founded in an entire misconception of the character and scope of what I have written concerning religion. I regard the Church of England as, in fact, a great national society for the promotion of what is commonly called *goodness*, and for promoting it through the most effectual means possible, the only means which are really and truly effectual for the object : through the means of the Christian religion and of the Bible. This plain practical object is undeniably the object of the Church of England and of the clergy. 'Our province,' says Butler, 'our province is virtue and religion, life and manners, the science of improving the temper and making the heart better. This is the field assigned us to cultivate ; how much it has lain neglected is indeed astonishing. He who should find out one rule to assist us in this work would deserve infinitely better of mankind than all the improvers of other knowledge put together.' This is indeed true religion, true Christianity.

And therefore the object of the Church, which is in large the promotion of goodness, and the business of the clergy, which is to teach men their duty and to assist them in the discharge of it, do really and truly interest me more, and do appear in my eyes as things more valuable and important, than the object and business pursued in those writings of mine which are in question, —writings which seek to put a new construction on much in the Bible, to alter the current criticism of it, to invalidate the conclusions of theologians from it. If the two are to conflict, I had rather that it should be the object and business of those writings which should have to give way. Most certainly the establishment of an improved biblical criticism, or the demolition of the systems of theologians, will never in itself avail to teach men their duty or to assist them in the discharge of it. Perhaps, even, no one can very much give himself to such objects without running some risk of over-valuing their importance and of being diverted by them from practice.—*Last Essays.*

THE CHURCH AND SOCIAL PROGRESS.

THE ideal of the working classes is a future,—a future on earth, not up in the sky,—which shall profoundly change and ameliorate things for them ; an immense social progress, nay, a social transformation ; in short, as their song goes, 'a good time coming.' And the Church is supposed to be an appendage to the Barbarians, as I have somewhere, in joke, called it ; an institution devoted above all to the landed gentry, but also to the propertied and satisfied classes generally ; favouring immobility, preaching submission, and reserving transformation in general for the other side of the grave.

Such a Church, I admit, cannot possibly nowadays attach the working classes, or be viewed with anything but disfavour by them. But certainly the superstitious worship of existing social facts, a devoted obsequiousness to the landed and propertied and satisfied classes, does not inhere in the Christian religion. The Church does not get it from the Bible. Exception is taken to its being said that there is communism in the Bible, because we see that communists are fierce, violent, insurrectionary people, with temper and actions abhorrent to the spirit of Christianity. But if we say, on the one hand, that the Bible utterly condemns all violence, revolt, fierceness, and self-assertion, then we may safely say, on the other hand, that there is certainly communism in the Bible. The truth is, the Bible enjoins endless self-sacrifice all round ; and to any one who has grasped this idea, the superstitious worship of property, the reverent devotedness to the propertied and satisfied classes, is impossible. And the Christian Church has, I boldly say, been the fruitful parent of men who, having grasped this idea, have been exempt from this superstition. Institutions are to be judged by their great men ; in the end, they take their line from their great men. The Christian Church, and the line which is natural to it and which will one day prevail in it, is to be judged from the saints and the tone of the saints. Now really, if there have been any people in the world free from illusions about the divine origin and divine sanctions of social facts just as they stand,— open, therefore, to the popular hopes of a profound renovation and a happier future,—it has been those inspired idiots, the poets and the saints. Nobody nowadays attends much to what the poets say, so I leave them on one side. But listen to a saint on the origin of property ; listen to Pascal. ' " This dog belongs to *me*," said these poor children ; "that place in the sun is *mine !*" Behold the beginning and the image of all usurpation upon earth ! '—*Last Essays.*

THE KINGDOM OF GOD.

IT is really well to consider, how entirely our religious teaching and preaching, and our creeds, and what passes with us for ' the gospel,' turn on quite other matters from the fundamental matter of the primitive gospel, or good news, of our Saviour himself. This gospel was the ideal of popular hope and longing, an immense renovation and transformation of things : *the kingdom of God.* ' Jesus came into Galilee proclaiming the good news of God and saying : The time is fulfilled and the kingdom of God is at hand ; repent and believe the good news.' Jesus went about the cities and villages 'proclaiming the good news of the kingdom.' The multitudes followed him, and he ' took them and talked to them about the kingdom of God.' He told his disciples to preach this. ' Go thou, and spread the news of the kingdom of God.' ' Into whatever city ye enter, say to them : The kingdom of God has come nigh unto you.' He told his disciples to pray for it. ' Thy kingdom come !' He told them to seek and study it before all things. ' Seek first God's righteousness and kingdom.'

It is a contracted and insufficient conception of the gospel which takes into view only the establishment of *righteousness*, and does not also take into view the establishment of *the kingdom.* And the establishment of the kingdom does imply an immense renovation and transformation of our actual state of things ; that is certain. This then, which is the ideal of the popular classes, of the multitude everywhere, is a legitimate ideal. And a Church of England devoted to the service and ideals of any class or classes,—however distinguished, wealthy, or powerful,—which are perfectly satisfied with things as they are, is not only out of sympathy with the ideal of the popular classes ; it is also out of sympathy with the gospel, of which the ideal does, in the main, coincide with theirs.—*Last Essays.*

TRUE STRENGTH OF THE CHURCH OF ENGLAND.

THIS is the real business of the Church : to make progress in grace and peace. Force the Church of England has certainly some ; perhaps a good deal. But its true strength is in relying, not on its powers of force, but on its powers of attractiveness. And by opening itself to the glow of the old and true ideal of the Christian Gospel, by fidelity to reason, by placing the stress of its religion on goodness, by cultivating grace and peace, it will inspire attachment, to which the attachment which it inspires now, deep though that is, will be as nothing ; it may last, such a Church may last, as long as this nation. —*Last Essays.*

EPIEIKEIA.

'I BESEECH you,' said Paul, '*by the mildness and gentleness of Christ.*'[1] The word which our Bible translates by 'gentleness' means more properly 'reasonableness with sweetness,' 'sweet reasonableness.' '*I beseech you by the mildness and sweet reasonableness of Christ.*' This mildness and sweet reasonableness it was, which, stamped with the individual charm they had in Jesus Christ, came to the world as something new, won its heart and conquered it. Every one had been asserting his ordinary self and was miserable ; to forbear to assert one's ordinary self, to place one's happiness in mildness and sweet reasonableness, was a revelation. As men followed this novel route to happiness, a living spring opened beside their way, the spring of charity ; and out of this spring arose those two heavenly visitants, Charis and Irene, *grace* and *peace*, which enraptured the poor wayfarer, and filled him with a joy which brought all the world after him. And still, whenever these visitants appear, as appear for a witness to the vitality of Christianity they daily do, it is from the same spring that they arise; and this spring is opened solely by the mildness and sweet reasonableness which forbears to assert our ordinary self, nay, which even takes pleasure in effacing it.—*St. Paul and Protestantism.*

[1] διὰ τῆς πραΰτητος καὶ ἐπιεικείας τοῦ Χριστοῦ.   *Cor.* II, x, 1.

THE RELIGIOUS SITUATION.

WHEN we consider the immense change which, in other matters where tradition and convention were the obstacles to all change, has befallen the thought of this country since the Continent was opened at the end of the great war, we cannot doubt that in religion, too, the mere barriers of tradition and convention will finally give way, that a common European level of thought will establish itself, and will spread to America also. Of course there will be backwaters, more or less strong, of superstition and obscurantism ; but I speak of the probable development of opinion in those classes which are to be called progressive and liberal. Such classes are undoubtedly the multiplying and prevailing body both here and in America. And I say that, if we judge the future from the past, these classes, in any matter where it is tradition and convention which at present isolates them from the common liberal opinion of Europe, will, with time, be drawn almost inevitably into that opinion.

The partisans of traditional religion in this country do not know, I think, how decisively the whole force of progressive and liberal opinion on the Continent has pronounced against the Christian religion. They do not know how surely the whole force of progressive and liberal opinion in this country tends to follow, so far as traditional religion is concerned, the opinion of the Continent.

They dream of patching up things unmendable, of retaining what can never be retained, of stopping change at a point where it can never be stopped. The undoubted tendency of liberal opinion is to reject the whole anthropomorphic and miraculous religion of tradition, as unsound and untenable. On the Continent such opinion has rejected it already. One cannot blame the rejection. 'Things are what they are,' and the religion of tradition, Catholic or Protestant, *is* unsound and untenable. A greater force of tradition in favour of religion is all which now prevents the liberal opinion in this country from following Continental opinion. That force is not of a nature to be permanent, and it will not, in fact, hold out long. But a very grave question is behind.

Rejecting, henceforth, all concern with the obsolete religion of tradition, the liberalism of the Continent rejects also, and on the like grounds, all concern with the Bible and Christianity. To claim for the Bible the direction, in any way, of modern life, is, we hear, as if Plato had sought to found his ideal republic 'upon a text of Hesiod.' The real question is, whether this conclusion, too, of modern liberalism is to be admitted, like the conclusion that traditionary religion is unsound and obsolete. And it does not find many gainsayers. Obscurantists are glad to see the question placed on this footing : that the cause of traditionary religion, and the cause of Christianity in general, must stand or fall together. For they see but very little way into the future ; and in the immediate present this way of putting the question tells, as they clearly perceive, in their favour.   In the immediate present many will be tempted to cling to the traditionary religion with their eyes shut, rather than accept the extinction of Christianity.   Other friends of religion are busy with fantastic projects, which can never come to anything, but which prevent their seeing the real character of the situation.   So the thesis of modern liberals on the Continent, that Christianity in general stands on the same footing as traditionary religion and must share its fate, meets with little direct discussion or opposition.   And liberal opinion everywhere will at last grow accustomed to finding that thesis put forward as certain, will become familiarised with it, will suppose that no one disputes it.   This in itself will tend to withhold men from any serious return upon their own minds in the matter.   Meanwhile the day will most certainly arrive, when the great body of liberal opinion in this country will adhere to the first half of the doctrine of Continental liberals ;—will admit that traditionary religion is utterly untenable.   And the danger is, that from the habits of their minds, and from seeing the thing treated as certain, and from hearing nothing urged against it, our liberals may admit as indisputable the second half of the doctrine too : that Christianity, also, is untenable.

And therefore is it so all-important to insist on what

I call the *natural truth* of Christianity, and to bring this out all we can.—*Last Essays.*

THE DISSENTERS AND THE CRISIS.

DISSENT, as a religious movement of our day, would be almost droll, if it were not, from the tempers and actions it excites, so extremely irreligious. But what is to be said for men, aspiring to deal with the cause of religion, who either cannot see that what the people now require is a religion of the Bible quite different from that which *any* of the churches or sects supply ; or who, seeing this, spend their energies in fiercely battling as to whether the Church should be a national institution or no? The question, at the present juncture, is in itself so absolutely unimportant ! The thing is, to recast religion. If this is done, the new religion will be the national one ; if it is not done, the separating the nation, in its collective and corporate character, from religion, will not do it. It is as if men's minds were much unsettled about mineralogy, and the teachers of it were at variance, and no teacher was convincing, and many people, therefore, were disposed to throw the study of mineralogy overboard altogether. What would naturally be the first business for every friend of the study? Surely, to establish on safe grounds the value of the study, and to put its claims in a new light where they could no longer be denied. But if he acted as our Dissenters act in religion, what would he do?

Give himself, heart and soul, to a furious crusade against keeping the Government School of Mines.—*Literature and Dogma*

RITUALISM.

THIS is the real objection both to the Catholic and to the Protestant doctrine as a basis for conduct ;—not that it is a degrading superstition, but that it is *not sure* ; that it assumes what cannot be *verified.*

For a long time this objection occurred to scarcely anybody. And there are still, and for a long time yet there will be, many to whom it does not occur. In particular, on those 'devout women' who in the history of religion have at all times played a part in many respects so beautiful but in some respects so mischievous,—on them, and on a certain number of men like them, it has and can as yet have, so far as one can see, no effect at all. Who that watches the energumens during the celebration of the Communion in some Ritualistic church, their gestures and behaviour, the floor of the church strewn with what seem to be the dying and the dead, progress to the altar almost barred by forms suddenly dropping as if they were shot in battle,—who that observes this delighted adoption of vehement rites, till yesterday unknown, adopted and practised now with all that absence of tact, measure, and correct perception in things of form and manner, all that slowness to see when they are making themselves ridiculous, which belongs to the people of our English race,—who, I say, that marks this can doubt, that for a not small portion of the religious community, a difficulty to the intelligence will for a long time yet be no difficulty at all? With their mental condition and habits, given a story to which their religious emotions can attach themselves, and the famous *Credo quia ineptum* will hold good with them still. To think they know what passed in the Council of the Trinity is not hard to them; they could easily think they even knew what were the hangings of the Trinity's council-chamber.—*Literature and Dogma.*

SIMPLETONS AND SAVAGES

To our English race, with its insularity, its profound faith in action, its contempt for dreamers and failers, inadequate ideals in life, manners, government, thought, religion, will always be a source of danger. Energetic action makes up, we think, for imperfect knowledge. We think that all is well, that a man is following 'a moral impulse,' if he pursues an end which he 'deems of supreme importance.' We impose neither on him nor on ourselves the duty of discerning whether he is *right* in deeming it so.

Hence our causes are often as small as our noise about them is great. To see people busy themselves about Ritualism, that question of not the most strong-minded portion of the clergy and laity, or to see them busy themselves about that 'burning question' of the fierce and acrimonious political Dissenters, the Burials Bill, leading up to the other 'burning question' of disestablishment,—to see people so eager about these things, one might sometimes fancy that the whole English nation, as in Chillingworth's time it was divided into two great hosts of Publicans and Sinners on the one side, Scribes and Pharisees on the other, so in ours it was going to divide itself into two vast camps of Simpletons here, under the command, suppose, of Mr. Beresford Hope, and of Savages there, under the command of Mr. Henry Richard. And it is so notorious that great movements are always led by aliens to the sort of people who make the mass of the movement,—by gifted outsiders,—that I shall not, I hope, be suspected of implying that Mr. Beresford Hope is a simpleton or Mr. Henry Richard a savage. But what we have to do is to raise and multiply in this country a third host, with the conviction that the ideals both of Simpletons and Savages are profoundly inadequate and profoundly unedifying, and with the resolve to win victory for a better ideal than that of either of them.—*Mixed Essays.*

FALSE HEBRAISERS.

It may be very well for born Hebraisers, like Mr. Spurgeon, to Hebraise ; but for Liberal statesmen to

Hebraise is surely unsafe, and to see poor old Liberal hacks Hebraising, whose real self belongs to a kind of negative Hellenism,—a state of moral indifferency without intellectual ardour,—is even painful.—*Culture and Anarchy.*

MESSRS. MOODY AND SANKEY.

I HEARD Mr. Moody preach to one of his vast audiences on a topic eternally attractive,—salvation by Jesus Christ. Mr. Moody's account of that salvation was exactly the old story, to which I have often adverted, of the contract in the Council of the Trinity. Justice puts in her claim, said Mr. Moody, for the punishment of guilty mankind ; God admits it. Jesus intercedes, undertakes to bear their punishment, and signs an undertaking to that effect. Thousands of years pass ; Jesus is on the cross on Calvary. Justice appears, and presents to him his signed undertaking. Jesus accepts it, bows his head, and expires. Christian salvation consists in the undoubting belief in the transaction here described, and in the hearty acceptance of the release offered by it.

Never let us deny to this story power and pathos, or treat with hostility ideas which have entered so deep into the life of Christendom. But the story is not true ; it never really happened. These personages never did meet together, and speak, and act, in the manner related. The personages of the Christian Heaven and their conversations are no more matter of fact than the personages of the Greek Olympus and their conversations. Sir Robert Phillimore seeks to tie up the Church of England to a belief in the personality of Satan, and he might as well seek to tie it up to a belief in the personality of Tisiphone. Satan and Tisiphone are alike not real persons, but shadows thrown by man's guilt and terrors. Mr. Moody's audiences are the last people who will come to perceive all this ; they are chiefly made up from the main body of lovers of our popular religion,—the serious and steady middle class, with its bounded horizons. To the more educated class above this, and to the more free class below it, the grave beliefs of the religious middle class in such stories as Mr. Moody's story of the Covenant of Redemption are impossible now ; to the religious middle class itself they will be impossible soon. Salvation by Jesus Christ, therefore, if it has any reality, must be placed somewhere else than in a hearty consent to Mr. Moody's story. Something Mr. Moody and his hearers have experienced from Jesus, let us own, which does them good ; but of this something they have not yet succeeded in getting the right history.—*God and the Bible.*

PROFESSOR CLIFFORD.

WE find a brilliant mathematician, Professor Clifford, launching invectives which, if they were just, would prove either that no religion at all has any right to mankind's regard, or that the Christian religion, at all events, has none. He calls Christianity 'that awful plague which has destroyed two civilisations and but barely failed to slay such promise of good as is now struggling to live amongst men.' He warns his fellow-men against showing any tenderness to 'the slender remnant of a system which has made its red mark on history and still lives to threaten mankind.' 'The grotesque forms of its intellectual be- lief,' he scornfully adds by way of finish, 'have survived the discredit of its moral teaching.'

But these are merely the crackling fireworks of youth- ful paradox. One reads it all, half sighing, half smiling, as the declamation of a clever and confident youth, with the hopeless inexperience, irredeemable by any clever- ness, of his age. Only when one is young and headstrong can one thus prefer bravado to experience, can one stand by the Sea of Time, and instead of listening to the solemn and rhythmical beat of its waves, choose to fill the air with one's own whoopings to start the echo. But the mass of plain people hear such talk with impatient indignation, and flock all the more eagerly to Messrs. Moody and Sankey. They feel that the brilliant free- thinker and revolutionist talks about their religion and yet is all abroad in it, does not know either that or the great facts of human life ; and they go to those who know them better. And the plain people are not wrong. · Compared with Professor Clifford, Messrs. Moody and

Sankey are masters of the philosophy of history.   Men are not mistaken in thinking that Christianity has done them good, in loving it, in wishing to listen to those who will talk to them about what they love, and will talk of it with admiration and gratitude, not contempt and hatred. Christianity is truly, as in ' Literature and Dogma ' I have called it, ' the greatest and happiest stroke ever yet made for human perfection.'   Men do not err, they are on firm ground of experience, when they say that they have practically found Christianity to be something incomparably beneficent.   Where they err, is in their way of accounting for this, and of assigning its causes.—*God and the Bible.*

PHILOSOPHICAL RADICALS.

IF the matter were not so serious, one could hardly help smiling at the chagrin and manifest perplexity of such of one's friends as happen to be philosophical radicals and secularists, at having to reckon with religion again when they thought its day was quite gone by, and that they need not study it any more or take account of it any more, but it was passing out, and a kind of new gospel, half Bentham half Cobden, in which they were themselves particularly strong, was coming in.   And perhaps there is no one who more deserves to be compassionated, than an elderly or middle-aged man of this kind, such as several of their Parliamentary spokesmen and respresentatives are. For perhaps the younger men of the party may take heart of grace, and acquaint themselves a little with religion, now that they see its day is by no means over. But, for the older ones, their mental habits are formed, and it is almost too late for them to begin such new studies. However, a wave of religious reaction *is* evidently passing over Europe ; due very much to our revolutionary and philosophical friends having insisted upon it that religion was gone by and unnecessary, when it was neither the one nor the other. Obedience, strange as it may sound, is a real need of human nature ;—above all, moral and religious obedience. Undoubtedly, there are in the popular classes of every country forces of piety and religion capable of being brought into an alliance with the Church, the national society for the promotion of goodness, in that country. And of no people may this be more certainly said than of ours.—*Last Essays.*

A HISTORICAL PARALLEL.

IT is often said : If Jesus Christ came now, his religion would be rejected. And this is only another way of saying that the world now, as the Jewish people formerly, has something which thwarts and confuses its perception of what righteousness really is. It is so ; and the thwarting cause is the same now as then :—the dogmatic system current, the so-called orthodox theology. This prevents now, as it did then, that which righteousness really is, the method and secret of Jesus, from being rightly received, from operating fully, and from accomplishing its due effect.

So true is this, that we have only to look at our own community to see the almost precise parallel, so far as religion is concerned, to the state of things presented in Judæa when Jesus Christ came. The multitudes are the same everywhere. The chief priests and elders of the people, and the scribes, are our bishops and dogmatists, with their pseudo-science of learned theology blinding their eyes, and always,—whenever simple souls are disposed to think that the method and secret of Jesus is true religion, and that the Great Personal First Cause and the Godhead of the Eternal Son have nothing to do with it,—eager to cry out : *This people that knoweth not the law are cursed !* The Pharisees, with their genuine concern for religion, but total want of perception of what religion really is, and by their temper, attitude, and aims doing their best to make religion impossible, are the Protestant Dissenters. The Sadducees are our friends the philosophical Liberals, who believe neither in angel nor spirit, but in Mr. Herbert Spencer. Even the Roman governor has his close parallel in our celebrated aristocracy, with its superficial good sense and good nature, its complete inaptitude for ideas, its profound helplessness in presence of all great spiritual movements. And the result is, that the splendid promises to righteousness made by the

Hebrew prophets, claimed by the Jews as the property of Judaism, claimed by us as the property of Christianity, are almost as ludicrously inapplicable to our religious state now, as to theirs then.—*Literature and Dogma.*

CHRISTIANITY WILL SURVIVE.

CHRISTIANITY will survive because of its natural truth. Those who fancied that they had done with it, those who had thrown it aside because what was presented to them under its name was so unreceivable, will have to return to it again, and to learn it better. The Latin nations,—even the southern Latin nations,—will have to acquaint themselves with that fundamental document of Christianity, the Bible, and to discover wherein it differs from 'a text of Hesiod.' Neither will the old forms of Christian worship be extinguished by the growth of a truer conception of their essential contents. Those forms, thrown out at dimly-grasped truth, approximative and provisional representations of it, and which are now surrounded with such an atmosphere of tender and profound sentiment, will not disappear. They will survive as poetry. Above all, among the Catholic nations will this be the case. And, indeed, one must wonder at the fatuity of the Roman Catholic Church, that she should not herself see what a future there is for her here. Will there never arise among Catholics some great soul, to perceive that the eternity and universality, which is vainly claimed for

Catholic dogma and the ultramontane system, might really be possible for Catholic worship? But to rule over the moment and the credulous has more attraction than to work for the future and the sane.

Christianity, however, will find the ways for its own future. What is certain is that it will not disappear. Whatever progress may be made in science, art, and literary culture,—however much higher, more general, and more effective than at present the value for them may become,—Christianity will be still there as what these rest against and imply ; as the indispensable background, the *three-fourths of life.* It is true, while 'the remaining fourth is ill-cared for, the three-fourths themselves must also suffer with it. But this does but bring us to the old and true Socratic thesis of the interdependence of virtue and knowledge.—*Last Essays.*

RELIGIOUS RECONSTRUCTION.

In the same spirit in which she judges Bishop Colenso, Miss Cobbe, like so many earnest liberals of our practical race, both here and in America, herself sets vigorously about a positive reconstruction of religion, about making a religion of the future out of hand, or at least setting about making it. We must not rest, she and they are always thinking and saying, in negative criticism, we must be creative and constructive ; hence we have such works as her recent 'Religious Duty,' and works still more considerable, perhaps, by others, which will be in every one's mind. These works often have much ability; they often spring out of sincere convictions, and a sincere wish to do good; and they sometimes, perhaps, do good. Their fault is (if I may be permitted to say so) one which they have in common with the British College of Health, in the New Road. Every one knows the British College of Health; it is that building with the lion and the statue of the Goddess Hygeia before it; at least, I am sure about the lion, though I am not absolutely certain about the Goddess Hygeia. This building does credit, perhaps, to the resources of Dr. Morrison and his disciples; but it falls a good deal short of one's idea of what a British College of Health ought to be. In England, where we hate public interference and love individual enterprise, we have a whole crop of places like the British College of Health; the grand name without the grand thing. Unluckily, creditable to individual enterprise as they are, they tend to impair our taste by making us forget what more grandiose, noble, or beautiful character properly belongs to a public institution. The same may be said of the religions of the future of Miss Cobbe and others. Creditable, like the British College of Health, to the resources of their authors, they yet tend to make us forget what more grandiose, noble, or beautiful character properly belongs to religious constructions.—*Essays in Criticism.*

INTERREGNUM.

MIRACLES, the mainstay of popular religion, are touched by Ithuriel's spear. They are beginning to dissolve ; but what are we to expect during the process ? Probably, amongst many religious people, vehement efforts at reaction, a recrudescence of superstition ; the passionate resolve to keep hold on what is slipping away from them, by giving up more and more the use of reason in religion, and by resting more and more on authority. The Church of Rome is the great upholder of authority as against reason in religion ; and it will be strange if in the coming time of transition the Church of Rome does not gain.

But for many more than those whom Rome attracts, there will be an interval, between the time when men take the religion of the Bible to be a thaumaturgy and the time when they perceive it to be something different, in which they will be prone to throw aside the religion of the Bible altogether as a delusion. And this, again, will be mainly the fault,—if fault that can be called which was an inevitable error,—of the religious people themselves, who, from the time of the Apostles downwards, have insisted upon it that religion shall be a thaumaturgy or nothing. For very many, therefore, when it cannot be a thaumaturgy, it will be nothing. And very likely there will come a day when there will be less religion than even now. For the religion of the Bible is so simple and powerful, that even those who make the Bible a thaumaturgy get hold of the religion, because they read the Bible ; but, if men do not read the Bible, they cannot get hold of the religion in it. And then will be fulfilled the saying of the prophet Amos : ' Behold, the days come, saith the Eternal, that I will send a famine in the land, not a famine of bread, nor a thirst for water, but of hearing the words of the Eternal ; and they shall wander from sea to sea, and from the north even to the east they shall run to and fro to seek the word of the Eternal, and shall not find it.'

Nevertheless, as after this mournful prophecy the herdsman of Tekoah goes on to say : ' *There shall yet not the least grain of Israel fall to the earth !* ' To the Bible men will return ; and why ? Because they cannot do without it. Because happiness is our being's end and aim, and happiness belongs to righteousness, and righteousness is revealed in the Bible. For this simple reason men will return to the Bible, just as a man who tried to give up food, thinking it was a vain thing and he could do without it, would return to food ; or a man who tried to give up sleep, thinking it was a vain thing and he could do without it, would return to sleep. Then there will come a time of reconstruction.--*Literature and Dogma.*

OBJECT OF 'LITERATURE AND DOGMA.'

THE freethinking of one age is the common-sense of the next, and the Christian world will certainly learn to transform beliefs which it now thinks to be untransformable. The way will be found. And the new Christianity will call forth more effort in the individual who uses it than the old, will require more open and instructed minds for its reception ; and this is progress. But we live at the beginning of a great transition, which cannot well be accomplished without confusion and distress. I do not pretend to operate a general change of religious opinion, such as can only come to pass through the operation of many labourers, working, all of them, towards a like end, and by the instrumentality, in a very considerable degree, of the clergy. *One man's life, what is it?* says Goethe ; but even one man in his short term may do something to ease a severe transition, to diminish violent shocks in it, and bitter pain. With this end in view, I have addressed myself to men such as are happily not rare in this country, men of free and active minds, who, though they may be profoundly dissatisfied with the received theology, are yet interested in religion, and more or less acquainted with the Bible. These I have endeavoured to help ; and they, if they are helped, will in their turn help others.—*God and the Bible.*

THE REPROACH OF PRESUMPTION.

THE charge of presumption, and of setting oneself up above all the great men of past days, above 'the wisdom of all nations,' which is often brought against those who pronounce the old view of our religion to be untenable, springs out of a failure to perceive how little the abandonment of certain long-current beliefs depends upon a man's own will, or even upon his sum of powers natural or acquired. Sir Matthew Hale was not inferior in force of mind to a modern Chief Justice because he believed in witchcraft. Nay, the more enlightened modern, who drops errors of his forefathers by help of that mass of experience which his forefathers aided in accumulating, may often be, according to the well-known saying, 'a dwarf on the giant's shoulders.' His merits may be small compared with those of the giant. Perhaps his only merit is, that he has had the good sense to get up on the giant's shoulders, instead of trotting contentedly along in his shadow. Yet even this, surely, is something.—*God and the Bible.*

INTELLECTUAL SERIOUSNESS.

IT is the habit of increased *intellectual seriousness*, bred of a wider experience and of a larger acquaintance with men's mental history, which is now transforming religion in our country. Intelligent people among the educated classes grow more and more sceptical of the miraculous data which supply the basis for our received theology. The habit is a conquest of the advancing human race; it spreads and spreads ; it cannot but be, and will be, on the whole and in the end, a boon to us. But many and many an individual it may find unprepared for it, and may act upon him injuriously. Goethe's saying is well known : 'All which merely frees our spirit, without giving us the command over ourselves, is deleterious.'[1] It is of small use by itself alone, however it may be in-dispensable, this one single current of intellectual serious-ness ;— of small use to those who are untouched by the great current of seriousness about conduct. To a frivo-lous and sensual upper class, to a raw and sensual lower class, to feel the greater current may be more than a compensation for not feeling the lesser. They do now feel the lesser current, however ; and it removes them farther than ever from the influence of the greater.—*God and the Bible.*

WEAK SIDE OF POPULAR CHRISTIANITY.

THE fault of popular Christianity, as an endeavour after *righteousness by Jesus Christ*, is not, like the fault of popu-lar Judaism as an endeavour after *salvation by righteous-ness*, first and foremost a moral fault. It is, much more, an

----

[1] Alles was unsern Geist befreit, ohne uns die Herrschaft über uns selbst zu geben, ist verderblich.

intellectual one. But it is not on that account insignifi-cant. Dr. Mozley urges, that 'no inquiry is obligatory upon religious minds in matters of the supernatural and miraculous,' because, says he, though 'the human mind must refuse to submit to anything contrary to moral sense in Scripture,' yet 'there is no moral question raised by the fact of a miracle, nor does a supernatural doctrine challenge any moral resistance.' As if there were no pos-sible resistance to religious doctrines but a resistance on the ground of their immorality ! As if intellectual resist-ance to them counted for nothing ! The objections to popular Christianity are not moral objections, but intel-lectual revolt against its demonstrations by miracle and metaphysics. To be intellectually convinced of a thing's want of conformity to truth and fact is surely an in-superable obstacle to receiving it, even though there be no moral obstacle added. And no moral advantages of a doctrine can avail to save it, in presence of the intellec-tual conviction of its want of conformity with truth and fact. And if the want of conformity exists, it is sure to be one day found out. 'Things are what they are, and the consequences of them will be what they will be ;' and one inevitable consequence of a thing's want of conformity with truth and fact is, that sooner or later the human mind perceives it. And whoever thinks that the ground-belief of Christians is true and indispensable, but that in the account they give of it, and of the reasons for holding it, there is a want of conformity with truth and fact, may well desire to find a better account and better reasons, and to prepare the way for their admission and for their acquiring some strength and consistency in men's minds, against the day when the old means of reliance fail.—*Last Essays.*

POPULAR SCIENCE OF RELIGION.

FOR the popular science of religion one has, or ought to have, an infinite tenderness.   It is the spontaneous work of nature.   It is the travail of the human mind to adapt to its grasp and employment great ideas, of which it feels the attraction, but for which, except as given to it by this travail, it would have been immature.   The imperfect science of the Bible, formulated in the so-called Apostles' Creed, was the only vehicle by which, to generation after generation of men, the method and secret of Jesus could gain any access ; and in this sense we may even call it, taking the point of view of popular theology, *Providential.* And this rude criticism is full of poetry, and in this poetry we have been all nursed.   To call it, as many of our philosophical Liberal friends are fond of calling it, 'a degrading superstition,' is as untrue as it is a poor compliment to human nature, which produced this criticism and used it.   It is an *Aberglaube,* or extra belief and fairy-tale, produced by taking certain great names and great promises too literally and materially ;

but it is not a degrading superstition.—*Literature and Dogma.*

MISSIONS.

THE non-Christian religions are not to the wise man mere monsters ; he knows they have much good and truth in them. He knows that Mahometanism, and Brahminism, and Buddhism, are not what the missionaries call them ; and he knows, too, how really unfit the missionaries in general are to cope with them. For any one who weighs the matter well, the missionary in clerical coat and gaiters whom one sees in woodcuts preaching to a group of picturesque Orientals, is, from the inadequacy of his criticism both of his hearers' religion and of his own, and his signal misunderstanding of the very Volume he holds in his hand, a hardly less grotesque object in his intellectual equipment for his task than in his outward attire. Yet everyone allows that this strange figure carries something of what is called European civilisation with him, and a good part of this is due to Christianity. But even the Christianity itself that he preaches, imbedded in a false theology though it be, cannot but contain, in a greater or lesser measure as it may happen, these three things : the all-importance of *righteousness*, the *method* of Jesus, the *secret* of Jesus. No Christianity that is ever preached but manages to carry something of these along with it.

And if it carries them to Mahometanism, they are carried where of the all-importance of righteousness there is a knowledge, but of the method and secret of Jesus, by which alone is righteousness possible, hardly any sense at all. If it carries them to Brahminism, they are carried where of the all-importance of righteousness, the foundation of the whole matter, there is a wholly insufficient sense ; and where religion is, above all, that metaphysical conception, or metaphysical play, so dear to the Aryan genius and to M. Emile Burnouf. If it carries them to Buddhism, they are carried to a religion to be saluted with respect, indeed; for it has not only the sense for righteousness, it has, even, it has the secret of Jesus. But it employs the secret ill, because greatly wanting in the method, because utterly wanting in the sweet reasonableness, the unerring balance, the *epieikeia.* Therefore to all whom it visits, the Christianity of our missions, inadequate as may be its criticism of the Bible, brings what may do them good. And if it brings the Bible itself, it brings what may not only help the good preached, but may also with time dissipate the erroneous criticism which accompanies this and impairs it.—*Literature and Dogma.*

MIRACLES COMING IN.

IT is almost impossible to exaggerate the proneness of the human mind to take miracles as evidence, and to seek for miracles as evidence ; or the extent to which religion, and religion of a true and admirable kind, has been, and is still, held in connexion with a reliance upon miracles. This reliance will long outlast the reliance on the supernatural prescience of prophecy, for it is not exposed to the same tests. To pick Scripture-miracles one by one to pieces is an odious and repulsive task ; it is also an unprofitable one, for whatever we may think of the affirmative demonstrations of them, a negative demonstration of them is, from the circumstances of the case, impossible. And yet the human mind is assuredly passing away, however slowly, from this hold of reliance also ; and those who make it their stay will more and more find it fail them, will more and more feel themselves disturbed shaken, distressed, and bewildered.

For it is what we call the *Time-Spirit* which is sapping the proof from miracles,—it is the 'Zeit-Geist' itself. Whether we attack them, or whether we defend them, does not much matter. The human mind, as its experience widens, is turning away from them. And for this reason : *it sees, as its experience widens, how they arise.* It sees that, under certain circumstances, they always do arise ; and that they have not more solidity in one case than another. Under certain circumstances, wherever men are found, there is, as Shakspeare says—

> No natural exhalation in the sky,
> No scape of nature, no distemper'd day,

> No common wind, no customed event,
> But they will pluck away his natural cause,
> And call them meteors, prodigies, and signs,
> Abortives, presages, and tongues of heaven.

Imposture is so far from being the general rule in these cases, that it is the rare exception. Signs and wonders men's minds will have, and they create them honestly and naturally; yet not so but that we can see *how* they create them.—*Literature and Dogma.*

MIRACLES GOING OUT.

IT was not to discredit miracles that 'Literature and Dogma' was written, but because miracles are so widely and deeply discredited already. And it is lost labour, I repeat, to be arguing for or against them. Mankind did not originally accept miracles because it had formal proof of them, but because its imperfect experience inclined it to them. Nor will mankind now drop miracles because it has formal proof against them, but because its more complete experience detaches it from them. The final result was inevitable, as soon as ever miracles began to embarrass people, began to be relegated,—especially the greater miracles,—to a certain limited period long ago over. Irenæus says, that people in his time had arisen from the dead, 'and abode with us a good number of years.'[1] One of his commentators, embarrassed by

[1] See Irenæus, *Adv. Hær.*, lib. ii, cap. xxxii, 4 ; with the note on the passage in Stieren's edition.

such stupendous miracles occurring outside of the Bible, makes an attempt to explain away this remarkable allegation; but the most recent editor of Irenæus points out, with truth, that the attempt is vain. Irenæus was as sure to want and to find miracles as the Bible-writers were. And sooner or later mankind was sure to see how universally and easily assertions like this of Irenæus arose, and that they arose with the Bible-writers just as they arose with Irenæus, and are not a whit more solid coming from them than from him.

A Catholic imagines that he gets over the difficulty by believing, or professing to believe, the miracles of Irenæus and Epiphanius and others, as well as those of the Bible-writers. But for him, too, even for him, the *Time-Spirit* is gradually becoming too strong. As we may say in general, that, although an educated Protestant may manage to retain for his own lifetime the belief in miracles in which he has been brought up, yet his children will lose it; so to an educated Catholic we may say, putting the change only a little farther off, that (unless some unforeseen deluge should overwhelm European civilisation, leaving everything to be begun anew) his grandchildren will lose it. They will lose it insensibly, as the eighteenth century saw the gradual extinction, among the educated classes, of that belief in witchcraft which in the century previous a man like Sir Matthew Hale could affirm to have the authority of Scripture and of the wisdom of all nations,—spoke of, in short, just as many religious people speak of miracles now. Witchcraft is but one department of the miraculous ; and it was comparatively easy, no doubt, to abandon one department, when men had all the rest of the region to fall back upon. Nevertheless the forces of experience, which have prevailed against witchcraft, will inevitably prevail also against miracles at large, and that by the mere progress of time.—*God and the Bible.*

'OFFENDICULUM' OF SCRUPULOUSNESS.

THE last of Butler's jottings in his memorandum-book is a prayer to be delivered 'from *offendiculum* of scrupulousness.' He was quite right. Religion is a matter where scrupulousness has been far too active, producing most serious mischief ; and where it is singularly out of place. I am the very last person to wish to deny it. Those, therefore, who declared their consent to the Articles long ago, and who are usefully engaged in the ministry of the Church, would in my opinion do exceedingly ill to disquiet themselves about having given a consent to the Articles formerly, when things had not moved to the point where they are now, and did not appear to men's minds as they now appear. 'Forgetting those things which are behind and reaching forth to those things which are before,' should in these cases be a man's motto. The Church is properly a national society for the promotion of goodness. For him it is such ; he ministers in it as such. He has never to use the Articles, never to rehearse them. He has to rehearse the prayers and services of the Church. Much of these he may rehearse as the literal, beautiful rendering of what he himself feels and believes. The rest he may rehearse as an approximative rendering of it ;—as language *thrown out* by other men, in other times, at immense objects which deeply engaged their affections and awe, and which deeply engage his also ; objects concerning which, moreover, adequate statement is impossible. To him, therefore, this approximative part of the prayers and services which he rehearses will be poetry. It is a great error to think that whatever is thus perceived to be poetry ceases to be available in religion. The noblest races are those which know how to make the most serious use of poetry.—*Last Essays.*

JESUS CHRIST USED POPULAR LANGUAGE.

THE great reason for continuing to use the familiar language of the religion around us as approximative language and as poetry, although we cannot take it literally, is that such was, likewise, the practice of Jesus. For evidently it was so. And evidently, again, the immense misapprehension of Jesus and of his meaning, by popular religion, comes in part from such having been his practice. But if Jesus used this way of speaking in spite of its plainly leading .

to such misapprehension, it must have been because it was the best way and the only one. For it was not by introducing a brand-new religious language, and by parting with all the old and cherished images, that popular religion could be transformed ; but by keeping the old language and images, and as far as possible conveying into them the soul of the new Christian ideal.

When Jesus talked of the Son of Man coming in his glory with the holy angels, setting the good on his right hand and the bad on his left, and sending away the bad into everlasting fire prepared for the devil and his angels, was he speaking literally ? Did Jesus mean that all this would actually happen ? Popular religion supposes so. Yet very many religious people, even now, suppose that Jesus was but using the figures of Messianic judgment familiar to his hearers, in order to impress upon them his main point :—what sort of spirit and of practice did really tend to salvation, and what did not. And surely almost every one must perceive, that when Jesus spoke to his disciples of their sitting on thrones judging the twelve tribes of Israel, or of their drinking new wine with him in the kingdom of God, he was adopting their material images and beliefs, and was not speaking literally. Yet their Master's thus adopting their material images and beliefs could not but confirm the disciples in them. And so it did, and Christendom, too, after them ; yet in this way, apparently, Jesus chose to proceed.

But some one may say, that Jesus used this language because he himself shared the materialistic notions of his disciples about the kingdom of God, and thought that coming upon the clouds, and sitting upon thrones, and drinking wine, would really occur in it, and was mistaken in thinking so. And yet there are plain signs that this cannot be the right account of the matter, and that Jesus did not really share the beliefs of his disciples or conceive the kingdom of God as they did. For they manifestly thought,—even the wisest of them, and after their Master's death as well as before it,—that this kingdom was to be a sudden, miraculous, outward transformation of things, which was to come about very soon and in their own life-time. Nevertheless they themselves report Jesus saying what is in direct contradiction to all this. They report him describing the kingdom of God as an inward change requiring to be spread over an immense time, and coming about by natural means and gradual growth, not suddenly, miraculously. Jesus compares the kingdom of God to a grain of mustard seed and to a handful of leaven. He says : 'So is the kingdom of God, as a man may cast seed in the ground, and may go to bed and get up night and day, and the seed shoots and extends he knoweth not how.' Jesus told his disciples, moreover, that the good news of the kingdom had to be preached *to the whole world.* The whole world must first be evangelised, no work of one generation, but of centuries and centuries;

and then, but not till then, should *the end*, the last day, the new world, the grand transformation of which Jewish heads were so full, finally come.   True, the disciples also make Jesus speak as if he fancied this end to be as near as they did.   But it is quite manifest that Jesus spoke to them, at different times, of two *ends* : one, the end of the Jewish state and nation, which any one who could 'discern the signs of that time' might foresee ; the other, the end of the world, the instatement of God's kingdom ;—and that they confused the two ends together.   Undeniably, therefore, Jesus saw things in a way very different from theirs, and much truer.   And if he uses their materialising language and imagery, then, it cannot have been because he shared their illusions.   Nevertheless, he uses it.—*Last Essays.*

AVOID VIOLENT REVOLUTION.

WE should avoid violent revolution in the words and externals of religion.   Profound sentiments are connected with them ; they are aimed at the highest good, however imperfectly apprehended.   Their form often gives them beauty, the associations which cluster around them give them always pathos and solemnity.   They are to be used as poetry ; while at the same time to purge and raise our view of that ideal, at which they are aimed, should be our incessant endeavour.   Else the use of them is mere dilettantism.   We should seek, therefore, to use them as Jesus did. How freely Jesus himself used them, we see. And yet what a difference between the meaning he put upon them, and the meaning put upon them by the Jews ! In how general a sense alone can it with truth be said, that he and even his disciples had the same aspirations, the same final aim ! How imperfectly did his disciples apprehend him ; how imperfectly must they have reported him ! But the result has justified his way of proceeding. For while he carried with him, so far as was possible, his disciples, and the world after them, and all who even now see him through the eyes of those first generations, he yet also marked his own real meaning so indelibly, that it shows and shines clearly out, to satisfy all whom,—as time goes on, and experience widens, and more things are known,—the old imperfect apprehension dissatisfies. And it is not to be supposed that a rejection of all the poetry of popular religion is necessary or advisable now, any more than when Jesus came. But it is an aim which may well indeed be pursued with enthusiasm, to make the true meaning of Jesus, in using that poetry, emerge and prevail. For the immense pathos, so perpetually enlarged upon, of his life and death, does really culminate here : that Christians have so profoundly misunderstood him.—*Last Essays.*

THE SCIENTIFIC BASIS.

IT is not that the scientific sense in us denies the rights of the poetic sense, which employs a figured and imaginative language. But the language of the dogmatic theology is not figurative and poetic language, it is scholastic and scientific language. Assertions in scientific language must stand the tests of scientific examination. Neither is it that the scientific sense in us refuses to admit willingly and reverently the name of God, as a point in which the religious and the scientific sense may meet, as the least inadequate name for that universal order which the intellect feels after as a law, and the heart feels after as a benefit. 'We, too,' might the men of science with truth say to the men of religion—'we, too, would gladly say *God*, if only, the moment one says *God*, you would not pester one with your pretensions of knowing all about him.' That *stream of tendency by which all things seek to fulfil the law of their being*, and which, inasmuch as our idea of real welfare resolves itself into this fulfilment of the law of one's being, man rightly deems the fountain of all goodness, and calls by the worthiest and most solemn name he can, which is *God*, science also might willingly own for the fountain of all goodness, and call God. But however much more than this the heart may with propriety put into its language respecting God, this is as much as science can with strictness put there.—*St. Paul and Protestantism.*

THE STREAM OF TENDENCY.

MANY excellent people are crying out every day, that all is lost in religion unless we can affirm that God is a person who thinks and loves. I say that, unless we can verify this, it is impossible to build religion successfully upon it; and it cannot be verified. Even if it could be shown that there is a low degree of probability for it, I say that it is a grave and fatal error to imagine that religion can be built on what has a low degree of probability. However, I do not think it can be said that there is even a low degree of probability for the assertion that God is a person who thinks and loves, properly and naturally though we may make him such in the language of feeling; the assertion deals with what is so utterly beyond us. But I maintain, that, starting from what may be verified about God,—that he is the Eternal which makes for righteousness,—and reading the Bible with this idea to govern us, we have here the elements for a religion more solid, serious, awe-inspiring, and profound, than any which the world has yet seen. True, it will not be just the same religion which prevails now; but who supposes that the religion now current can go on always, or ought to go on? Nay and even of that much-decried idea of God as *the stream of tendency by which all things seek to fulfil the law of their being*, it may be said with confidence that it has in it the elements of a religion new, indeed, but in the highest degree serious, hopeful, solemn, and profound.—*God and the Bible.*

THE 'NOT OURSELVES.'

In the first place, we did not make ourselves and our nature, or make conduct to be the object of three-fourths of that nature ; we did not provide that happiness should follow conduct, as it undeniably does ; that the sense of succeeding, going right, hitting the mark, in conduct, should give satisfaction, and a very high satisfaction, just as really as the sense of doing well in his work gives pleasure to a poet or painter, or accomplishing what he tries gives pleasure to a man who is learning to ride or to shoot ; or as satisfying his hunger, also, gives pleasure to a man who is hungry.

All this we did not make ; and, in the next place, our dealing with it at all, when it is made, is not wholly, or even nearly wholly, in our own power. Our conduct is capable, irrespective of what we can ourselves certainly answer for, of almost infinitely different degrees of force and energy in the performance of it, of lucidity and vividness in the perception of it, of fulness in the satisfaction from it ; and these degrees may vary from day to day, and quite incalculably. Facilities and felicities,— whence do they come ? suggestions and stimulations,— where do they tend ? hardly a day passes but we have some experience of them. And so Henry More was led to say, that 'there was something about us that knew better, often, what we would be at than we ourselves.' For instance : everyone can understand how health and freedom from pain may give energy for conduct, and how a neuralgia, suppose, may diminish it. It does not depend on ourselves, indeed, whether we have the neuralgia or not, but we can understand its impairing our spirit. But the strange thing is, that with the same neuralgia we may find ourselves one day without spirit and energy for conduct, and another day with them. So that we may most truly say : 'Left to ourselves, we sink and perish ; visited, we lift up our heads and live.'[1] And we may well give ourselves, in grateful and devout self-surrender, to that by which we are thus visited. So much is there incalculable, so much that belongs to *not ourselves*, in conduct ; and the more we attend to conduct, and the more we value it, the more we shall feel this.— *Literature and Dogma.*

CONDUCT THREE-FOURTHS OF LIFE.

SURELY, if there be anything with which metaphysics have nothing to do, and where a plain man, without skill to walk in the arduous paths of abstruse reasoning, may yet find himself at home, it is religion. For the object of religion is *conduct* ; and conduct is really, however men may overlay it with philosophical disquisitions,

---

[1] Relicti mergimur et perimus, visitati vero erigimur et vivimus.

the simplest thing in the world.   That is to say, it is the simplest thing in the world as far as *understanding* is concerned ; as regards *doing*, it is the hardest thing in the world.   Here is the difficulty,—to *do* what we very well know ought to be done ; and instead of facing this, men have searched out another with which they occupy themselves by preference,—the origin of what is called the moral sense, the genesis and physiology of conscience, and so on.   No one denies that here, too, is difficulty, or that the difficulty is a proper object for the human faculties to be exercised upon ; but the difficulty here is speculative   It is not the difficulty of religion, which is a practical one ; and it often tends to divert attention from this.   Yet surely the difficulty of religion is great enough by itself, if men would but consider it, to satisfy the most voracious appetite for difficulties.   It extends to rightness in the whole range of what we call *conduct* ; in three-fourths, therefore, at the very lowest computation, of human life.   The only doubt is whether we ought not to make the range of conduct wider still, and to say it is four-fifths of human life, or five-sixths.   But it is better to be under the mark than over it ; so let us be content with reckoning conduct as three-fourths of human life.—*Literature and Dogma*

MORALITY TOUCHED BY EMOTION.

THE antithesis between *ethical* and *religious* is quite a false one. Ethical means *practical*, it relates to practice or conduct passing into habit or disposition. Religious also means *practical*, but practical in a still higher degree ; and the right antithesis to both ethical and religious, is the same as the right antithesis to practical : namely, *theoretical.*

Now, propositions about the Godhead of the Eternal Son are theoretical, and they therefore are very properly opposed to propositions which are moral or ethical ; but they are with equal propriety opposed to propositions which are religious. They differ in kind from what is religious, while what is ethical agrees in kind with it. But is there, therefore, no difference between what is ethical, or morality, and religion ? There *is* a difference ; a difference of degreee. Religion, if we allow the intention of human thought and human language in the use of the word, is ethics heightened, enkindled, lit up by feeling ; the passage from morality to religion is made when to morality is applied emotion. And the true meaning of religion is thus, not simply *morality*, but *morality touched by emotion.* And this new elevation and inspiration of morality is well marked by the word ‘righteousness.’ Conduct is the word of common life, morality is the word of philosophical disquisition, righteousness is the word of religion.—*Literature and Dogma.*

NATURAL AND REVEALED RELIGION.

As we have pointed out the falseness of the common antithesis between *ethical* and *religious*, let us anticipate the objection that the religion here spoken of is but natural religion, by pointing out the falseness of the common antithesis, also, between *natural* and *revealed*. For that in us which is really natural is, in truth, *revealed*. We awake to the consciousness of it, we are aware of it coming forth in our mind ; but we feel that we did not make it, that it is discovered to us, that it is what it is whether we will or no. If we are little concerned about it, we say it is *natural* ; if much, we say it is *revealed*. But the difference between the two is not one of kind, only of degree. The real antithesis, to natural and revealed alike, is *invented, artificial.* Religion springing out of an experience of the power, the grandeur, the necessity of righteousness, is revealed religion, whether we find it in Sophocles or in Isaiah. 'The will of mortal men did not beget it, neither shall oblivion ever lay it to sleep.' A system of theological notions about personality, essence, existence, consubstantiality, is *artificial* religion, and is the proper opposite to *revealed* ; since it is a religion which comes forth in no one's consciousness, but is invented by theologians,—able men with uncommon talents for abstruse reasoning. This religion is in no sense revealed, just because it is in no sense natural. And revealed religion is properly so named, just in proportion as it is in a pre-eminent degree natural.

The religion of the Bible, therefore, is well said to be *revealed*, because the great natural truth, that 'righteousness tendeth to life,' is seized and exhibited there with such incomparable force and efficacy. All, or very nearly all, the nations of mankind have recognised the importance of conduct, and have attributed to it a natural obligation. They, however, looked at conduct, not as something full of happiness and joy, but as something one could not manage to do without. But : ' Sion heard of it and *rejoiced*, and the daughters of Judah were *glad*, because of thy judgments, O Eternal !' Happiness is our being's end and aim, and no one has ever come near Israel in feeling, and in making others feel, that *to righteousness belongs happiness !* The prodigies and the marvellous of Bible-religion are common to it with all religions ; the love of righteousness, in this eminency, is its own.—*Literature and Dogma.*

THE WITNESS OF ISRAEL.

CLEARLY, unless a sense or endowment of human nature, however in itself real and beneficent, has some signal representative among mankind, it tends to be pressed upon by other senses and endowments, to suffer from its own want of energy, and to be more and more pushed out of sight. Anyone, for instance, who will go to the Potteries, and will look at the tawdry, glaring, ill-proportioned ware which is being made there for certain American and colonial markets, will easily convince himself how, in our people and kindred, the sense for the arts of design, though it is certainly planted in human nature, might dwindle and sink to almost nothing, if it were not for the witness borne to this sense, and the protest offered against its extinction, by the brilliant æsthetic endowment and artistic work of ancient Greece. And one cannot look out over the world without seeing that the same sort of thing might very well befall conduct, too, if it were not for the signal witness borne by Israel.

Then there is the practical force of the example ; and this is even more important. Everyone is aware how those, who want to cultivate any sense or endowment in themselves, must be habitually conversant with the works of people who have been eminent for that sense, must study them, catch inspiration from them. Only in this way, indeed, can progress be made. And as long as the world lasts, all who want to make progress in righteousness will come to Israel for inspiration, as to the people who have had the sense for righteousness most glowing and strongest ; and in hearing and reading the words Israel has uttered for us, carers for conduct will find a glow and a force they will find nowhere else. As well imagine a man with a sense for sculpture not cultivating it by the help of the remains of Greek art, or a man with a sense for poetry not cultivating it by the help of Homer and Shakspeare, as a man with a sense for conduct not cultivating it by the help of the Bible ! And this sense, in the satisfying of which we come naturally to the Bible, is a sense which the generality of men have far more decidedly than they have the sense for art or for science. At any rate, whether this or that man has it decidedly or not, it is the sense which has to do with three-fourths of human life.

This does truly constitute for Israel a most extraordinary distinction. In spite of all which in them and in their character is unattractive, nay, repellent,—in spite of their shortcomings even in religion itself and their insignificance in everything else,—this petty, unsuccessful, unamiable people, without politics, without science, without art, without charm, deserve their great place in the world's regard, and are likely to have it more, as the world goes on, rather than less. It is secured to them by the facts of human nature, and by the unalterable constitution of things. ' God hath given commandment to bless, and he hath blessed, and we cannot reverse it ; he hath not seen iniquity in Jacob, and he hath not seen perverseness in Israel ; the Eternal, his God, is with him.'—*Literature and Dogma.*

GREECE AND ISRAEL.

WHAT the Greeks were, and what they accomplished, and how brilliant a course they ran, we know ; and with that knowledge we shall not be forward to utter against them hard censures. But thus much, at least, we may say, notwithstanding all the glory and genius of Greece, notwithstanding all the failure and fanaticism of Israel ;—thus much we may well say, as often as we contrast the heart and mind of the Græco-Roman world in its maturity with the interior joys of Israel : *They that run after another God shall have great trouble.*

For Israel advanced from the God of Abraham, the Mighty who requires integrity of heart and innocency of hands, to the God of Moses, the Eternal who makes for righteousness unalterably. Then the law in its primitive shape, an organism having for its heart the Ten Commandments, arose. It formulated, with authentic voice and for ever, the religion of Israel as a religion in which ideas of moral order and of right were paramount. And so things went on from Moses to Samuel, and from Samuel to David, and from David to the great prophets of the eighth century and to the Captivity, and from that to the Restoration, and from the Restoration to Antiochus and the invasion of Greek culture, to the Maccabees and the Book of Daniel, and from thence to the Roman conquest, and from that to

John the Baptist ;—until all the wonderful history received its solution and consummation in Jesus Christ. Through progress and backsliding, amid infectious contact with idolatry, amid survival of old growths of superstition, of the crude practices of the past ; amid multiplication of new precepts and observances, of formalism and cere- monial ; amid the solicitation of new aspects of life ; in material prosperity, and in material ruin ;—more and more the great governing characteristics of the religion of Israel accentuated and asserted themselves, and forced themselves on the world's attention : the God of this religion, with his eternal summons to keep judgment and do justice ; the mission of this religion, to bring in everlasting righteousness.—*God and the Bible.*

THE DECALOGUE BY EVOLUTION.

SUPPOSE that our moral perceptions and rules are all to be traced up, as evolutionists say, to habits due to one or other of two main instincts,—the reproductive instinct and the instinct of self-preservation. Let us take an example of a moral rule due to each instinct. For a moral rule traceable, on our present supposition, to the instinct of self-preservation, we cannot do better than to take 'the first commandment with promise :' *Honour thy father and thy mother.* I say that it makes not the smallest difference to religion, whether we suppose this commandment to be thus traceable or not.

For let it be thus traceable, and suppose the original natural affection of the young to their parents to be due to a sense of dependence upon them, and of benefit from them. And then, when the dependence and benefit end, when the young can shift for themselves, the natural affection seems in the lower animals, as they are called, to pass away. But in man it is not thus evanescent. For at first, perhaps, there were some who from weakness or from accident felt the dependence and received the benefit longer than others, and in such was formed a more deep and strong tie of attachment. And while their neighbours, so soon as they were of adult vigour, heedlessly left the side of their parents, and troubled themselves about them no more, and let them perish if so it might happen, these few remained with their parents, and grew used to them more and more, and finally even fed and tended them when they grew helpless. Presently they began to be shocked at their neighbours' callous neglect of those who had begotten them and borne them ; and they expostulated with their neighbours, and entreated and pleaded that their own way was best. Some suffered, perhaps, for their interference ; some had to fight for their parents to hinder their neighbours maltreating them ; and all the more fixed in their new feelings did these primitive gropers after the Fifth Commandment become.

Meanwhile this extending of the family-bond, this

conquering of a little district from the mere animal life, this limiting of the reign of blind, selfish impulse, brought, we may well believe, more order into the homes of those who practised it, and with more order more well-doing, and with both more happiness. And when the reformers solicited their more inhuman neighbours to change their ways, they must always have had to back them the remembrance, more or less alive in every man, of an early link of affection with his parents ; but now they had their improved manner of life and heightened well-being to back them too. So the usage of the minority gradually became the usage of the majority. And we may end this long chapter of suppositions by supposing that thus there grew at last to be communities which honoured their fathers and mothers, instead of, —as, perhaps, if one went back far enough, one would find to have been the original practice,—eating them.

But all this took place during that which was, in truth, a twilight ante-natal life of humanity, almost as much as the life which each man passes in the womb before he is born. The history of man as man proper, and as distinguished from the other animals,—the real history of our race, and of its institutions,—does not begin until stages such as that which we have been describing are passed, and feelings such as that of which we have been tracing the growth are formed. Man and his history begin, I say, when he becomes distinctly conscious of feelings which, in a long preparatory period of obscure growth, he may have been forming. Then he calls his habit, acquired by a process which he does not recollect, *nature*; and he gives effect to it in fixed customs, rules, laws, and institutions. His religion consists in acknowledging and reverencing the awful sanctions with which this right way for man has, he believes, been invested by the mighty *not ourselves* which surrounds us. And the more emphatically he places a feeling under the guardianship of these sanctions, the more impressive is his testimony to the hold it has upon him. When Israel fixed the feeling of a child's natural attachment to its parents by the commandment, *Honour thy father and thy mother, that thy days may be long in the land which the Eternal thy God giveth thee*, he showed that he had risen to regard this feeling,—slowly and precariously acquired though by our supposition it may have been,— as a sure, solid, and sacred part of the constitution of human nature.

But, as well as the supposition of a moral habit and rule evolved out of the instinct of self-preservation, we are to take the supposition of a moral habit and rule evolved out of the reproductive instinct. And here, indeed, in the relations between the sexes, we are on ground where to walk right is of vital concern to men, and where disasters are plentiful. Who first, in the early and tentative up-struggling of our race, who first discerned them, this peril of disaster, this necessity for taking heed to one's steps? Who was he, that, amid the promiscuous concubinage of man's commencements,—if we are to suppose that out of the sheer animal life human life had to evolve itself and to rise,—who was he that first, through attachment to his chance companion or through attachment to his supposed offspring, gathered himself together, put a bridle on his vague appetites, marked off himself and his, drew the imperfect outline of the circle of home, and fixed for the time to come the rudiments of the family? Who first, amid the loose solicitations of sense, obeyed (for create it he did not) the mighty *not ourselves* which makes for moral order, the stream of tendency which was here carrying him, and our embryo race along with him, towards the fulfilment of the true law of their being?—became aware of it, and obeyed it? Whoever he was, he would soon have had imitators; for never was a more decisive step taken towards bringing into human life greater order, and, with greater order, greater well-doing and greater happiness. So the example was followed, and a habit grew up, and marriage was instituted.

And thus, again, we are brought to the point where history and religion begin. And at this point we first find the Hebrew people, with polygamy still clinging to it as a survival from the times of ignorance, but with the marriage-tie solidly established, strict and sacred, as we see it between Abraham and Sara. Presently this same Hebrew people, with that aptitude which, as I say, characterised it for being profoundly impressed by ideas of moral order, placed in the Decalogue the marriage-tie under the express and solemn sanction of the Eternal, by the Seventh Commandment: *Thou shalt not commit adultery.—God and the Bible.*

PERSISTENCY OF ISRAEL'S FAITH.

MOST remarkable, indeed, is the inward travail to which, in the six hundred years that followed the age of David and Solomon, the many and rude shocks befalling Israel's fundamental idea, *Righteousness tendeth to life*, gave occasion. 'Wherefore do the wicked live,' asks Job, 'become old, yea, are mighty in power? their houses are safe from fear, neither is the rod of God upon them?' Job himself is righteous, and yet : 'On mine eyelids is the shadow of death, not for any injustice in mine hands.' All through the Book of Job, the question, how this can be, is over and over again asked and never answered ; inadequate solutions are offered and repelled, but an adequate solution is never reached. The only solution reached is that of silence before the insoluble : 'I will lay mine hand upon my mouth.' The two perceptions, *Righteousness tendeth to life*, and, *The ungodly prosper in the world*, are left confronting one another like Kantian antinomies. ' *The earth is given under the hand of the wicked !* ' and yet : ' *The counsel of the wicked is far from me ; God rewardeth him, and he shall know it !* ' And this last, the original perception, remains indestructible. The Book of Ecclesiastes has been called sceptical, epicurean ; it is certainly without the glow and hope which animate the Bible in general. It belongs, probably, to the fourth century before Christ, to the latter and worse days of the Persian power ; with difficulties pressing the Jewish community on all sides, with a Persian governor lording it in Jerusalem, with resources light and taxes heavy, with the cancer of poverty eating into the mass of the people, with the rich estranged from the poor and from the national traditions, with the priesthood slack, insincere, and worthless. Composed under such circumstances, the book has been said, and with justice, to' breathe *resignation at the grave of Israel.* Its author sees ' the tears of the oppressed, and they had no comforter, and on the side of their oppressors there was power ; wherefore I praised the dead which are already dead more than the living which are yet alive.' He sees ' all things come alike to all, there is one event to the righteous and to the wicked.' Attempts at a philosophic indifference appear, at a sceptical suspension of judgment, at an easy *ne quid nimis* : ' Be not righteous overmuch, neither make thyself overwise ! why shouldst thou destroy thyself?' Vain attempts, even at a moment which favoured them ! shows of scepticism, vanishing as soon as uttered before the intractable conscientiousness of Israel ! For the Preacher makes answer against himself : 'Though a sinner do evil a hundred times and his days be prolonged, yet surely I know that it shall be well with them that fear God ; but it shall not be well with the wicked, because he feareth not before God.'

Malachi, probably almost contemporary with the Preacher, felt the pressure of the same circumstances, had the same occasions of despondency. All around him people were saying : 'Every one that doeth evil is good in the sight of the Eternal, and he delighteth in them ; where is the God of judgment? it is vain to serve God, and what profit is it that we have kept his ordinance ?' What a change from the clear certitude of the golden age : 'As the whirlwind passeth, so is the wicked no more ; but the righteous is an everlasting foundation ! ' But yet, with all the certitude of this happier past, Malachi answers on behalf of the Eternal : 'Unto you that fear my name shall the sun of righteousness arise with healing in his wings ! '—*Literature and Dogma.*

'*COGITAVI VIAS MEAS.*'

' *Cogitavi vias meas, et converti pedes meos in testimonia Tua* ; I called mine own ways to remembrance, and turned my feet unto Thy testimonies.' Israel is the great, standing, unsilenceable, unshaken witness to the necessity of minding one's ways, of conduct. And whatever else he may have done, or not done, he can assuredly plead : *Cogitavi vias meas.* 'Sacrifices mark a conception in which morality has no part,' says one of my critics ; 'sacrifices existed in Israel *ab origine.*' Even in his historic time there hung, we are told, about Israel traces of an inchoate and dark stage, remains of an early 'conception of God as an unseen but powerful foe, whose enmity might be averted by the death of victims.' It may have been so. But still, Israel can answer, still, all hampered with these survivals of a lower world, *cogitavi vias meas !* 'Though righteousness,' pursues our critic, ' entered largely into Israel's conception of the Eternal, yet that conception contained much that conflicts with righteousness. The God of Israel often appears as more patriotic than righteous ; blesses Jael, for instance, for the treacherous murder of Sisera.' ' Israel's God,' this objector goes on, ' is a magnified and non-natural man, not impassive and uniform like a law of nature, but angry and then repenting him, jealous and then soothed.' True, Israel may again answer ; but nevertheless, with all this mixture, and with this crude anthropomorphic conception of God, *cogitavi vias meas !* ' Israel's religion deals in ecstasy, enthusiasm, evocations of the dead.' *Cogitavi vias meas!* 'The current idea of righteousness in Israel was largely made up of ceremonial observances.' *Cogitavi vias meas !* Finally, in spite of all this thinking upon his ways, Israel misdirected them. 'The Bible,' cries our anti-Israelitish critic, 'failed to turn the hearts of those to whom it was addressed ; what a commentary is afforded by Israel's history on the value of the Bible !' True, as Israel managed his profession of faith, he did not walk by it aright, it did not save him ;—but did he on that account drop it? *Cogitavi, cogitavi vias meas !—God and the Bible.*

'*ABERGLAUBE.*'

IN one sense, the lofty Messianic ideas of 'the great and notable day of the Eternal,' 'the consolation of Israel,' 'the restitution of all things,' are even more important than the solid but humbler idea, *righteousness tendeth to life*, out of which they arose. In another sense they are much less important. They are more important, because they are the development of this idea and prove its strength. It might have been crushed and baffled by the falsification events seemed to delight in giving to it ; that, instead of being crushed and baffled, it took this magnificent flight, shows its innate power. Moreover, the Messianic ideas do in a wonderful manner attract emotion to the ideas of conduct and morality, attract it to them and combine it with them. On the other hand, the idea that *righteousness tendeth to life* has a firm, experimental ground, which the Messianic ideas have not. And the day comes when the possession of such a ground is invaluable.

That the spirit of man should entertain hopes and anticipations, beyond what it actually knows and can verify, is quite natural. Human life could not have the scope, and depth, and progress it has, were this otherwise. It is natural, too, to make these hopes and anticipations give in their turn support to the simple and humble experience which was their original ground. Israel, therefore, who originally followed righteousness because he felt that it tended to life, might and did naturally come at last to follow it because it would enable him to stand before the Son of Man at his coming, and to share in the triumph of the saints of the Most High.

But this latter belief has not the same character as the belief which it is thus set to confirm. It is a kind of fairy-tale, which a man tells himself, which no one, we grant, can prove impossible to turn out true, but which no one, also, can prove certain to turn out true. It is exactly what is expressed by the German word 'Aber-glaube,' *extra-belief*, belief beyond what is certain and verifiable. Our word 'superstition' had by its derivation this same meaning, but it has come to be used in a merely bad sense, and to mean a childish and craven religiosity. With the German word it is not so ; therefore Goethe can say with propriety and truth : ' *Aberglaube* is the poetry of life,—*der Aberglaube ist die Poesie des Lebens.*' It is so. *Extra-belief*, that which we hope, augur, imagine, is the poetry of life, and has the rights of poetry. But it is not science ; and yet it tends always to imagine itself science, to substitute itself for science, to make itself the ground of the very science out of which it has grown. The Messianic ideas, which were the poetry of life to Israel in the age when Jesus Christ came, did this ; and it is the more important to mark that they did it, because similar ideas have so signally done the same thing with popular Christianity.—*Literature and Dogma.*

WHAT JESUS CHRIST EFFECTED.

SIGNS there are, without doubt, of others, before Jesus Christ, trying to identify the Messiah of popular Jewish hope,—the triumphant Root of David, the mystic Son of Man,—with an ideal of meekness, inwardness, patience, and self-denial. And well might reformers try to effect this identification, for the true line of Israel's progress lay through it ! But not he who tries makes an epoch, but he who effects ; and the identification which was needed Jesus Christ effected. Henceforth the true Israelite was, undoubtedly, he who allied himself with this identification ; who perceived its incomparable fruitfulness, its continuance of the real tradition of Israel, its correspondence with the ruling idea of the Hebrew spirit, *Through righteousness to happiness !* or, in Bible words : *To him that ordereth his conversation right shall be shown the salvation of God !* That the Jewish nation at large, and its rulers, refused to accept the identification, shows only that want of power to penetrate through wraps and appearances to the essence of things, which the majority of mankind always display. The national and social character of their theocracy was everything to the Jews, and they could see no blessings in a revolution which annulled it.—*Literature and Dogma.*

'EPIEIKEIA' AGAIN.

JESUS Christ's new and different way of putting things was the secret of his succeeding where the prophets failed. And this new way he had of putting things is what is indicated by the expression *epieikeia,*—an expression best rendered, as I have elsewhere said, by these two words: 'sweet reasonableness.' For that which is *epieikes* is that which has an air of truth and likelihood ; and that which has an air of truth and likelihood is prepossessing. Now, never were there utterances concerning conduct and righteousness,—Israel's master-concern, and the master-topic of the New Testament as well as of the Old, —which so carried with them an air of consummate truth and likelihood as Jesus Christ's did ; and never, therefore, were any utterances so irresistibly prepossessing. He put things in such a way that his hearer was led to take each rule or fact of conduct by its inward side, its effect on the heart and character ; then the reason of the thing, the meaning of what had been mere matter of blind rule, flashed upon him. The hearer could distinguish between

what was only ceremony, and what was *conduct* ; and the
hardest rule of conduct came to appear to him infinitely
reasonable and natural, and therefore infinitely prepossess=
ing.　A return upon themselves, and a consequent intuition of the truth and reason of the matter of conduct in
question, gave men for right action the clearness, spirit,
energy, happiness, they had lost.—*Literature and Dogma.*

MORAL THERAPEUTICS.

IN one respect alone have the miracles of Jesus Christ
a more real ground than the mass of miracles of
which we have the relation.　Medical science has never
gauged,—never, perhaps, enough set itself to gauge,—the
intimate connexion between moral fault and disease.　To
what extent, or in how many cases, what is called *illness*
is due to moral springs having been used amiss,—whether
by being over-used or by not being used sufficiently,—we
hardly at all know, and we too little inquire.　Certainly
it is due to this very much more than we commonly think ;
and the more it is due to this, the more do moral therapeutics rise in possibility and importance.[1]　The bringer
of light and happiness, the calmer and pacifier, or invigo-
rator and stimulator, is one of the chiefest of doctors.
Such a doctor was Jesus ; such an operator, by an effica-

---

[1] Consult the *Charmides* of Plato (chap. v.) for a remarkable
account of the theory of such a treatment, attributed by Socrates to
Zamolxis, the god-king of the Thracians.

cious and real, though little observed and little employed agency, upon what we, in the language of popular superstition, call the *unclean spirits*, but which are to be designated more literally and more correctly as the *uncleared, unpurified spirits*, which came raging and madding before him. This his own language shows, if we know how to read it. '*What does it matter whether I say, Thy sins are forgiven thee! or whether I say, Arise and walk!*' And again : '*Thou art made whole; sin no more, lest a worse thing befall thee.*' His reporters, we must remember, are men who saw thaumaturgy in all that Jesus did, and who saw in all sickness and disaster visitations from God, and they bend his language accordingly. But indications enough remain to show the line of the Master, his perception of the large part of moral cause in many kinds of disease, and his method of addressing to this part his cure.

It would never have done, indeed, to have men pronouncing right and left that this and that was a judgment, and how, and for what, and on whom. And so, when the disciples, seeing an afflicted person, asked whether this man had done sin or his parents, Jesus checked them and said : 'Neither the one nor the other, but that the works of God might be made manifest in him.' Not the less clear is the belief of Jesus himself in the moral root of much physical disease, and in moral therapeutics ; and it is important to note well the instances of miracles where this belief comes in.   For the action of Jesus in these instances, however it may be amplified in the reports, was real ; but it is not, therefore, as popular religion fancies, thaumaturgy,—it is not what people are fond of calling the *supernatural*, but what is better called the *non-natural*. It is, on the contrary, like the grace of Raphael, or the grand style of Phidias, eminently natural ; but it is above common, low-pitched nature ; it is a line of nature not yet mastered or followed out.—*Literature and Dogma.*

THE NEW TESTAMENT PRESENTATION OF JESUS CHRIST.

THE New Testament contains all that we know of a wonderful spirit, far above the heads of his reporters, still farther above the head of our popular theology, which has added its own misunderstanding of the reporters to the reporters' misunderstanding of Jesus.   And it was quite inevitable that anything so superior and so profound should be imperfectly understood by those amongst whom it first appeared, and for a very long time afterwards ; and that it should come at last gradually to stand out clearer only by time,—*Time*, as the Greek maxim says, *the wisest of all things, for he is the unfailing discoverer.*

Yet, however much is discovered, the object of our scrutiny must still be beyond us, must still transcend our adequate knowledge, if for no other reason, because of the character of the first and only records of him.   But in the view now taken we have at least a wonderful figure transcending his time, transcending his disciples,—attaching them but transcending them; in very much that **he** uttered going far above their heads, treating Scripture and prophecy like a master while they treated it like children, resting his doctrine on internal evidence while they rested it on miracles ; and yet, by his incomparable lucidity and penetrativeness, planting his profound veins of thought in their memory along with their own notions and prepossessions, to come out all mixed up together, but still distinguishable one day and separable ;—and leaving his word thus to bear fruit for the future.—*Literature and Dogma.*

JESUS CHRIST AND SOCRATES.

A GREAT solicitude is always shown by popular Christianity to establish a radical difference between Jésus and a teacher like Socrates. Ordinary theologians establish this difference by transcendental distinctions into which plain people cannot follow them. But what really does make the radical difference between Jesus and Socrates is, that such a conception as Paul's conception of *faith* would, if applied to Socrates, be out of place and ineffective. Socrates inspired boundless friendship and esteem ; but a penetrating enthusiasm of love, sympathy, pity, adoration, reinforcing the inspiration of reason and duty where this inspiration is of insufficient power, does not belong to Socrates. With Jesus it is different. On this point it is needless to argue ; history has proved. In the midst of errors the most prosaic, the most immoral, the most unscriptural, concerning God, Christ, and righteousness, the immense emotion of love and sympathy inspired by the person and character of Jesus has had to work almost alone by itself for righteousness ; and it has worked wonders. The surpassing religious grandeur of Paul's conception of faith is that it seizes a real salutary emotional force of incalculable magnitude, and reinforces moral effort with it.—*St. Paul and Protestantism.*

THE MARVELLOUS WORK AND WONDER.

THE 'marvellous work and wonder' about the saving truth which the simple receive is, not that, being difficult to the reason, it is yet got hold of by the unlettered and not by the wise ; but that, being so simple, it should yet be so immense, important, indispensable ; and that, being so immense, important, indispensable, it should yet so often be followed by quite unlettered people, and neglected by such very clever. ones. The clever are attending to other things,—things which *do* task the reason and intelligence, and in which the unlettered have no skill and no voice : these things however are, at most, only one-fourth of life. And this absurdity, for such it really is, we see every day ;—people attending to the difficult *science* of matters where the plain *practice* they quite let slip. How many people will be now[1] busy with Mr. Darwin's new book, so admirably ingenious, on the natural history of the emotions, who yet are always using their own emotions in the worst possible manner ! They are eager to know how their emotions arose, how these came to express themselves as they do ; yet there the emotions now are, and have for a long time been, and the first thing for any sane man to do is to make a proper use of them, and to know how to make a proper use is not difficult ;— but all this we never think of, but investigate zealously how they arose ! Such persons are just like those learned inquirers the Cynic laughed at, who were so busy about the strayings of Ulysses, so inattentive to their own.

And Israel's greatness was that he was so impatient of trifling of this kind, of being busy with one-fourth of life while the three-fourths, conduct, was forgotten. And Israel boldly said : 'They that seek the Eternal understand *all things* ;' that is, they are occupied with conduct, righteousness, which truly is, as we have seen, at least three-fourths of life, and which Israel thought the whole of it. They have a hold on three-fourths of life, while it may be that their great, clever, and accomplished neighbours have a hold on only one-fourth, or part of one-fourth, of life. Which is the solid and sensible man, which understands most, which *lives* most ? Compare a Metho-

---

[1] Written in 1872.

dist day-labourer with some dissolute, gifted, brilliant grandee, who thinks nothing of him !—but the first deals successfully with nearly the whole of life, while the second is all abroad in it. Compare some simple and pious monk, at Rome, with one of those frivolous men of taste whom we have all seen there !—each knows nothing of what interests the other ; but which is the more vital concern for a man : conduct, or arts and antiquities ?

Nay, and however false even his Biblical criticism, the believer who applies the method and the secret of Jesus has a width of range and sureness of foothold in life, which the best scientific and literary critic of the Bible, who applies them not, is without ; because the first is right in what affects three-fourths of life, and the second in what affects but one-fourth, or even but one-eighth. Each has a secret of which the other, who has no experience of it, does not know the value ; but the value of the learned man's secret is ridiculously least. This, I say, is the very glory and marvel of the religion of the true Israel, and what makes this religion, as Jesus called it, 'the good news to the *poor* ;' that it covers nearly the whole of life, and yet is so simple.—*Literature and Dogma.*

THE SPIRIT OF TRUTH.

When Jesus was going away, and his disciples were to be thrown on themselves and left to use his method of inwardness more deeply and thoroughly, not having him to go to,—then they would find, he said, a new power come to their help ; a power of insight such as they had never had before, and which was none of their making, but came from God as Jesus did, and said nothing of itself, but only what God said or Jesus said ; a ' Paraclete,' or reinforcement working in aid of God and Jesus : *even the Spirit of Truth.* While Jesus was with them, the disciples had lived in contact with *aletheia,* or reality; and they were promised now an *intuition of reality* within themselves.

Now, will it be believed, that the Athanasian Creed, and our bishops, and the clergymen who write to the 'Guardian,' and dogmatic theology in general, should have imagined that Jesus Christ here meant to convey to us the 'blessed doctrine' that this Spirit of truth, too, 'is a PERSON'? The force of metaphysical talent out-running literary experience could really, we say, no farther go ! The Muse, who visited Hesiod when he was tending his sheep on the side of Helicon, and 'breathed into him a divine voice, and taught him the things to come and the former things,' might every bit as well be made, with much display of metaphysical apparatus, 'a PERSON.' The influence which visited Hesiod was a *real* one,—that is as much metaphysics as we can without error, in a case of this sort, apply. Whoever applies more, falls into absurdity.

T

The spiritual visitant, indeed, which rejoiced the wise poet of Ascra, was not the Paraclete of Jesus.   No, it was the Muse of art and science, the Muse of the gifted few, the Muse who brings to the ingenious and learned among mankind ' a forgetfulness,' as Hesiod sings, ' of evils and a truce from cares.'   The Paraclete that Jesus promised, on the other hand, was the Muse of *righteousness* ; the Muse of the work-day, care-crossed, toil-stained millions of men,—the Muse of humanity.   To all who live, for all that concerns three-fourths of life, this divine Muse offers ' a forgetfulness of evils and a truce from cares.' That is why this Muse is far more real, and far greater, than the Muse of Hesiod ; not from any metaphysical personality.—*Literature and Dogma.*

ST. PAUL AND THE 'NOT OURSELVES.'

THE element in which we live and move and have our being, which stretches around and beyond the strictly moral element in us, around and beyond the finite sphere of what is originated, measured, and controlled by our own understanding and will,—this infinite element is very present to Paul's thoughts, and makes a profound impression on them.   By this element we are receptive and influenced, not originative and influencing ; now, we all of us receive far more than we originate.   Our plea- sure from a spring day we do not make ; our pleasure, even, from an approving conscience we do not make.

And yet we feel that both the one pleasure and the other can, and often do, work with us in a wonderful way for our good.   So we get the thought of an impulsion outside ourselves which is at once awful and beneficent. ' No man,' as the Hebrew psalm says, 'hath quickened his own soul.'   'I know,' says Jeremiah, 'that the way of man is not in himself ; it is not in man that walketh to direct his steps.'   Most true and natural is this feeling ; and the greater men are, the more natural is this feeling to them.   Great men like Sylla and Napoleon have loved to attribute their success to their fortune, their star ; religious great men have loved to say that their sufficiency was of God.   But through every great spirit runs a train of feeling of this sort ; and the power and depth, which there undoubtedly is in Calvinism, comes from Calvinism's being overwhelmed by it.   Paul is not, like Calvinism, overwhelmed by it ; but it is always before his mind and strongly agitates his thoughts.   The voluntary, rational, and human world, of righteousness, moral choice, effort, filled a large place in his spirit. But the necessary, mystical, and divine world, of influence, sympathy, emotion, filled an even larger ; and he could pass naturally from the one world to the other.   The presence in Paul of this twofold feeling acted irresistibly upon his doctrine.   What he calls 'the power that worketh in us,' and that produces results transcending all our expectations and calculations, he instinctively sought to

combine with our personal agencies of reason and conscience.—*St. Paul and Protestantism.*

THE PAULINE ‘NECROSIS.’

IT is impossible to be in presence of the Pauline conception of *faith*, without remarking on the incomparable
power of edification which it contains.   It is at once
mystical and rational ; and it enlists in its service the
best forces of both worlds,—the world of reason and
morals, and the world of sympathy and emotion.   The
world of reason and duty has an excellent clue to action,
but wants motive-power.; the world of sympathy and
influence has an irresistible force of motive-power, but
wants a clue for directing its exertion.   The danger of
the one world is weariness in well-doing ; the danger
of the other is sterile raptures and immoral fanaticism.
Paul takes from both worlds what can help him, and
leaves what cannot.   The elemental power of sympathy
and emotion in us, a power which extends beyond the
limits of our own will and conscious activity, which we
cannot measure and control, and which in each of us differs immensely in force, volume, and mode of manifestation, he calls into full play, and sets it to work with all its
strength and in all its variety.   But one unalterable object
is assigned by him to this power; *to die with Christ to
the law of the flesh, to live with Christ to the law of the
mind.*

This is the doctrine of the *necrosis*,[1]—Paul's central doctrine, and the doctrine which makes his profoundness and originality.—*St. Paul and Protestantism.*

PREDESTINATION.

WE have seen how strong was Paul's consciousness of that power, not ourselves, in which we live and move and have our being. The sense of life, peace, and joy, which comes through identification with Christ, brings with it a deep and grateful consciousness that this sense is none of our own getting and making. No, it is grace, it is the free gift of God, who gives abundantly beyond all that we ask or think, and calls things that are not as though they were. ' It is not of him that willeth or of him that runneth, but of God that showeth mercy.' As moral agents, for whom alone exist all the predicaments of merit and de-merit, praise and blame, effort and failure, vice and virtue, we are impotent and lost ;—we are saved through that in us which is passive and involuntary ; we are saved through our affections; it is by an *influence*, and the emotion from it, that we are saved ! Well might Paul cry out, as this mystical but profound and beneficent conception filled his soul : ' All things work together for good to them that love God, to them who are the called according to his purpose.' Well might he say, in the gratitude which cannot find words enough to express its sense of bound-

[1] II *Cor.*, iv., 10.

less favour, that those who reached peace with God through identification with Christ were vessels of mercy, marked from endless ages ; that they had been foreknown, predestinated, called, justified, glorified.—*St. Paul and Protestantism.*

ATONEMENT.

THE substantial basis of the notion of atonement, so far as we ourselves are concerned, is the bitter experience that the habit of wrong-doing, of blindly obeying selfish impulse, so affects our temper and powers, that to withstand selfish impulse, to do right, when the sense of right awakens in us, requires an effort out of all proportion to the actual present emergency. We have not only the difficulty of the present act in itself, we have the resistance of all our past. Fire and the knife, cautery and amputation, are often necessary in order to induce a vital action, which, if it were not for our corrupting past, we might have obtained from the natural healthful vigour of our moral organs. This is the real basis of our personal sense of the need of expiating, and thus it is that man expiates.

Not so the Just, who is man's ideal. He has no indurated habit of wrong, no perverse temper, no enfeebled powers, no resisting past, no spiritual organs gangrened, no need of the knife and fire ; smoothly and inevitably he follows the eternal order, and hereto belongs happiness. What sins, then, has the just to expiate ?—*ours.*

In truth, men's habitual unrighteousness, their hard and careless breaking of the moral law, do so tend to reduce and impair the standard of goodness, that, in order to keep this standard pure and unimpaired, the righteous must actually labour and suffer far more than would be necessary if men were better. In the first place, he has to undergo our hatred and persecution for his justice. In the second place, he has to make up for the harm caused by our continual shortcomings, to step between us foolish transgressors and the destructive natural consequences of our transgression, and, by a superhuman example, a spending himself without stint, a more than mortal scale of justice and purity, to save the ideal of human life and conduct from the deterioration with which men's ordinary practice threatens it. In this way Jesus Christ truly 'was sacrificed as a blameless lamb to redeem us from the vain conversation which had become our second nature;' in this way, 'he was made to be sin for us, who knew no sin.' Such, according to that true and profound perception of the import of Christ's sufferings, which, in all St. Paul's writings, and in the inestimable First Epistle of St. Peter, is presented to us, is the atonement of Christ.—*St. Paul and Protestantism.*

JOHN WESLEY.

WESLEY, with his genius for godliness, struggled all his life for some deeper and more edifying account of that faith, which he felt working wonders in his own soul, than that it was a hearty consent to the covenant of grace and an acceptance of the benefit of Christ's imputed righteous-ness. Yet this amiable and gracious spirit, but intellectually slight and shallow compared to Paul, beat his wings in vain. Paul, nevertheless, had solved the problem for him, if only he could have had eyes to see Paul's solution.—*St. Paul and Protestantism.*

ST. PAUL AND THE PURITANS.

PAUL'S figures our Puritans have taken literally, while for his central idea they have substituted another which is not his. And his central idea they have turned into a figure, and have let it almost disappear out of their mind. His essential idea lost, his figures misused, an idea essentially not his substituted for his,—the unedifying patch-work thus made, Puritanism has stamped with Paul's name, and called *the gospel.* It thunders at Romanism for not preaching it, it casts off Anglicanism for not setting it forth alone and unreservedly, it founds organisations of its own to give full effect to it ; these organisations guide politics, govern statesmen, destroy institutions ;—and they are based upon a blunder !

It is to Protestantism, and to this its Puritan gospel, that the reproaches thrown on St. Paul, for sophisticating religion of the heart into theories of the head about election and justification, rightly attach. St. Paul himself begins with seeking righteousness and ends with finding it ; from first to last, the practical religious sense never deserts him. If he could have seen and heard our preachers of predestination and justification, they are just the people he would have called ' diseased about questions and word-battlings.' He would have told Puritanism that every Sunday, when in all its countless chapels it reads him and preaches from him, the veil is upon its heart. The moment it reads him right, a veil will seem to be taken away from its heart ; it will feel as though scales were fallen from its eyes.—*St. Paul and Protestantism.*

SAN PAOLO FUORI LE MURA.

PAUL died, and men's familiar fancies of bargain and appeasement, from which, by a prodigy of religious insight, he had been able to disengage the death of Jesus, fastened on it and made it their own. Back rolled over the human soul the mist which the fires of Paul's spiritual genius had dispersed for a few short years. The mind of the whole world was imbrued in the idea of blood, and only through the false idea of sacrifice did men reach Paul's true one. Paul's idea of dying with Christ the

' Imitation ' elevates more conspicuously than any Protestant treatise elevates it ; but it elevates it environed and dominated by the idea of appeasement ;—of the magnified and non-natural man in Heaven, wrath-filled and blood-exacting ; of the human victim adding his piacular sufferings to those of the divine. Meanwhile another danger was preparing. Gifted men had brought to the study of St. Paul the habits of the Greek and Roman schools, and philosophised where Paul Orientalised. Augustine, a great genius, who can doubt it ?—nay a great religious genius, but unlike Paul in this, and inferior to him, that he confused the boundaries of metaphysics and religion, which Paul never did,—Augustine set the example of finding in Paul's eastern speech, just as it stood, the formal propositions of western dialectics. Last came the interpreter in whose slowly relaxing grasp we still lie,—the heavy-handed Protestant Philistine. Sincere, gross of perception, prosaic, he saw in Paul's mystical idea of man's investiture with the righteousness of God nothing but a strict legal transaction, and reserved all his imagination for Hell and the New Jerusalem and his foretaste of them. A so-called Pauline doctrine was in all men's mouths, but the ideas of the true Paul lay lost and buried.

Every one who has been at Rome has been taken to see the Church of St. Paul, rebuilt after a destruction by fire some forty years ago. The church stands a mile or

two out of the city, on the way to Ostia and the desert.
The interior has all the costly magnificence of Italian
churches ; on the ceiling is written in gilded letters :
'*Doctor Gentium.*' Gold glitters and marbles gleam, but
man and his movement are not there. The traveller has
left at a distance the *fumum et opes strepitumque Romæ* ;
around him reigns solitude. There is Paul, with the
mystery which was hidden from ages and from generations, which was uncovered by him for some half score
years, and which then was buried with him in his grave !
Not in our day will he re-live, with his incessant effort to
find a moral side for miracle, with his incessant effort to
make the intellect follow and secure all the workings of
the religious perception. Of those who care for religion,
the multitude of us want the materialism of the Apocalypse ; the few want a vague religiosity. Science, which
more and more teaches us to find in the unapparent the
real, will gradually serve to conquer the materialism of
popular religion. The friends of vague religiosity, on
the other hand, will be more and more taught by experience that a theology, a scientific appreciation of the
facts of religion, is wanted for religion ; but a theology
which is a true theology, not a false. Both these influences will work for Paul's re-emergence. The doctrine
of Paul will arise out of the tomb where for centuries it
has lain buried. It will edify the church of the future ;
it will have the consent of happier generations, the

applause of less superstitious ages.   All will be too little, to pay the debt which the church of God owes to this 'least of the apostles, who was not fit to be called an apostle, because he persecuted the church of God.'— *St. Paul and Protestantism.*

THE BRIDGE WHICH CARRIES US OVER.

THE method and the secret of Jesus have been always prized.   The Catholic Church from the first held aloft the secret of Jesus ; the monastic orders were founded, we may say, in homage to it.   And from time to time, through the course of ages, there have arisen men who threw themselves on the method and secret of Jesus with extraordinary force, with intuitive sense that here was salvation ; and who really cared for nothing else, though ecclesiastical dogma, too, they professed to believe, and sincerely thought they did believe,—but their heart was elsewhere.   These are they who 'received the kingdom of God as a little child,' who perceived how simple a thing Christianity was, though so inexhaustible, and who are therefore 'the greatest in the kingdom of God.'   And they, not the theological doctors, are the true lights of the Christian Church ; not Augustine, Luther, Bossuet, Butler, but the nameless author of the ' Imitation,' but Tauler, but St. Francis of Sales, Wilson of Sodor and Man.   Yet not only these men, but the whole body of Christian churches and sects always, have all at least professed the method and secret of Jesus, and to some extent used them. And whenever these were used, they have borne their natural fruits of joy and life ; and this joy and this life have been taken to flow from the ecclesiastical dogma held along with them, and to sanction and prove it. And people, eager to praise the bridge which carried them over from death to life, have taken this dogma for the bridge, or part of the bridge, that carried them over, and have eagerly praised it. Thus religion has been made to stand on its apex instead of its base. Righteousness is supported on ecclesiastical dogma, instead of ecclesiastical dogma being supported on righteousness.—*Literature and Dogma.*

CATHOLICISM AND PROTESTANTISM.

CATHOLICISM, we have said, laid hold on the 'secret' of Jesus, and strenuously, however blindly, employed it ; this is the grandeur and the glory of Catholicism. In like manner Protestantism laid hold on his 'method,' and strenuously, however blindly, employed it ; and herein is the greatness of Protestantism. The preliminary labour of inwardness and sincerity in the conscience of each individual man, which was the method of Jesus and the indispensable discipline for learning to employ his secret aright, had fallen too much out of view ; *obedience* had in a manner superseded it. Protestantism drew it into light and prominence again ;

was even, one may say, over-absorbed by it, so as to leave too much out of view the 'secret.' This, if one would be just both to Catholicism and to Protestantism, is the thing to bear in mind :—Protestantism had hold of Jesus Christ's method of inwardness and sincerity, Catholicism had hold of his secret of self-renouncement. The chief word with Protestantism is the word of the method : *repentance, conversion* ; the chief word with Catholicism is the word of the secret : *peace, joy.*

And since, though the method and the secret are equally indispensable, the secret may be said to have in it more of practice and conduct, Catholicism may claim perhaps to have more of religion. On the other hand, Protestantism has more light ; and, as the method of inwardness and sincerity, once gained, is of general application, and a power for all the purposes of life, Protestantism, we can see, has been accompanied by most prosperity. And here is the answer to Mr. Buckle's famous parallel between Spain and Scotland, that parallel which everyone feels to be a sophism. Scotland has had, to make her different from Spain, the 'method' of Jesus ; and though, in theology, Scotland may have turned it to no great account, she has found her account in it in almost everything else. Catholicism, again, has had, perhaps, most happiness. When one thinks of the bitter and contentious temper of Puritanism,—temper being, nevertheless, such a vast part of *conduct*,—and then thinks of St. Theresa and her sweetness, her never-sleeping hatred of 'detraction,' one is tempted almost to say, that there was more of Jesus in St. Theresa's little finger than in John Knox's whole body.   Protestantism has the method of Jesus with his secret too much left out of mind ; Catholicism has his secret with his method too much left out of mind.   Neither has his unerring balance, his intuition, his *sweet reasonableness.*   But both have hold of a great truth, and get from it a great power.

And many of the reproaches cast by one on the other are idle.   If Catholicism is reproached with being indifferent to much that is called *civilisation*, it must be answered : So was Jesus.   If Protestantism, with its private judgment, is accused of opening a wide field for individual fancies and mistakes, it must be answered : So did Jesus when he introduced his method.   Private judgment, *'the fundamental and insensate doctrine of Protestantism,'* as Joseph de Maistre calls it, is in truth but the necessary method, the eternally incumbent duty, imposed by Jesus himself, when he said : 'Judge not according to the appearance, but judge righteous judgment.'   'Judge *righteous* judgment' is, however, the duty imposed ; and the duty is not, whatever many Protestants may seem to think, fulfilled if the judgment be *wrong*.   But the duty of inwardly judging is the very entrance into the way and walk of Jesus.—*Literature and Dogma.*

CRITICISM WITHIN THE CHURCH.

THE Christian religion has practice for its great end and aim ; but it raises, as any one can see, and as Church-history proves, numerous and great questions of philosophy and of scientific criticism. Well, for the true elucidation of such questions, and for their final solution, time and favourable developing conditions are confessedly necessary. From the end of the apostolic age and of the great fontal burst of Christianity down to the present time, have such conditions ever existed, in the Christian communities, for determining adequately the questions of philosophy and scientific criticism which the Christian religion starts? *God, creation, will, evil, propitiation, immortality,*—these terms and many more of the same kind, however much they might in the Bible be used in a concrete and practical manner, yet plainly had in themselves a provocation to abstract thought, carried with them the occasions of a criticism and a philosophy, which must sooner or later make its appearance in the Church. It did make its appearance, and the question is whether it has ever yet appeared there under conditions favourable to its true development. Surely this is best elucidated by considering whether questions of criticism and philosophy, in general, ever had one of their happy moments, their times for successful development, in the early and middle ages of Christendom at all, or have had one of them in the Christian churches, as such, since. All these questions hang together, and the time that is improper for solving one sort of them truly, is improper for solving the others.

Well, surely, historic criticism, criticism of style, criticism of nature, no one would go to the early or middle ages of the Church for illumination on these matters. How then should those ages develop successfully a philosophy of theology, or in other words, a criticism of physics and metaphysics, which involves the three other criticisms and more besides? Church-theology is an elaborate attempt at a philosophy of theology, at a philosophical criticism. In Greece, before Christianity appeared, there had been a favouring period for the development of such a criticism ; a considerable movement of it took place, and considerable results were reached. When Christianity began, this movement was in decadence ; it declined more and more till it died quite out ; it revived very slowly, and as it waxed, the mediæval Church waned. The doctrine of universals is a question of philosophy discussed in Greece, and re-discussed in the middle ages. Whatever light this doctrine receives from Plato's treatment of it, or Aristotle's, in whatever state they left it, will any one say that the Nominalists and Realists brought any more light to it, that they developed it in any way, or could develop it? For the same reason, St. Augustine's criticism of God's eternal decrees, original sin, and justification, the criticism of St. Thomas Aquinas on them, the decisions of the Church on them, are of necessity, and from the very nature of things, inadequate, because, being philosophical developments, they are made in an age when the forces for true philosophical development are waning or wanting.

So when Hooker says most truly : ' Our belief in the Trinity, the co-eternity of the Son of God with his Father, the proceeding of the Spirit from the Father and the Son, with other principal points the necessity whereof is by none denied, are notwithstanding in Scripture nowhere to be found by express literal mention, only deduced they are out of Scripture by collection ; '—when Hooker thus points out, what is undoubtedly the truth, that these Church-doctrines are developments, we may add this other truth equally undoubted,—that, being *philosophical* developments, they are developments of a kind which the Church has never yet had the right conditions for making adequately, any more than it has had the conditions for developing out of what is said in the Book of Genesis a true philosophy of nature, or out of what is said in the Book of Daniel, a true philosophy of history. It matters nothing whether the scientific truth was there, and the problem was to extract it ; or not there, and the problem was to understand why it was not there, and the relation borne by what *was* there to the scientific truth. The Church had no means of solving either the one problem or the other. And this from no fault at all of the Church, but for the same reason that she was unfitted to solve a difficulty in Aristotle's 'Physics' or Plato's 'Timæus,' and to determine the historical value of Herodotus or Livy ; simply from the natural operation of the law of development, which for success in philosophy and criticism requires certain conditions, which in the early and mediæval Church were not to be found.

And when the movement of philosophy and criticism came with the Renascence, this movement was almost entirely outside the Churches, whether Catholic or Protestant, and not inside them. It worked in men like Descartes and Bacon, and not in men like Luther and Calvin ; so that the doctrine of these two eminent personages, Luther and Calvin, so far as it was a philosophical and critical development from Scripture, had no more likelihood of being an adequate development than the doctrine of the Council of Trent. And so it has gone on to this day. Philosophy and criticism have become a great power in the world, and inevitably tend to alter and develop Church-doctrine, so far as this doctrine is, as to a great extent it is, philosophical and critical. Yet the seat of the developing force is not in the Church itself, but elsewhere ; its influences filter strugglingly into the Church, and the Church slowly absorbs and incorporates them. And whatever hinders their filtering in and becoming incorporated, hinders truth and the natural progress of things.—*St. Paul and Protestantism.*

'SECURUS JUDICAT.'

CARDINAL NEWMAN has told us what an impression was once, made upon his mind by the sentence : *Securus judicat orbis terrarum.* We have endeavoured to show, how, for matters of philosophical judgment, not yet settled but requiring development to clear them, the consent of the world, at a time when this clearing development cannot have happened, seems to carry little or no weight at all ; indeed, as to judgment on these points, we should rather be inclined to lay down the very contrary of Cardinal Newman's affirmation, and to say : *Securus delirat orbis terrarum.* But points of speculative theology being out of the question, and the practical ground and purpose of man's religion being broadly and plainly fixed, we should be quite disposed to concede to Cardinal Newman, that *securus* colit *orbis terrarum ;*—those pursue the purpose of *worship* best, who pursue it together. For unless prevented by extraneous causes, they manifestly tend, as the history of the Church's growth shows, to pursue it together.—*St. Paul and Protestantism.*

MORALITY AND RELIGION.

MORAL rules, apprehended as ideas first, and then rigorously followed as laws, are, and must be, for the sage only. The mass of mankind have neither force of intellect enough to apprehend them clearly as ideas, nor force of character enough to follow them strictly as laws. The mass of mankind can be carried along a course full of hardship for the natural man, can be borne over the thousand impediments of the narrow way, only by the tide of a joyful and bounding emotion. It is impossible to rise from reading Epictetus or Marcus Aurelius without a sense of constraint and melancholy, without feeling that the burden laid upon man is well-nigh greater than he can bear. Honour to the sages who have felt this, and yet have borne it ! Yet, even for the sage, this sense of labour and sorrow in his march towards the goal constitutes a relative inferiority ; the noblest souls of whatever creed, the pagan Empedocles as well as the Christian Paul, have insisted on the necessity of an inspiration, a joyful emotion, to make moral action perfect. An obscure indication of this necessity is the one drop of truth in the ocean of verbiage with which the controversy on justification by faith has flooded the world. But, for the ordinary man, this sense of labour and sorrow constitutes an absolute disqualification ; it paralyses him ; under the weight of it, he cannot make way towards the goal at all. The paramount virtue of religion is, that it has *lighted up* morality ; that it has supplied the emotion and inspiration needful for carrying the sage along the narrow way perfectly, for carrying the ordinary man along it at all.

Even the religions with most dross in them have had something of this virtue ; but the Christian religion manifests it with unexampled splendour.—*Essays in Criticism.*

CHRISTIANITY AND THE ANTONINES.

THE Christianity which the Antonines aimed at repressing was, in their conception of it, something philosophically contemptible, politically subversive, and morally abominable. As men, they sincerely regarded it much as well-conditioned people, with us, regard Mormonism ; as rulers, they regarded it much as Liberal statesmen, with us, regard the Jesuits. A kind of Mormonism, constituted as a vast secret society, with obscure aims of political and social subversion, was what Antoninus Pius and Marcus Aurelius believed themselves to be repressing when they punished Christians. The early Christian apologists again and again declare to us under what odious imputations the Christians lay, how general was the belief that these imputations were well-grounded, how sincere was the horror which the belief inspired. The multitude, convinced that the Christians were atheists who ate human flesh and thought incest no crime, displayed against them a fury so passionate as to embarrass and alarm their rulers. The severe expressions of Tacitus, *exitiabilis superstitio—odio humani generis convicti,* show how deeply the prejudices of the multitude imbued the educated class also. One asks oneself with astonishment how a doctrine so benign as that of Jesus Christ can have incurred misrepresentation so monstrous. The inner and moving cause of the misrepresentation lay, no doubt, in this,—that Christianity was a new spirit in the Roman world, destined to act in that world as its dissolvent ; and it was inevitable that Christianity in the Roman world, like democracy in the modern world, like every new spirit with a similar mission assigned to it, should at its first appearance occasion an instinctive shrinking and repugnance in the world which it was to dissolve. The outer and palpable causes of the misrepresentation were, for the Roman public at large, the confounding of the Christians with the Jews, that isolated, fierce, and stubborn race, whose stubbornness, fierceness, and isolation, real as they were, the fancy of a civilised Roman yet further exaggerated ; the atmosphere of mystery and novelty which surrounded the Christian rites ; the very simplicity of Christian theism. For the Roman statesman, the cause of mistake lay in that character of secret assemblages which the meetings of the Christian community wore, under a State-system as jealous of unauthorised associations as the State-system of modern France.

A Roman of Marcus Aurelius's time and position could not well see the Christians except through the mist of these prejudices. Seen through such a mist, the Christians appeared with a thousand faults not their own ;

but it has not been sufficiently remarked that faults really their own many of them assuredly appeared with besides, faults especially likely to strike such an observer as Marcus Aurelius, and to confirm him in the prejudices of his race, station, and rearing. We look back upon Christianity after it has proved what a future it bore within it, and for us the sole representatives of its early struggles are the pure and devoted spirits through whom it proved this ; Marcus Aurelius saw it with its future yet unshown, and with the tares among its professed progeny not less conspicuous than the wheat. Who can doubt that among the professing Christians of the second century, as among the professing Christians of the nineteenth, there was plenty of folly, plenty of rabid nonsense, plenty of gross fanaticism ? Who will even venture to affirm, that, separated in great measure from the intellect and civilisation of the world for one or two centuries, Christianity, wonderful as have been its fruits, had the development perfectly worthy of its inestimable germ ? Who will venture to affirm, that, by the alliance of Christianity with the virtue and intelligence of men like the Antonines,— of the best product of Greek and Roman civilisation, while Greek and Roman civilisation had yet life and power,—Christianity and the world, as well as the Antonines themselves, would not have been gainers ? That alliance was not to be. The Antonines lived and died with an utter misconception of Christianity ; Christianity grew up in the Catacombs, not on the Palatine. And Marcus Aurelius incurs no grave moral reproach by having authorised the punishment of the Christians ; he does not thereby become in the least what we mean by a *persecutor.* One may concede that it was impossible for him to see Christianity as it really was ;—as impossible as for even the moderate and sensible Fleury to see the Antonines as they really were ;—one may concede that the point of view from which Christianity appeared something anti-civil and anti-social, which the State had the faculty to judge and the duty to suppress, was inevitably his. Still, however, it remains true that this sage, who made perfection his aim and reason his law, did Christianity an immense injustice, and rested in an idea of State-attributes which was illusive. And this is, in truth, characteristic of Marcus Aurelius,—that he is blameless, yet, in a certain sense, unfortunate ; in his character, beautiful as it is, there is something melancholy, circumscribed, and ineffectual.—*Essays in Criticism.*

MARCUS AURELIUS.

MARCUS AURELIUS is perhaps the most beautiful character in history. He is one of those consoling and hope-inspiring marks, which stand for ever to remind our weak and easily discouraged race how high human goodness and perseverance have once been carried, and may be carried again. The interest of mankind is peculiarly attracted by examples of signal goodness in high places ; for that testimony to the worth of goodness is the most striking, which is borne by those to whom all the means of pleasure and self-indulgence lay open, by those who had at their command the kingdoms of the world and the glory of them.   Marcus Aurelius was the ruler of the grandest of empires ; and he was one of the best of men.   Besides him, history presents one or two other sovereigns eminent for their goodness, such as Saint Louis or Alfred.   But Marcus Aurelius has, for us moderns, this great superiority in interest over Saint Louis or Alfred, that he lived and acted in a state of society modern by its essential characteristics, in an epoch akin to our own, in a brilliant centre of civilisation.   Trajan talks of 'our enlightened age' just as glibly as the 'Times' talks of it.   Marcus Aurelius thus becomes for us a man like ourselves, a man in all things tempted as we are.   Saint Louis inhabits an atmosphere of mediæval Catholicism, which the man of the nineteenth century may admire indeed, may even passionately wish to inhabit, but which, strive as he will, he cannot really inhabit.   Alfred belongs to a state of society (I say it with all deference to the 'Saturday Review' critic who keeps such jealous watch over the honour of our Saxon ancestors) half barbarous.   Neither Alfred nor Saint Louis can be morally and intellectually as near to us as Marcus Aurelius.

The record of the outward life of this admirable man

has in it little of striking incident. He was born at Rome on the 26th of April, in the year 121 of the Christian era. He was nephew and son-in-law to his predecessor on the throne, Antoninus Pius. When Antoninus died, he was forty years old, but from the time of his earliest manhood he had assisted in administering public affairs. Then, after his uncle's death in 161, for nineteen years he reigned as emperor. The barbarians were pressing on the Roman frontier, and a great part of Marcus Aurelius's nineteen years of reign was passed in campaigning. His absences from Rome were numerous and long. We hear of him in Asia Minor, Syria, Egypt, Greece ; but, above all, in the countries on the Danube, where the war with the barbarians was going on,—in Austria, Moravia, Hungary. In these countries much of his Journal seems to have been written ; parts of it are dated from them ; and there, a few weeks before his fifty-ninth birthday, he fell sick and died.[1] The record of him on which his fame chiefly rests is the record of his inward life,—his ' Journal,' or ' Commentaries,' or ' Meditations,' or ' Thoughts,' for by all these names has the work been called.

Of the records of his outward life perhaps the most interesting is that which the first book of this work supplies, where he gives an account of his education, recites the names of those to whom he is indebted for it, and enumerates his obligations to each of them. It is a re-

---

[1] He died on the 17th of March, A.D. 180.

freshing and consoling picture, a priceless treasure for those, who, sick of the 'wild and dreamlike trade of blood and guile,' which seems to be nearly the whole of what history has to offer to our view, seek eagerly for that substratum of right thinking and well doing which in all ages must surely have somewhere existed, for without it the continued life of humanity would have been impossible. 'From my mother I learnt piety and beneficence, and abstinence not only from evil deeds but even from evil thoughts ; and further, simplicity in my way of living, far removed from the habits of the rich.' Let us remember that, the next time we are reading the sixth satire of Juvenal. 'From my tutor I learnt' (hear it, ye tutors of princes!) 'endurance of labour, and to want little, and to work with my own hands, and not to meddle with other people's affairs, and not to be ready to listen to slander.' The vices and foibles of the Greek sophist or rhetorician, —the *Græculus esuriens,*—are in everybody's mind ; but he who reads Marcus Aurelius's account of his Greek teachers and masters, will understand how it is that, in spite of the vices and foibles of individual *Græculi,* the education of the human race owes to Greece a debt which can never be overrated. Again, the vague and colourless praise of history leaves on the mind hardly any impression of Antoninus Pius : it is only from the private memoranda of his nephew that we learn what a disciplined, hard-working, gentle, wise, virtuous man he was ;

a man who, perhaps, interests mankind less than his immortal nephew only because he has left in writing no record of his inner life,—*caret quia vate sacro.*

Of the outward life and circumstances of Marcus Aurelius, beyond these notices which he has himself supplied, there are few of much interest and importance. There is the fine anecdote of his speech when he heard of the assassination of the revolted Avidius Cassius, against whom he was marching ; *he was sorry*, he said, *to be deprived of the pleasure of pardoning him.* And there are one or two more anecdotes of him which show the same spirit. But the great record for the outward life of a man who has left such a record of his lofty inward aspirations as that which Marcus Aurelius has left, is the clear consenting voice of all his contemporaries,—high and low, friend and enemy, pagan and Christian,—in praise of his sincerity, purity, justice, and goodness. The world's charity does not err on the side of excess, and here was a man occupying the most conspicuous station in the world, and professing the highest possible standard of conduct ;—yet the world was obliged to declare that he walked worthily of his profession. Long after his death, his bust was to be seen in the houses of private men throughout the wide Roman empire. It may be the vulgar part of human nature which busies itself with the semblance and doings of living sovereigns, it is its nobler part which busies itself with those of the dead; these busts of Marcus Aurelius, in the homes of Gaul, Britain, Spain, and Italy, bear witness, not to the inmates' frivolous curiosity about princes and palaces, but to their reverential memory of the passage of a great man upon the earth.—*Essays in Criticism.*

MARCUS AURELIUS AND CHRISTIANITY.

MARCUS AURELIUS remains the especial friend and comforter of all clear-headed and scrupulous, yet pure-hearted and upward-striving men, in those ages most especially that walk by sight, not by faith, but have, nevertheless, no open vision. He cannot give such souls, perhaps, all they yearn for, but he gives them much; and what he gives them, they can receive.

Yet no, it is not for what he thus gives them that such souls love him most! it is rather because of the emotion which lends to his voice so touching an accent, it is because he too yearns as they do for something unattained by him. What an affinity for Christianity had this persecutor of the Christians! The effusion of Christianity, its relieving tears, its happy self-sacrifice, were the very element, one feels, for which his soul longed; they were near him, they brushed him, he touched them, he passed them by. One feels, too, that the Marcus Aurelius one reads must still have remained, even had Christianity been fully known to him, in a

great measure himself; he would have been no Justin;—
but how would Christianity have affected him? in what
measure would it have changed him? Granted that he
might have found, like the *Alogi* of modern times, in
the most beautiful of the Gospels, the Gospel which has
leavened Christendom most powerfully, the Gospel of
St. John, too much Greek metaphysics, too much *gnosis*;
granted that this Gospel might have looked too like what
he knew already to be a total surprise to him : what, then,
would he have said to the Sermon on the Mount, to
the twenty-sixth chapter of St. Matthew? What would
have become of his notions of the *exitiabilis superstitio*,
of the 'obstinacy of the Christians'? Vain question !
yet the greatest charm of Marcus Aurelius is that he
makes us ask it. We see him wise, just, self-governed,
tender, thankful, blameless ; yet, with all this, agitated,
stretching out his arms for something beyond,—*tenden-
temque manus ripæ ulterioris amore.—Essays in Criticism.*

THE IMAMS.

ABNEGATION and mildness, based on the depth of the
inner life, and visited by unmerited misfortune, made the
power of the first and famous Imams, Ali, Hassan, and
Hussein, over the popular imagination. 'O brother,'
said Hassan, as he was dying of poison, to Hussein, who
sought to find out and punish his murderer, 'O brother,

let him alone till he and I meet together before God !' So his father Ali had stood back from his rights instead of clutching at them. So of Hussein himself it was said by his successful rival, the usurping Caliph Yezid : 'God loved Hussein, *but he would not suffer him to attain to anything.*' They might attain to nothing, they were too pure, these great ones of the world as by birth they were ; but the people, which itself also can attain to so little, loved them all the better on that account, loved them for their abnegation and mildness, felt that they were dear to God, that God loved them, and that they and their lives filled a void in the severe religion of Mahomet. These saintly self-deniers, these resigned sufferers, who would not strive nor cry, supplied a tender and pathetic side in Islam. The conquered Persians, a more mobile, more impressionable, and gentler race than their concen-trated, narrow, and austere Semitic conquerors, felt the need of it most, and gave most prominence to the ideals which satisfied the need ; but in Arabs and Turks also, and in all the Mahometan world, Ali and his sons excite enthusiasm and affection. Round the central sufferer, Hussein, has come to group itself everything which is most tender and touching. His person brings to the Mussulman's mind the most human side of Mahomet himself, his fondness for children,—for Mahomet had loved to nurse the little Hussein on his knee, and to show him from the pulpit to his people. The Family of

the Tent is full of women and children, and of their devotion and sufferings,—blameless and saintly women, lovely
and innocent children. There, too, are lovers and their
story, lovers lit with the beauty and the love of youth;
all follow the attraction of the pure and resigned Imam,
all die for him. The tender pathos from all these flows
into the pathos from him and enhances it, until finally
there arises for the popular imagination an immense
ideal of mildness and self-sacrifice, melting and over-
powering the soul.

Even for us, to whom almost all the names are
strange, whose interest in the places and persons is faint,
who have them before us for a moment to-day, to see
them again, probably, no more for ever,—even for us, unless I err greatly, the power and pathos of this ideal are
recognisable. What must they be for those to whom
every name is familiar, and calls up the most solemn and
cherished associations; who have had their adoring gaze
fixed all their lives upon this exemplar of self-denial
and gentleness, and who have no other?—*Essays in
Criticism.*

SPINOZA.

THE lonely precursor of German philosophy, Spinoza still
shines, while the light of his successors is fading away;
they had celebrity, Spinoza has fame. Not because his
peculiar system of philosophy has had more adherents

than theirs ; on the contrary, it has had fewer. But schools of philosophy arise and fall ; their .bands of adherents inevitably dwindle ; no master can long persuade a large body of disciples that they give to themselves just the same account of the world as he does ; it is only the very young and the very enthusiastic who can think themselves sure that they possess the whole mind of Plato, or Spinoza, or Hegel, at all. The very mature and the very sober can even hardly believe that these philosophers possessed it themselves enough to put it all into their works, and to let us know entirely how the world seemed to them. What a remarkable philosopher really does for human thought, is to throw into circulation a certain number of new and striking ideas and expressions, and to stimulate with them the thought and imagination of his century or of after-times. So Spinoza has made his distinction between adequate and inadequate ideas a current notion for educated Europe. So Hegel seized a single pregnant sentence of Heracleitus, and cast it, with a thousand striking applications, into the world of modern thought. But to do this is only enough to make a philosopher noteworthy ; it is not enough to make him great. To be great, he must have something in him which can influence character, which is edifying ; he must, in short, have a noble and lofty character himself, a character,—to recur to that much-criticised expression of mine,—*in the grand style.* This is what Spinoza had ; and because he had it, he stands out from the multitude of philosophers, and has been able to inspire in powerful minds a feeling which the most remarkable philosophers, without this grandiose character, could not inspire. 'There is no possible view of life but Spinoza's,' said Lessing. Goethe has told us how he was calmed and edified by him in his youth, and how he again went to him for support in his maturity. Heine, the man (in spite of his faults) of truest genius that Germany has produced since Goethe,—a man with faults, as I have said, immense faults, the greatest of them being that he could reverence so little,—reverenced Spinoza. Hegel's influence ran off him like water : 'I have seen Hegel,' he cries, 'seated with his doleful air of a hatching hen upon his unhappy eggs, and I have heard his dismal clucking. How easily one can cheat oneself into thinking that one understands everything, when one has learnt only how to construct dialectical formulas !' But of Spinoza, Heine said : 'His life was a copy of the life of his divine kinsman, Jesus Christ.'— *Essays in Criticism.*

TURGOT AND BUTLER.

LOOK at a contemporary of Butler in France,—a man who, more than any one else, reminds me of Butler,— the great French statesman, the greatest, in my opinion, that France has ever had ; look at Turgot. Turgot was like Butler in his mental energy, in his deep moral and intellectual ardour, his strenuousness. 'Every science, every language, every literature, every business,' says Michelet, 'interested Turgot.' But that in which Turgot most resembled Butler was what Michelet calls his *férocité,* —what I should rather call his *sæva indignatio.* Like Butler, Turgot was filled with an astonished, awful, oppressive sense of 'the immoral thoughtlessness' of men ; of the heedless, hazardous way in which they deal with things of the greatest moment to them ; of the immense, incalculable misery which is due to this cause. 'The greatest evils in life,' Turgot held, just as Butler did, 'have had their rise from somewhat which was thought of too little importance to be attended to.' And for these serious natures religion, one would think, is the line of labour which would naturally first suggest itself. And Turgot was destined for the Church ; he prepared to take orders, like Butler. But in 1752, when Butler lay dying at Bath, Turgot,—the true spiritual yoke-fellow of Butler, with Butler's sacred horror at men's frivolity, with Butler's sacred ardour for rescuing them from the consequences of it,—Turgot, at the age of twenty-five, could stand religion, as in France religion then presented itself to him, no longer. '*Il jeta ce masque,*' says Michelet, adopting an expression of Turgot's own ; 'he flung away that mask.' He took to the work of civil government ; in what spirit we many of us know, and whoever of us does not know should make it his business to learn.

Nine years afterwards began his glorious administration as Intendant of the Limousin, in which for thirteen years he showed what manner of spirit he was of. When, in 1774, he became Minister and Controller-General, he showed the same thing on a more conspicuous stage. ' Whatsoever things are true, whatsoever things are nobly serious, whatsoever things are just, whatsoever things are pure, whatsoever things are of good report,'—that is the history of Turgot's administration ! He was a Joseph Butler in government. True, his work, though done as secular administration, has in fact and reality a religious character ; all work like his has a religious character. But the point to seize is here : that in our country, in the middle of the eighteenth century, a man like Butler is still possible in religion ; in France he is only possible in civil government. And that is what I call a true ' decay of religion, the influence of it more and more wearing out of the minds of men.' The very existence and work of Butler proves, in spite of his own desponding words, that matters had not in his time gone so far as this in England.—*Last Essays.*

BUTLER'S PSYCHOLOGY.

WHAT he calls our instincts and principles of action, which are in truth the most obscure, changing, inter-dependent of phenomena, Butler takes as if they were things as separate, fixed, and palpable as the bodily

organs which the dissector has on his table before him.
He takes them as if, just as he now finds them, there
they had always been, and there they must always be ;
as if benevolence had always gone on secreting love of
our neighbour, and compassion a desire to relieve misery,
and conscience right verdicts, just as the liver secretes
bile. Butler's error is that of the early chemists, who
imagined things to be elements which were not, but were
capable of being resolved and decomposed much farther.
And a man who is thrown fairly upon himself, and will
have the naked truth, must feel that it is with Butler's
principles and affections as it was with the elements of
the early chemists ;—they are capable of being resolved
and decomposed much farther, and solid ground is not
reached until they are thus decomposed. ‘There is this
principle of reflexion or conscience in mankind.’—‘True,’
the student may answer ; ‘but what and whence is it ?
It had a genesis of some kind, and your account of its
genesis is fantastic. What is its natural genesis, and
what the natural genesis of your benevolence, compassion,
resentment, and all the rest of them ? Till I know this,
I do not know where I am in talking about them.’—But
into this vast, dimly lighted, primordial region of the
natural genesis of man's affections and principles, Butler
never enters.

Yet in this laboratory arose those wonderful com-
pounds with which Butler deals, and the source of his

ruling faculty of conscience is to be traced back thither.—
Last Essays.

BUTLER'S ARGUMENT FROM ANALOGY.

I DO not remember to have anywhere seen pointed out the precise break-down, which a cool inquirer must, it seems to me, be conscious of in Butler's argument from analogy. The argument is of this kind :—The reality of the laws of moral government of *this* world, says Butler, implies, by analogy, a like reality of laws of moral government in the second world, where we shall be hereafter. - The analogy is, in truth, used to prove not only the probable continuance of the laws of moral government, but also the probable existence of that future world in which they will be manifested. It *does* only prove the probable continuance of the laws of moral government in the future world, *supposing* that second world to exist. But for that existence it supplies no probability whatever. For it is not the laws of moral government which give us proof of this present world in which they are manifested ; it is the experience that this present world actually exists, and is a place in which these laws are manifested. Show us, we may say to Butler, that a like place presents itself over again after we are dead, and we will allow that by analogy the same moral laws will probably continue to govern it. But this is all which analogy can prove in the matter. The positive existence of the world to come must be **proved**, like the positive existence of the present world, by *experience*. And of this experience Butler's argument furnishes, and can furnish, nct one tittle.

There may be other reasons for believing in a second life beyond the grave. Christians in general consider that they get such grounds from revelation. And people who come to Butler with the belief already established, are not likely to ask themselves very closely what Butler's analogical reasoning on its behalf is good for. The reasoning is exercised in support of a thesis which does not require to be made out for them. But whoever comes to Butler in a state of genuine uncertainty, and has to lean with his whole weight on Butler's reasonings for support, will soon discover their fundamental weakness. The weakness goes through the 'Analogy' from beginning to end. For example :—

The states of life in which we ourselves existed formerly, in the womb and in our infancy, are almost as different from our present in mature age as it is possible to conceive any two states or degrees of life can be. Therefore, that we are to exist hereafter in a state as different (suppose) from our present as this is from the former, is but according to the analogy of nature.

There it is in the first chapter ! But we have *experience* of the several different states succeeding one another in man's present life ; that is what makes us believe in their succeeding one another here. We have no experience of a further different state beyond the limits of this life. If we had, we might freely admit that analogy renders it probable that that state may be as unlike to our actual state, as our actual state is to our state in the womb or in infancy. But that there *is* the further different state must first, for the argument from analogy to take effect, be proved from experience.—*Last Essays.*

BUTLER'S APPEAL TO OUR IGNORANCE.

BUTLER appeals, and no man ever appealed more impressively than he, to the sense we must have of our ignorance. Difficulties alleged against the truth of religion, he says, 'are so apparently and wholly founded in our ignorance, that it is wonderful they should be insisted upon by any but such as are weak enough to think they are acquainted with the whole system of things.' And he speaks of 'that infinitely absurd supposition that we know the whole of the case.' But does not the common account of God by theologians, does not Butler's own assertion of the all-foreseeing, quasi-human designer, with a will and a character, go upon the supposition that we know, at any rate, a very great deal, and more than we actually do know, of the case? And are not the difficulties alleged created by that supposition? And is not the appeal to our ignorance in fact an appeal to us, having taken a great deal for granted, to take something more for granted :—namely, that what we at first took for granted has a satisfactory solution somewhere beyond the reach of our knowledge ?—*Last Essays.*

RESULT OF THE 'ANALOGY.'

THE wonderful thing about the 'Analogy' is the poor insignificant result, even in Butler's own judgment,—the puny total outcome,—of all this accumulated evidence from analogy, metaphysics, and Bible-history. It is, after all, only 'evidence which keeps the mind in doubt, perhaps in perplexity.' The utmost it is calculated to beget is, 'a serious doubting apprehension that it *may* be true.' However, 'in the daily course of life,' says Butler, 'our nature and condition necessarily require us to act upon evidence much lower than what is commonly called probable.' In a matter, then, of such immense practical importance as religion, where the bad consequences of a mistake may be so incalculable, we ought, he says, unhesitatingly to act upon imperfect evidence. 'It ought, in all reason, considering its infinite importance, to have nearly the same influence upon practice, as if it were thoroughly believed !' And such is, really, the upshot of the 'Analogy.' Such is, when all is done, the 'happy alliance' achieved by it 'between faith and philosophy.'

But we *do* not, in the daily course of life, act upon evidence which *we ourselves conceive* to be much lower than what is commonly called probable. If I am going to take a walk out of Edinburgh, and thought of choosing the Portobello road, and a travelling menagerie is taking the same road, it is certainly possible that a tiger may escape from the menagerie and devour me if I take that road ; but the evidence that he will is certainly, also, much lower than what is commonly called probable. Well, I do not, on that low degree of evidence, avoid the Portobello road and take another. But the duty of acting on such a sort of evidence is really made by Butler the motive for a man's following the road of religion,— the way of peace.

How utterly unlike is this motive to the motive always supposed in the book itself of our religion, in the Bible ! After reading the ' Analogy,' one goes instinctively to bathe one's spirit in the Bible again, to be refreshed by its boundless certitude and exhilaration. ' The Eternal is the strength of my life !' 'the foundation of God standeth sure ! '—that is the constant tone of religion in the Bible. ' If I tell you the *truth*, why do ye not believe me ?—the *evident* truth, that whoever comes to me has life ; and evident, because whoever *does* come, gets it !' That is the evidence to constrain our practice which is offered by Christianity.—*Last Essays.*

THE 'ANALOGY' TO-DAY.

LET us, then, confess it to ourselves plainly. The ' Analogy,' the great work on which such immense praise has been lavished, is, for all real intents and purposes now, a failure ; it does not serve. It seemed once to have a spell and a power ; but the *Zeit-Geist* breathes upon it, and we rub our eyes, and it has the spell and the power no longer. It has the effect upon me, as I contemplate it, of a stately and severe fortress, with thick and high walls, built of old to control the kingdom of evil ;— but the gates are open, and the guards gone.—*Last Essays.*

GREATNESS OF BUTLER.

AND yet, in spite of his gloom, in spite of the failure of his 'Analogy' to serve our needs, Butler remains a personage of real grandeur for us. This pathetic figure, with its earnestness, its strenuous rectitude, its firm faith both in religion and in reason, does in some measure help us, does point the way for us. Butler's profound sense, that inattention to religion implies 'a dissolute immoral temper of mind,' engraves itself upon his readers' thoughts also, and comes to govern them. His conviction, that religion and Christianity do somehow 'in themselves entirely fall in with our natural sense of things,' that they are true, and that their truth, moreover, is somehow to be established and justified on plain grounds of reason,— this wholesome and invaluable conviction, also, gains upon us as we read him. The ordinary religionists of Butler's day might well be startled, as they were, by this bishop with the strange, novel, and unhallowed notion, full of dangerous consequence, of 'referring mankind to a law of nature or virtue, written on their hearts.' The pamphleteer, who accused Butler of dying a Papist, declares plainly that he for his part 'has no better opinion of the certainty, clearness, uniformity, universality, &c., of this law, than he has of the importance of external religion.' But Butler *did* believe in the certainty of this law. It was the real foundation of things for him. With awful reverence, he saluted, and he set himself to study and to follow, this 'course of life marked out for man by nature, whatever that nature be.' And he was for perfect fairness of mind in considering the evidence for this law, or for anything else. 'It is fit things be stated and considered as they really are.' 'Things are what they are, and the consequences of them will be what they will be ; why, then, should we desire to be deceived?' And he believed in reason. 'I express myself with caution, lest I should be mistaken to vilify reason, which is indeed the only faculty we have wherewith to judge concerning anything, even religion itself.' Such was Butler's fidelity to that sacred light to which religion makes too many people false,—reason.—*Last Essays.*

BISHOP WILSON'S 'MAXIMS.'

BISHOP WILSON's 'Maxims of Piety and Christianity' deserve to be circulated as a religious book, not only by comparison with the cartloads of rubbish circulated at present under this sort of designation, but for their own sake, and even by comparison with the other works of the same author. Over the far better known 'Sacra Privata' they have this advantage, that they were prepared by him for his own private use, while the 'Sacra Privata' were prepared by him for the use of the public. The 'Maxims' were never meant to be printed, and have on that account,—like a work of, doubtless, far deeper emotion and power, the 'Meditations' of Marcus Aurelius,—something peculiarly sincere and first-hand about them. Some of the best things from the 'Maxims' have passed into the 'Sacra Privata.' Still, in the 'Maxims,' we have them as they first arose ; and whereas, too, in the 'Sacra Privata' the writer speaks very often as one of the clergy, and as addressing the clergy, in the 'Maxims' he almost always speaks only as a man. I am not saying a word against the 'Sacra Privata,' for which I have the highest respect ; only the 'Maxims' seem to me a better and more edifying book still. They should be read, as Joubert says Nicole should be read, with a direct aim at practice. The reader will leave on one side things which, from the change of time and from the changed point of view which the change of time inevitably brings with it, no longer suit him ; enough will remain to serve as a sample of the very best, perhaps, which our nation and race can do in the way of direct religious writing. M. Michelet makes it a reproach to us that, in all the doubts as to the real author of the ' Imitation,' no one has ever dreamed of ascribing that work to an Englishman. It is true, the ' Imitation ' could not well have been written by an Englishman ; the religious delicacy and the profound asceticism of that admirable book are hardly in our nature. This would be more of a reproach to us, if in poetry, which requires, no less than religion, a true delicacy of spiritual perception, our race had not done great things ; and if the "Imitation,' exquisite as it is, did not, as I have elsewhere remarked, belong to a class of works in which the perfect balance of human nature is lost, and which have therefore, as spiritual productions, in their contents something excessive and morbid, in their form something not thoroughly sound. On a lower range than the ' Imitation,' and awakening in our nature chords less poetical and delicate, the ' Maxims ' of Bishop Wilson are, as a religious work, far more solid. To the most sincere ardour and unction, Bishop Wilson unites, in these ' Maxims,' that downright honesty and plain good sense which our English race has so powerfully applied to the divine impossibilities of religion ; by which it has brought religion so much into practical life, and has so faithfully striven to do its allotted part in promoting upon earth the kingdom of God.—*Culture and Anarchy.*

THE NEW RELIGIOUS PROSPECT.

WE have to renounce impossible attempts to receive the
legendary and miraculous matter of Scripture as grave
historical and scientific fact. We have to accustom ourselves to regard henceforth all this part as poetry and
legend. In the Old Testament, as an immense poetry
growing round and investing an immortal truth, 'the
secret of the Eternal:' *Righteousness is salvation.* In
the New, as an immense poetry growing round and investing an immortal truth, the secret of Jesus: *He that
will save his life shall lose it, he that will lose his life shall
save it.*

The best friends of mankind are those who can
lead it to feel animation and hope in presence of the religious prospect thus profoundly transformed. The way
to effect this is by bringing men to see that our religion,
in this altered view of it, does but at last become again
that religion which Jesus Christ really endeavoured to
found, and of which the truth and grandeur are indestructible. We should do Christians generally a great
injustice, if we thought that the entire force of their
Christianity lay in the fascination and subjugation of their
spirits by the miracles which they suppose Jesus to have
worked, or by the materialistic promises of heaven which
they suppose him to have offered. Far more does the
vital force of their Christianity lie in the boundless con-

fidence, consolation, and attachment, which the whole being and discourse of Jesus inspire. What Jesus, then, himself thought sufficient, Christians too may bring themselves to accept with good courage as enough for them. What Jesus himself dismissed as chimerical, Christians too may bring themselves to put aside without dismay.

The central aim of Jesus was to transform for every religious soul the popular Messias-ideal of his time, the ideal of happiness and salvation of the Jewish people ; to disengage religion, one may say, from the materialism of the Book of Daniel. Fifty years had not gone by after his death, when the Apocalypse replunged religion in this materialism ; where, indeed, it was from the first mani-fest that replunged by the followers of Jesus religion must be. It *was* replunged there, but with an addition of inestimable value and of incalculable working,—the figure and influence of Jesus. Slowly this influence emerges, transforms the turbid elements amid which it was thrown, brings back the imperishable ideal of its author. To the mind of Jesus, his own resurrection after a short sojourn in the grave was the victory of his cause after his death, and at the price of his death. His dis-ciples materialised his resurrection ; and their version of the matter falls day by day to ruin. But no ruin or con-tradiction befalls-the version of Jesus himself. He *has* risen, his cause has conquered ; the course of events continually attests his resurrection and victory. The manifest unsoundness of popular Christianity inclines at present many persons to throw doubts on the truth and permanence of Christianity in general. Creeds are discredited, religion is proclaimed to be in danger, the pious quake, the world laughs. Nevertheless, *the prince of this world is judged* ;[1] the victory of Jesus is won and sure. Conscience and self-renouncement, the method and the secret of Jesus, are set up as a leaven in the world, nevermore to cease working there until the world is leavened. That this is so, that the resurrection and re-emergent life of Jesus are in this sense undeniable, and that in this sense Jesus himself predicted them, may in time, surely, encourage Christians to lay hold on this sense as Jesus did.

So, too, with the hope of immortality. Our common materialistic notions about the resurrection of the body and the world to come are, no doubt, natural and attractive to ordinary human nature. But they are in direct conflict with the new and loftier conceptions of life and death which Jesus himself strove to establish. His secret, *He that will save his life shall lose it, he that will lose his life shall save it*, is of universal application. It judges, not only the life to which men cling here, but, just as much, the life we love to promise to ourselves in the New Jerusalem. The immortality propounded by Jesus must

[1] John, xvi. 11.

be looked for elsewhere than in the materialistic aspirations of our popular religion. *He lived in the eternal order, and the eternal order never dies ;*—this, if we may try to formulate in one sentence the result of the sayings of Jesus about life and death, is the sense in which, according to him, we can rightly conceive of the righteous man as immortal, and aspire to be immortal ourselves. And this conception we shall find to stand us in good stead, when the popular materialistic version of our future life fails us. So that here again, too, the version which, unfamiliar and novel as it may now be to us, has the merit of standing fast and holding good while other versions break down, is at the same time the version of Jesus.—*God and the Bible.*

REPROACH OF A SUBLIMATED CHRISTIANITY.

PEOPLE talk scornfully of 'a sublimated Christianity,' as if the Christianity of Jesus Christ himself had been a materialistic fairy-tale like that of Messrs. Moody and Sankey. On the contrary, insensibly to lift us out of all this sort of materialism was Jesus Christ's perpetual endeavour. The parable of the king, who made a marriage for his son, ends with the episode of the guest who had not on a wedding garment, and was cast out.[1] And here, as usual, the Tübingen critics detect *tendence.* They see in the episode a deliberate invention of the Evangelists,

[1] Matth., xxii, 1–14.

a stroke of Jewish particularism, indemnifying itself for having had to relate, that salvation was preached in the highways. We have disagreed often with the Tübingen critics, and we shall venture finally to disagree with them here. We receive the episode as genuine ; but what did Jesus mean by it ? Shall we not do well in thinking, that he, whose lucidity was so incomparable, and who indicated so much which was to be seized not by the present but by the future, here marked and meant to mark, although but incidentally and in passing, the profound, the utter insufficiency of popular religion ? Through the turbid phase of popular religion the religion of Jesus had to pass. Good and bad it was to bear along with it ; the gross and ignorant were to be swept in, by wholesale, from the highways ; *the wedding was to be furnished with guests.* On this wise must Christianity needs develop itself, and the necessary law of its development was to be accepted. Vain to be too nice about the unpreparedness of the guests in general, about their inevitable misuse of the favours which they were admitted to enjoy ! What could have been the end of such a fastidious scrutiny ? To turn them all out into the highways again. But the king's design was, that *the wedding should be furnished with guests.* So the guests shall all stay and fall to ;—popular Christianity is founded. But presently, almost as if by accident, a guest even more unprepared and gross than the common, a guest 'not having on a wedding garment,' comes under the king's eye, and is ejected. Only one is noted for decisive ejection ; but ah ! how many of those guests are as really unapt to seize and to follow God's designs for them as he ! *Many are called, few chosen.* The conspicuous delinquent, however, is sentenced to be bound hand and foot, and to be taken away, and cast into outer darkness.

In the severity of this sentence, Jesus marks how utterly those who are gathered to his feast may fail to know him. The misapprehending and materialising of his religion, the long and turbid stage of popular Christianity, was, indeed, inevitable. But, to give light and impulsion to future times, Jesus stamps this Christianity, even from the very moment of its birth, as, though inevitable, not worthy of its name ; as ignorant and transient, and requiring all who would be truly children of the kingdom to rise beyond it.—*God and the Bible.*

THE TRUE JERUSALEM.

ISRAEL'S visible Jerusalem is in ruins ; and how, then, shall men 'call Jerusalem the throne of the Eternal, and all the nations shall be gathered unto it'? But the true Israel was Israel the bringer-in and defender of the idea of *conduct,* Israel the lifter-up to the nations of the banner of *righteousness.* The true Jerusalem was the city of this ideal Israel. And this ideal Israel could not and cannot perish, so long as its idea, righteousness and its necessity, does not perish, but prevails. Now, that it does prevail, the whole course of the world proves, and the fall of the actual Israel is of itself witness. Thus, therefore, the ideal Israel for ever lives and prospers ; and its city is the city whereto all nations and languages, after endless trials of everything else except conduct, after incessantly attempting to do without righteousness and failing, are slowly but surely gathered.

To this Israel are the promises, and to this Israel they are fulfilled. 'The nation and kingdom that will not serve thee shall perish, yea, those nations shall be utterly wasted.' It is so ; since all history is an accumulation of experiences that what men and nations fall by is want of *conduct.* To call it by this plain name is often not amiss, for the thing is never more great than when it is looked at in its simplicity and reality. Yet the true name to touch the soul is the name Israel gave : *righteousness.* And to Israel, as the representative of this imperishable and saving idea of righteousness, all the promises come true, and the language of none of them is pitched too high. *The Eternal,* Israel says truly, *is on my side.* 'Fear not, thou worm Jacob, and thou handful Israel ! I will help thee, saith the Eternal. The Eternal hath chosen Zion ; men shall call Jerusalem "the throne of the Eternal," and all the nations shall be gathered unto it. And he will destroy in this mountain the face of the covering cast over all people, and the veil that is spread over all nations ; he will swallow up death in victory.'— *Literature and Dogma.*

ISRAEL AND HIS REVELATION.

THE whole history of the world to this day is in truth one continual establishing of the Old Testament revelation : *O ye that love the Eternal, see that ye hate the thing that is evil ! to him that ordereth his conversation right, shall be shown the salvation of God.* And whether we consider this revelation in respect to human affairs at large, or in respect to individual happiness, in either case its importance is so immense, that the people to whom it was given, and whose record is in the Bible, deserve fully to be singled out as the Bible singles them. ' Behold, darkness shall cover the earth, and gross darkness the nations ; but the Eternal shall arise upon *thee*, and his glory shall be seen upon thee !' For, while other nations had the misleading idea that this or that, other than righteousness, is saving, and it is not ; that this or that, other than conduct, brings happiness, and it does not ; Israel had the true idea that *righteousness* is saving, that to *conduct* belongs happiness.

Nor let it be said that other nations, too, had at least something of this idea. They had, but they were not *possessed* with it ; and to feel it enough to make the world feel it, it was necessary to be possessed with it. It is not sufficient to have been visited by such an idea at times, to have had it forced occasionally on one's mind by the teachings of experience. No ; *he that hath the bride is the bridegroom* ; the idea belongs to him who has most *loved* it. Common prudence can say : Honesty is the best policy ; morality can say : To conduct belongs happiness. But Israel and the Bible are filled with religious joy, and rise higher and say : '*Righteousness is salvation !*'—and this is what is inspiring. ' I have *stuck* unto thy testimonies ! Eternal, what *love* have I unto thy law ! *all the day long* is my study in it. Thy testimonies have I claimed as *mine heritage for ever*, and why ? *they are the very ·joy of my heart !*' This is why the testimonies of righteousness are Israel's heritage for ever, because they were *the very joy of his heart.* Herein Israel stood alone, the friend and elect of the Eternal. ' He showeth his word unto *Jacob*, his statutes and ordinances unto *Israel.* He hath not dealt so with any nation, neither have the heathen knowledge of his laws.'

Poor Israel ! poor 'ancient people' ! It was revealed to thee that righteousness is salvation ; the question, *what* righteousness is, was thy stumbling-stone. Seer of the vision of peace, that yet couldst not see the things which belong unto thy peace ! with that blindness thy solitary pre-eminence ended, and the new Israel, made up out of all nations and languages, took thy room. But, thy visitation complete, thy temple in ruins, thy reign over, thine office done, thy children dispersed, thy teeth drawn, thy shekels of silver and gold plundered, did there yet stay with thee any remembrance of thy primitive intuition, simple and sublime, of *the Eternal that loveth righteousness?* Perhaps not ; the Talmudists were fully as well able to efface it as the Fathers. But if there did, what punishment can have been to thee like the punishment of watching the performances of the Aryan genius upon the foundation which thou hadst given to it ?—to behold this terrible and triumphant philosopher, with his monotheistic idea and his metaphysical Trinity, ' neither confounding the Persons nor dividing the Substance'? Like the torture for a poet to hear people laying down the law about poetry who have not the sense what poetry is,—a sense with which *he* was born ! like the affliction to a man of science to hear people talk of things as *proved*, who do not even know what constitutes a fact ! From the Council of Nicæa down to Convocation and our two bishops 'doing something' for the Godhead of the Eternal Son, what must thou have had to suffer !—*Literature and Dogma.*

GRANDEUR OF CHRISTIANITY.

THE grandeur of Christianity, and the imposing and impressive attestation of it, if one could but worthily bring the thing out, is here : in that immense experimental proof of the necessity of it, which the whole course of the world has steadily accumulated, and indicates to us as still continuing and extending.   Men will not admit assumptions, the popular legend they call a fairy-tale, the metaphysical demonstrations do not demonstrate, nothing but experimental proof will go down ; and here is an experimental proof which never fails, and which at the same time is infinitely grander, by the vastness of its scale, the scope of its duration, the gravity of its results, than the machinery of the popular fairy-tale.   Walking on the water, multiplying loaves, raising corpses, a heavenly judge appearing with trumpets in the clouds while we are yet alive,—what is this compared to the real experience offered as witness to us by Christianity?   It is like the difference between the grandeur of an extravaganza and the grandeur of the sea or the sky,—immense objects which dwarf us, but where we are in contact with reality, and a reality of which we can gradually, though very slowly, trace the laws.—*Literature and Dogma.*

IMMORTALITY.

By what futilities the demonstration of our immortality may be attempted, is to be seen in Plato's ' Phædo.' Man's natural desire for continuance, however little it may be worth as a scientific proof of our immortality, is at least a proof a thousand times stronger than any such demonstration.   The want of solidity in such argument is so palpable, that one scarcely cares to turn a steady regard upon it at all.   And even of the common Christian conception of immortality the want of solidity is, perhaps, most conclusively shown, by the impossibility of so framing it as that it will at all support a steady regard turned upon it. In our English popular religion, for instance, the common conception of a future state of bliss is just that of the Vision of Mirza : ' Persons dressed in glorious habits with garlands on their heads, passing among the trees, lying down by the fountains, or resting on beds of flowers, amid a confused harmony of singing birds, falling waters, human voices, and musical instruments.' Or, even, with many, it is that of a kind of perfected middle-class home, with labour ended, the table spread, goodness all around, the lost ones restored, hymnody incessant. '*Poor fragments all of this low earth !*' Keble might well say. That this conception of immortality cannot possibly be true, we feel, the moment we consider it seriously. And yet who can devise any conception of a future state of bliss, which shall bear close examination better?

Here, again, it is far best to take what is experimentally true, and nothing else, as our foundation, and afterwards to let hope and aspiration grow, if so it may be, out of this. Israel had said : 'In the way of righteousness is life, and in the pathway thereof there is no death.' He had said : 'The righteous hath hope in his death.' He had cried to his *Eternal that loveth righteousness* : 'Thou wilt not leave my soul in the grave, neither wilt thou suffer thy faithful servant to see corruption ! thou wilt show me the path of life ! ’   And by a kind of short cut to the conclusion thus laid down, the Jews constructed their fairy-tale of an advent, judgment, and resurrection, as we find it in the Book of Daniel.   Jesus, again, had said : ‘ If a man keep my word, he shall never see death.’ And by a kind of short cut to the conclusion thus laid down, Christians constructed their fairy-tale of the second advent, the resurrection of the body, the New Jerusalem. But, instead of fairy-tales, let us begin, at least, with certainties.

And a certainty is the sense of *life*, of being truly *alive*, which accompanies righteousness.   If this experimental sense does not rise to be stronger in us, does not rise to the sense of being inextinguishable, that is probably because our experience of righteousness is really so very small.   Here, therefore, we may well permit ourselves to trust Jesus, whose practice and intuition, both of them, went, in these matters, so far deeper than ours.   At any rate, we have in our experience this strong sense of *life from righteousness* to start with ; capable of being developed, apparently, by progress in righteousness into something immeasurably stronger.   Here is the true basis for all religious aspiration after immortality.   And it is an experimental basis ; and therefore, as to grandeur, it is again, when compared with the popular *Aberglaube,* grand with all the superior grandeur, on a subject of the highest seriousness, of reality over fantasy.

At present, the fantasy hides the grandeur of the reality. But when all the *Aberglaube* of the second advent, with its signs in the sky, its sounding trumpets and opening graves, is cleared away, then and not till then will come out the profound truth and grandeur of words of Jesus like these : ' The hour is coming, and now is, when the dead shall hear the voice of the Son of God ; and they that hear shall *live.'—Literature and Dogma.*